Anonymous

Results of the magnetical and meteorological observations

Made at the Royal Observatory, Greenwich, in the year 1876-82 -Vol. 6

Anonymous

Results of the magnetical and meteorological observations
Made at the Royal Observatory, Greenwich, in the year 1876-82 -Vol. 6

ISBN/EAN: 9783337869380

Printed in Europe, USA, Canada, Australia, Japan

Cover: Foto ©ninafisch / pixelio.de

More available books at **www.hansebooks.com**

RESULTS

OF THE

MAGNETICAL AND METEOROLOGICAL OBSERVATIONS

MADE AT

THE ROYAL OBSERVATORY, GREENWICH,

IN THE YEAR

1882:

UNDER THE DIRECTION OF

W. H. M. CHRISTIE, M.A. F.R.S.

ASTRONOMER ROYAL.

PUBLISHED BY ORDER OF THE BOARD OF ADMIRALTY

IN OBEDIENCE TO HER MAJESTY'S COMMAND.

LONDON.

PRINTED BY EYRE AND SPOTTISWOODE,

PRINTERS TO THE QUEEN'S MOST EXCELLENT MAJESTY.

FOR HER MAJESTY'S STATIONERY OFFICE.

1884.

INDEX.

PAGE

INDEX.

INDEX.

ROYAL OBSERVATORY, GREENWICH.

RESULTS

OF

MAGNETICAL AND METEOROLOGICAL OBSERVATIONS.

1882.

GREENWICH MAGNETICAL AND METEOROLOGICAL OBSERVATIONS, 1882.

INTRODUCTION.

§ 1. *Personal Establishment and Arrangements.*

During the year 1882 the establishment of Assistants in the Magnetical and Meteorological Department of the Royal Observatory consisted of William Ellis, Superintendent, and William Carpenter Nash, Assistant, who had the aid usually of four Computers. The names of the Computers who were employed at different times during the year are, John A. Greengrass, William Hugo, Ernest E. McClellan, William J. Sanders, and Frank Finch.

Mr. Ellis controls and superintends the whole of the work of the Department. Mr. Nash is charged generally with the instrumental adjustments, the determination of the values of instrumental constants, and the more delicate magnetic observations. He also specially superintends the Meteorological Reductions. The routine magnetical and meteorological observations have been in general made by the Computers.

§ 2. *General Description of the Buildings and Instruments of the Magnetical and Meteorological Observatory.*

The Magnetical and Meteorological Observatory was erected in the year 1838. Its northern face is distant about 170 feet south-south-east from the nearest point of the South-East Dome, and about 35 feet south from the carpenters' workshop. On its east stands the New Library (erected at the end of the year 1881), in the construction of which non-magnetic bricks were used, and every care was taken to exclude iron. The Magnetical and Meteorological Observatory is based on concrete and built of wood, united for the most part by pegs of bamboo: no iron was intentionally admitted in its construction, or in subsequent alterations. Its form is that of a cross, the arms of the cross being nearly in the directions of the cardinal magnetic points as they were in 1838. The northern arm is longer than the others, and is separated from them by a partition, and used as a computing room; the stove which warms this room, and its flue, are of copper. The remaining portion, consisting of the eastern, southern and western arms, is known as the Upper Magnet Room. The upper declination magnet and its theodolite for determination of absolute declination, are placed in the southern arm, an opening in the roof allowing circumpolar stars to be observed by the theodolite for determination of the position of the astronomical meridian. Both the magnet and its theodolite are supported on piers built from the ground. In the eastern arm is placed the Thomson electrometer for photographic record of the variations of atmospheric electricity, its water cistern being supported by a platform fixed to the western side of the southern arm, near the ceiling. The Standard barometer is suspended near the point of junction of the southern and western arms. The Sidereal clock, Grimalde and Johnson, is fixed at the junction of the eastern and southern arms, and there is in addition a mean solar chronometer, McCabe No. 649, for general use.

Until the year 1863 the horizontal and vertical force magnets were also located in the Upper Magnet Room, the upper declination magnet being up to that time employed for photographic record of the variations of declination, as well as for absolute measure of the element. But experience having shown that the horizontal and vertical force magnets were subject in the upper room to too great variations of temperature, a room known as the Magnet Basement was in the year 1864 excavated below the Upper Magnet Room, and the horizontal and vertical force magnets, as well as a new declination magnet for photographic record of declination, were mounted therein, in order that they might be less exposed to changes of temperature. The Magnet Basement is of the same dimensions as the Upper Magnet Room. The lower declination magnet and the horizontal force and vertical force magnets, as now located in the Basement, are used entirely for record of the variations of the respective magnetic elements. The declination magnet is suspended in the southern arm, immediately under the upper declination magnet, in order that the position of the latter should not be affected thereby; the horizontal and vertical force magnets are placed in the eastern and western arms respectively, in positions nearly underneath those which they occupied when in the Upper Magnet Room. All are mounted on or suspended from supports carried by piers built from the ground. A photographic barometer is fixed to the northern wall of the Basement, and an apparatus for photographic registration of earth currents is placed near the southern wall of the eastern arm. A clock of peculiar construction for interruption of the photographic traces at each hour is fixed to the pier which supports the upper declination theodolite. The mean-time clock is attached to the western wall of the southern arm. On the northern wall, near the photographic barometer, is fixed the Sidereal standard clock of the Astronomical Observatory, Dent 1906, communicating with the chronograph and with clocks of the Astronomical Department by means of underground wires. This clock is placed in the Magnet Basement, because of its nearly uniform temperature.

The Basement is warmed when necessary by a gas stove (of copper), and ventilated by means of a large copper tube nearly two feet in diameter, which receives the flues from the stove and all gas-lights and passes through the Upper Magnet Room to a revolving cowl above the roof. Each of the arms of the Basement has a well window facing the south, but these wells are usually closely stopped.

A platform erected above the roof of the Magnet House is used for the observation of meteors. The sunshine instrument and a rain gauge are placed on a table on this platform.

An apparatus for naphthalizing the gas used for the photographic registration is mounted in a small detached zinc-built room adjacent to the computing room on its western side.

To the south of the Magnet House, in what is known as the Magnet Ground, is an open shed, consisting principally of a roof supported on four posts, under which is placed the photographic dry-bulb and wet-bulb thermometer apparatus. On the roof of this shed there is fixed an ozone box and a rain gauge, and close to its north-western corner are placed the earth thermometers, the upper portions of which, projecting above the ground, are protected by a small wooden hut. About 25 feet to the west of the photographic thermometers is situated the thermometer stand carrying the thermometers used for eye observations, and adjacent thereto on the north side are several rain gauges.

The Magnet Ground is bounded on its south side by a range of seven rooms, known as the Magnet Offices. No. 1 is used as a general store room, and in it is placed the Watchman's Clock; Nos. 2, 3, and 4 are used for photographic purposes in connexion with the Photoheliograph, placed in a dome adjoining No. 3, on its south side; Nos. 5 and 6 are store rooms. In No. 7 are placed the Dip Instrument and Deflexion apparatus.

To the south of the Magnet Offices, in what is known as the South Ground, are placed the thermometers for solar and terrestrial radiation; they are laid on short grass, and freely exposed to the sky. On 1882 March 4 these thermometers were removed to the position in the Magnet Ground which they had occupied up to 1880 January 31.

Two Anemometers, Osler's, giving continuous record of direction and pressure of wind and amount of rain, and Robinson's, giving continuous record of velocity, are fixed, the former above the north-western turret of the Octagon Room (the ancient part of the Observatory), the latter above the small building on the roof of the Octagon Room.

Regular observation of the principal magnetical and meteorological elements was commenced in the autumn of the year 1840, and has been continued, with some additions to the subjects of observation, to the present time. Until the end of the year 1847 observations were in general made every two hours, but at the beginning of the year 1848 these were superseded by the introduction of the method of photographic registration, by which means a continuous record of the various elements is obtained.

For information on many particulars concerning the history of the Magnetical and Meteorological Observatory, especially in regard to alterations not recited in this volume, which from time to time have been made, the reader is referred to the Introduction to the Magnetical and Meteorological Observations for the year 1880 and previous years, and to the Descriptions of the Buildings and Grounds, with accompanying Plans, given in the Volumes of Astronomical Observations for the years 1845 and 1862.

§ 3. *Subjects of Observation in the year 1882.*

These comprise determinations of absolute magnetic declination, horizontal force, and dip; continuous photographic record of the variations of declination, horizontal force, and vertical force, and of the earth currents indicated in two distinct lines of wire; eye observation of the ordinary meteorological instruments, including the barometer, dry and wet bulb thermometers, and radiation and earth thermometers; continuous photographic record of the variations of the barometer, dry and wet bulb thermometers, and electrometer (for atmospheric electricity); continuous automatic record of the direction, pressure, and velocity of the wind, and of the amount of rain; registration of the duration of sunshine, and amount of ozone; observation of some of the principal meteor showers; general record of ordinary atmospheric changes of weather, including numerical estimation of the amount of cloud; and other occasional phenomena.

§ 4. *Magnetic Instruments.*

UPPER DECLINATION MAGNET AND ITS THEODOLITE.—The upper declination magnet is by Meyerstein of Göttingen; it is a bar of hard steel, 2 feet long, 1½ inch broad, and about ¼ inch thick, and is employed solely for the determination of absolute declination. The magnet carrier was also made by Meyerstein, since however altered by Troughton and Simms; the magnet is fixed therein by two pinching screws. To a stalk extending upwards from the magnet carrier is attached the torsion circle, which consists of two circular brass discs, one turning independently on the other on their common vertical axis, the lower and graduated portion being firmly fixed to the stalk of the magnet carrier; to the upper portion carrying the vernier is attached, by a hook, the suspension skein. This is of silk, and consists of several fibres united by juxtaposition, without apparent twist; its length is about 6 feet.

The magnet, with its suspending skein, &c., is carried by a braced wooden tripod stand, whose feet rest on slates covering brick piers, built from the ground and rising through the Magnet Basement nearly to the roof. The upper end of the suspension skein is attached to a short square wooden rod, sliding in the corresponding square hole of a fixed wooden bracket. To the upper end of the rod is fixed a leather strap, which, passing over two brass pulleys carried by the upper portion of the tripod stand, is attached to a cord which passes down to a small windlass fixed to the stand. Thus in raising or lowering the magnet, an operation necessary in determinations of its collimation error, no alteration is made in the length of the suspension skein. The magnet is inclosed in a double rectangular wooden box (one box within another), both boxes being covered with gilt paper on their exterior and interior sides, and having holes at their south and north ends, for illumination of the magnet-collimator and for viewing the collimator by the theodolite telescope respectively. The holes in the outer box are covered with glass. The magnet-collimator is formed by a diagonally placed cobweb cross, and a lens of 13 inches focal length and nearly 2 inches aperture, carried respectively by two sliding frames fixed by pinching screws to the south and north arms of the magnet. The cobweb cross is in the principal focus of the lens, and its image in the theodolite telescope is well seen. From the lower side of the magnet carrier a rod extends downwards, terminating below the magnet box in a horizontal brass bar immersed in water, for the purpose of checking small vibrations of the magnet.

On September 10 the suspension skein gave way. A new skein was attached on September 11, and on September 12 observations were recommenced.

The theodolite, by which the position of the upper declination magnet is observed, is by Troughton and Simms. It is planted about 7 feet north of the magnet. The radius of its horizontal circle is 8·3 inches, and the circle is divided to 5′, and read, by three verniers, to 5″. The theodolite has three foot-screws, which rest in brass channels let into the stone pier placed upon the brick pier which rises from the ground through the Magnet Basement. The length of the telescope is 21 inches, and the aperture of its object glass 2 inches: it is carried by a horizontal transit axis $10\frac{1}{2}$ inches long, supported on Y's carried by the central vertical axis of the theodolite. The eye-piece has one fixed horizontal wire and one vertical wire moved by a micrometer-screw, the field of view in the observation of stars being illuminated through the pivot of the transit-axis on that side of the telescope which carries the micrometer-head. The value of one division of the striding level is considered to be equal to 1″·05. The opening in the roof of the Magnet House permits of observation of circumpolar stars as high as δ Ursæ Minoris above the pole and as low as 51 Cephei below the pole. A fixed mark, consisting of a small hole in a plate of metal, placed on one of the buildings of the Astronomical Observatory, at a distance of about 270 feet from the theodolite, is, in addition, provided by which to check the continued steadiness of the theodolite.

The inequality of the pivots of the axis of the theodolite telescope was found from several independent determinations made at different times to be very small. It appears that when the level indicates the axis to be horizontal the pivot at the illuminated end of the axis is really too low by $1^{div}\cdot3$, equivalent to 1″·4.

The value in arc of one revolution of the telescope-micrometer is 1′. 34″·2.

The reading for the line of collimation of the theodolite telescope was found, by ten double observations, 1882 January 31, to be $100^{r}\cdot221$, and by ten double observations, 1882 September 14, $100^{r}\cdot297$. The value used throughout the year 1882 was $100^{r}\cdot250$.

The effect of the plane glass in front of the outer box of the declination-magnet at that end of the box towards the theodolite was determined by ten double observations made on 1881 September 8, which showed that in the ordinary position of the glass the theodolite readings were diminished by 18″·6. Another set of observations, made on 1882 September 14, gave 20″·1. The mean of these, 19″·4, has been added to all readings throughout the year 1882.

The error of collimation of the magnet collimator is found by observing the position of the magnet, first with its collimator in the usual position (above the magnet), then with the collimator reversed (or with the magnet placed in its carrier with the collimator below), repeating the observations several times. The value used during the year 1882 was 26′. 9″·3, being the mean of determinations made on 1878 December 10, 1879 December 9, 1880 October 26, 1881 September 8, and 1882 September 12, giving respectively 26′. 13″·6, 26′. 2″·2, 25′. 56″·6, 26′. 18″·9, and 26′. 15″·0. With the collimator in its usual position, above the magnet, the amount has to be subtracted from all readings.

The effect of torsion of the suspending skein is eliminated by turning the lower portion of the torsion-circle until a brass bar (of the same size as the magnet, and weighted with lead weights to be also of equal weight), inserted in place of the magnet, rests in the plane of the magnetic meridian. The brass bar is thus inserted usually about once a month, and whenever the adjustment is found not to have been sufficiently close, the observed positions of the magnet are corrected for the amount by which the magnet is deflected from the meridian by the torsion force of the skein. Such correction is determined experimentally, with the magnet in position, by changing the reading of the torsion circle by a definite amount, usually 90°, thus giving the skein the same amount of azimuthal twist, and observing, by the theodolite, the displacement in the position of the magnet thereby produced, from which is derived the ratio of the torsion force of the skein to the earth's magnetic force. In this way the torsion force of the skein was, on 1879 December 9, found to be [illegible]th part of the earth's magnetic force: on 1881 September 8, it was found to be $\frac{1}{171}$th part, and on 1882 September 13 (after renewal of the suspension skein, see page *vii*), $\frac{1}{120}$th part. In general during the year 1882 the plane in which the suspension skein was free from torsion so nearly coincided with the magnetic meridian that corrections for the effect of torsion were required only during portions of the six months from May to October. On collecting the results, however, it appeared that there was a break of continuity between the values of absolute declination given with the old skein, in use up to September 10, and those found from the new skein mounted on September 11, the mean values given with the new suspension being about 3′ less than the values deduced with the old suspension. In regard to this it is to be remarked that the photographic trace of the lower declination magnet conclusively shows that no such change occurred at this time. There seems thus to be no doubt that the later values obtained with the old suspension of the upper magnet were in some manner influenced by the failing thread, indeed this had been suspected before the suspension gave way, from the character of the resulting mean declination curve, which indicates that this influence became sensible from about the month of June. Corrections proportional to the time have therefore been applied to the old suspension results as follows, in June −0′·7, July −1′·5, August −2′·2, and from September 1 to 10 −3′·0. Though a little uncertainty may thus attach to the absolute declination values intermediate between June and September, the diurnal variations and the changes from day to day would not be affected.

The time of vibration of the upper declination magnet under the influence of terrestrial magnetism was found on 1880 December 29 to be $30^{s}\cdot78$, on 1881 September 9, $31^{s}\cdot30$, and on 1882 September 14, $31^{s}\cdot20$.

The reading of the azimuthal circle of the theodolite corresponding to the astronomical meridian is determined about once in each month by observation of the stars Polaris and δ Ursæ Minoris. The fixed mark is usually observed weekly. The concluded mean reading of the circle for the south astronomical meridian (deduced entirely from the observations of the polar stars), used during the year 1882 for reduction of the observations of the declination magnet, was 27°. 3′. 16″·8.

In regard to the manner of making and reducing observations made with the upper declination magnet, the observer on looking into the theodolite telescope sees the image of the diagonally placed cross of the magnet collimator vibrating alternately right and left. The time of vibration of the magnet being about 30 seconds, the observer first applies his eye to the telescope about one minute, or two vibrations, before the pre-arranged time of observation, and, with the vertical wire carried by the telescope-micrometer, bisects the magnet-cross at its next extreme limit of vibration, reading the micrometer. He similarly observes the next following extreme vibration, in the opposite direction, and so on, taking in all four readings. The mean of each pair of adjacent readings of the micrometer is taken, giving three means, and the mean of these three is taken as the adopted reading. In practice this is done by adding the first and fourth readings to twice the second and third, and dividing the sum by 6. Should the magnet be nearly free from vibration, two bisections only of the cross are made, one at the vibration next before the pre-arranged time, the other at the vibration following. The verniers of the theodolite-circle are then read. The excess of the adopted micrometer-reading above the reading for the line of collimation of the telescope being converted into arc and applied to the mean circle-reading, and also the corrections for collimation of the magnet and for collimation of the plane glass in front of its box, the concluded circle-reading corresponding to the position of the magnet is found. The difference between this reading and the adopted reading of the circle for the south astronomical meridian gives, when, as is usually the case, no correction for torsion of the skein is necessary, the observed value of absolute declination, afterwards used for determining the value of the photographed base line on the photographic register of the lower declination magnet. The times of observation of the upper declination magnet are usually $1^h. 5^m$, $3^h. 5^m$, $9^h. 5^m$, and $21^h. 5^m$ of Greenwich mean time.

LOWER DECLINATION MAGNET.—The lower declination magnet is used simply for the purpose of obtaining photographic register of the variations of magnetic declination. It is by Troughton and Simms, and is of the same dimensions as the upper declination magnet, being 2 feet long, $1\frac{1}{2}$ inch broad, and $\frac{1}{4}$ inch thick. The magnet is suspended, in the Magnet Basement, immediately below the upper declination magnet, in order that the absolute measure of declination by the upper magnet should not be affected by the proximity of the lower magnet.

The manner of suspension of the magnet is in general similar to that of the upper declination magnet, the suspension pulleys being carried by a small pier built on one of the crossed slates resting on the brick piers rising up from the ground. The length of free suspending skein is about 6 feet, but, unlike the arrangement adopted for the upper magnet, the skein is itself carried over the suspension pulleys. The position of the azimuthal plane in which the brass bar rests, when substituted for the magnet, is examined from time to time, and adjustment made as necessary, to keep this plane in or near the magnetic meridian, such exact adjustment as is required for the upper declination-magnet not being necessary in this case.

To destroy the small accidental vibrations to which the magnet would be otherwise liable, it is encircled by a damper consisting of a copper bar, about 1 inch square, which is bent into a long oval form, the plane of the oval being vertical; a lateral bend is made in the upper bar of the oval to avoid interference with the suspension piece of the magnet. The effect of the damper is to reduce the amplitude of the oscillation after every complete or double vibration of the magnet in the proportion of 5 : 2 nearly.

In regard to photographic arrangements, it may be convenient, before proceeding to speak of the details peculiar to each instrument, to remark that the general principle adopted for obtaining continuous photographic record is the same for all instruments. For the register of each indication an accurately turned cylinder of ebonite is provided, the axis of the cylinder being placed parallel to the direction of the change of indication to be registered. If, as is usually the case, there are two indications whose movements are in the same direction, both may be registered on the same cylinder: thus the movements in the case of magnetic declination and horizontal magnetic force, being both horizontal, can be registered on different parts of one cylinder with axis horizontal: so also can two different galvanic earth currents. The movements in the case of vertical magnetic force, and of the barometer, being both vertical, can similarly be registered on different parts of one cylinder having its axis vertical, as also can the indications of the dry-bulb and wet-bulb thermometers. In the electrometer the movement is horizontal, for which a horizontal cylinder is provided, no other register being made on this cylinder.

The cylinder is in each case driven by chronometer or accurate clock-work to ensure uniform motion. The pivots of the horizontal cylinders turn on anti-friction wheels: the vertical cylinders rest on a circular plate turning on anti-friction wheels, the driving mechanism being placed below. A sheet of sensitized paper being wrapped round the cylinder, and a cylindrical glass cover, open at one end, slipped over it, the cylinder so prepared is placed in position, and connected with the clock-movement: it is then ready to receive the photographic record, the optical arrangements for producing which will be found explained in the special description of each particular instrument. The sheets are removed from the cylinders and fresh sheets supplied every day, usually at noon. On each sheet, where necessary, a reference line is also photographed, the arrangements for which will be more particularly described in each special case. All parts of the apparatus and all parts of the paths of light are protected, as found necessary, by wood or zinc casings or tubes, blackened on the inside, in order to prevent stray exterior light from reaching the photographic paper.

In June 1882 the photographic process for so many years employed, as described in the concluding section of the Introduction to previous volumes, was discarded, and a dry paper process introduced, the argentic-gelatino-bromide-paper, as prepared by Messrs. Morgan and Kidd of Richmond (Surrey) being used with ferrous oxalate development. The greater sensitiveness of this paper permits diminution of the effective surface of the magnet mirrors, and allows also the use of smaller gas flames. In the case of the vertical force magnet the old and comparatively heavy mirror has been replaced by a small and light mirror with manifest advantage, as will be seen in the description of the vertical force magnet. The new paper works equally well at all seasons of the year, and any loss of register on account of photographic failure is now extremely rare.

Referring now specially to the lower declination magnet, there is attached to the magnet carrier, for the purpose of obtaining photographic register of the motions of the magnet, a concave mirror of speculum metal, 5 inches in diameter, (reduced by a stop, on the introduction of the new photographic paper, to an effective diameter of about 1 inch), which thus receives all the angular movements of the magnet. The revolving ebonite cylinder is 11½ inches long and 14¼ inches in circumference: it is supported, in an approximately east and west position, on brass uprights carried by a metal plate, the whole being planted on a firm wooden platform, the supports of which rest on blocks driven into the ground. The platform is placed midway between the declination and horizontal force magnets, in order that the variations of magnetic declination and horizontal force may both be registered on the same cylinder, which makes one complete revolution in 26 hours.

The light used for obtaining the photographic record is that given by a flame of coal gas, charged with the vapour of coal naphtha. A vertical slit about $0^{in}\cdot3$ long and $0^{in}\cdot01$ wide, placed close to the light, is firmly supported on the pier which carries the magnet. It stands slightly out of the straight line joining the mirror and the registering cylinder, and its distance from the concave mirror of the magnet is about 25 inches. The distance of the axis of the registering cylinder from the concave mirror is 134·4 inches. Immediately above the cylinder, and parallel to its axis, are placed two long reflecting prisms (each 11 inches in length) facing opposite ways towards the mirrors carried by the declination and horizontal force magnets respectively. The front surface of each prism is convex, being a portion of a horizontal cylinder. The light of the declination lamp, after passing through the vertical slit, falls on the concave mirror, and is thence reflected as a converging beam to form an image of the slit on the convex surface of the reflecting prism, by the action of which it is reflected downwards to the paper on the cylinder as a small spot of light. A small azimuthal adjustment of the concave mirror allows the position of the spot to be so adjusted that it shall fall not at the centre of the cylinder but rather towards its western side, in order that the declination trace shall not become mixed with that of horizontal force, which is made to fall towards the eastern side of the cylinder. The special advantage of the arrangement here described is that the registers of both magnets are made at the same part of the circumference of the cylinder, a line joining the two spots being parallel to its axis, so that when the traces on the paper are developed, the parts of the two registers which appear in juxtaposition correspond to the same Greenwich time.

By means of a small prism, fixed near to the registering cylinder, the light from another lamp is made to form a spot of light in a fixed position on the cylinder, so that, as the cylinder revolves, a reference or base line is traced out on the paper, from which, in the interpretation of the records, the curve ordinates are measured.

A clock of special construction, arranged by Messrs. E. Dent and Co., acting upon a small shutter placed near the declination slit, cuts off the light from the mirror two minutes before each hour, and lets it in again two minutes after the hour, thus producing at each hour a visible interruption in the trace, and so ensuring accuracy as regards time scale. By means of another shutter the observer occasionally cuts off the light for a few minutes, registering the times at which it was cut off and at which it was again let in. The visible interruptions thus made at definite times in the trace obviate any possibility of error being made by wrong numeration of the hourly breaks.

The usual hour of changing the photographic sheet is noon, but on Sundays, and occasionally on other days, this rule is in some measure departed from. To obviate any uncertainty that might on such occasions arise from the mixing on the paper of the two ends of a trace slightly longer than 24 hours, it was, as has been mentioned, arranged that one revolution of the cylinder should be made in 26 hours. The actual length of 24 hours on the sheet is about 13·3 inches.

The scale for measurement of ordinates of the photographic curve is thus determined. The distance from the concave mirror to the surface of the cylinder, in the actual path of the ray of light through the prism, is practically the same as the horizontal distance of the centre of the cylinder from the mirror, 134·4 inches. A movement of 1° of the mirror produces a movement of 2° in the reflected ray. From this it is found that 1° of movement of the mirror, representing a change of 1° of magnetic declination, is equal to 4·691 inches on the photographic paper. A small scale of pasteboard is therefore prepared, graduated on this unit to degrees and minutes. The ordinates of the curve as referred to the base line being measured for the times at which absolute values of declination were determined by the upper declination magnet, usually four times daily, the apparent value of the base line, as inferred from each observation, is found. The process assumes that the movements of the upper and lower declination magnets are precisely similar. The separate base line values being divided into groups, usually monthly, a mean base line value is adopted for use through each group. This adopted base line value is written upon every sheet. Then, by the same pasteboard scale, there is laid down, conveniently near to the photographic trace, a new base line, whose ordinate represents some whole number of degrees or other convenient quantity. Thus every sheet carries its own scale of magnetic measure.

HORIZONTAL FORCE MAGNET.—The horizontal force magnet, for measure of the variations of horizontal magnetic force, was furnished by Meyerstein of Göttingen, and like the two declination magnets, is 2 feet long, 1½ inch broad, and about ¼ inch thick. For support of its suspension skein the back and sides of its brick pier rise through the eastern arm of the Magnet Basement to the Upper Magnet Room, being there covered by a slate slab, to the top of which a brass plate is attached, carrying, immediately above the magnet, two brass pulleys, with their axes in the same east and west line; and at the back of the pier, and opposite to these pulleys, two others, with their axes similarly in an east and west line: these constitute the upper suspension piece, and support the upper portions of the two branches of the suspension skein. The two lower pulleys, having their axes in the same horizontal plane, and their grooves in the same vertical plane, are attached to a small horizontal bar which forms the upper portion of the torsion circle: it carries the verniers for reading the torsion circle, and can be turned independently of the lower and graduated portion of the torsion circle, below which, and in rigid connexion with it, is the magnet carrier.

The suspension skein is led under the two pulleys carried by the upper portion of the torsion circle, its two branches then rise up and pass over the front pulleys of the upper suspension piece, thence to and over the back pulleys, thence descending to a single pulley, round which the two branches are tied: from this pulley a cord goes to a small windlass fixed to the back of the pier. The effective length of each of the two branches of the suspension skein is about $7^{ft}\ 6^{in}$. The distance between the branches of the skein, where they pass over the upper pulleys, is $1^{in}\cdot 14$; at the lower pulleys the distance between the branches is $0^{in}\cdot 80$. The two branches are not intended to hang in one plane, but are to be so twisted that their torsion force will maintain the magnet in a direction very nearly east and west magnetic, the marked end being west. In this state an increase of horizontal magnetic force draws the marked end of the magnet towards the north, whilst a diminution of horizontal force allows the torsion force to draw the marked end towards the south. An oval copper bar, exactly similar to that used with the lower declination magnet, is applied also to the horizontal force magnet, for the purpose of diminishing the small accidental vibrations.

Below the magnet carrier there is attached a small plane mirror to which is directed a small telescope for the purpose of observing by reflexion the graduations of a horizontal opal glass scale, attached to the southern wall of the eastern arm of the basement. The magnet, with its plane mirror, hangs within a double rectangular box, covered with gilt paper in the same way as was described for the upper declination magnet. The numbers of the fixed scale increase from east to west, so that when the magnet is inserted in its usual position, with its marked end towards the west, increasing readings of the scale, as seen in the telescope, denote increasing horizontal force. The normal to the scale that meets the centre of the plane mirror is situated at the division 51 of the scale nearly, the distance of the scale from the centre of the plane mirror being 90·84 inches. The angle between the normal to the scale, which coincides nearly with the normal to the axis of the magnet, and the axis of the fixed telescope is about 38°, the plane of the mirror is therefore inclined to the axis of the magnet by about 19°.

To adjust the magnet so that it shall be truly transverse to the magnetic meridian, which position is necessary in order that the indications of the instrument may apply truly to changes in the magnitude of horizontal magnetic force, without regard to changes of direction, the time of vibration of the magnet and the reading of the fixed scale are determined for different readings of the torsion circle. In regard to the interpretation of such experiments the following explanation may be premised.

Suppose that the magnet is suspended in its carrier with its marked end in a magnetic westerly direction, not exactly west but in any westerly direction, and suppose that, by means of the fixed telescope, the reading of the scale is taken. The position of the axis of the magnet is thereby defined. Now let the magnet be taken out of its carrier, and replaced with its marked end easterly. The terrestrial magnetic force will now act, as regards torsion, in the direction opposite to that in which it acted before, and the magnet will take up a different position. But by turning the torsion circle, and thereby changing the amount and direction of the torsion force produced by the oblique tension of the two branches of the suspending skein, the magnet may be made to take the same position as before, but with reversed direction of poles, which will be proved by the reading of the scale, as seen in the fixed telescope, being the same. The reading of the torsion circle will now be different, the effect of the operation being to give the difference of torsion circle reading for the same position of the magnet axis, but with the marked end opposite ways, without however affording any information as to whether the magnet axis is accurately transverse to the magnetic meridian, inasmuch as the same operation can be performed whether the magnet axis be transverse or not.

But there is another observation which will indicate whether the magnet axis is or is not accurately transverse. Let the time of vibration be, in addition, taken in each position of the magnet. Resolve the terrestrial magnetic force acting on the poles of the magnet into two parts, one transverse to the magnet, the other longitudinal.

In the two positions of the magnet, marked end westerly and marked end easterly, the magnitude of the transversal force is the same, and the changes which the torsion undergoes in a vibration of given extent are the same, and, if there were no other force, the time of vibration would also be the same. But there is another force, the longitudinal force, and when the marked end is northerly this tends from the centre of the magnet's length, and when it is southerly it tends towards the centre of the magnet's length, and in a vibration of given extent this produces force, in one case increasing that due to the torsion, and in the other case diminishing it. The times of vibration will therefore be different. There is only one exception to this, which is when the magnet axis is transverse to the magnetic meridian, in which case the longitudinal force vanishes.

The criterion then of the position truly transverse to the meridian is this. Find the readings of the torsion circle which, with the magnet in reversed positions, will give the same readings of the scale and the same time of vibration for the magnet. With such readings of the torsion circle the magnet is, in either position, transverse to the meridian, and the difference of readings is the difference between the position in which the terrestrial magnetism acting on the magnet twists it one way and the position in which the same force twists it the opposite way, and is therefore double of the angle due to the torsion force of the suspending lines when they, in either position, neutralize the force of terrestrial magnetism.

The present suspension skein was mounted on 1880 December 30, and on December 31 the following observations were made:—

1880. Day.	The Marked End of the Magnet. West. Torsion-Circle Reading.	Scale Reading.	Difference of Scale Readings for change of 1° of Torsion-Circle Reading.	Mean of the Times of Vibration.	East. Torsion-Circle Reading.	Scale Reading.	Difference of Scale Readings for change of 1° of Torsion-Circle Reading.	Mean of the Times of Vibration.
	°	div.	div.	s	°	div.	div.	s
Dec. 31	144	36·80	8·46	21·30	227	32·52	7·55	20·50
	145	45·26	7·89	21·12	228	40·07	7·28	20·62
	146	53·15	8·94	20·94	229	47·35	7·97	20·76
	147	62·09	8·06	20·74	230	55·32	7·94	20·90
	148	70·15		20·54	231	63·26	8·67	21·00
					232	71·93		21·12

From these observations it appeared that the times of vibration and scale readings were sensibly the same when the torsion circle read 148° . 15′, marked end west, and

230°. 0′, marked end east, the difference being 83 . 45′. Half this difference, or 41°. 52′·5, is therefore the angle of torsion when the magnet is transverse to the meridian. The values similarly found from other sets of observations made on 1882 January 3, 1883 February 16, and 1883 December 31 were respectively 42°. 9′, 41°. 56′, and 42°. 1′·5. The value adopted in the reduction of the observations during the year 1882 was 42°. 0′.

The adopted reading of torsion-circle, for transverse position of the magnet, the marked end being west, was 146° throughout the year.

The angle through which the magnet turns to produce a change of one division of scale reading, and the corresponding variation of horizontal force in terms of the whole horizontal force, is thus found.

The length of 30^div·85 of the fixed scale is exactly 12 inches, and the distance of the centre of the face of the plane mirror from the scale 90·84 inches; consequently the angle at the mirror subtended by one division of the scale is 14′. 43″·2, or for change of one division of scale-reading the magnet is turned through an angle of 7′. 21″·6.

The variation of horizontal force, in terms of the whole horizontal force, producing angular motion of the magnet corresponding to change of one division of scale reading = cotan. angle of torsion × value of one division in terms of radius. Using the numbers above given, the change of horizontal force corresponding to change of one division of scale-reading was found to be 0·000237S, which value has been used throughout the year 1882 for conversion of the observed scale-readings into parts of the whole horizontal force.

In regard to the manner of making observations with the horizontal force magnet. —A fine vertical wire is fixed in the field of view of the observing telescope, across which the graduations of the fixed scale, as reflected by the plane mirror carried by the magnet, are seen to pass alternately right and left as the magnet oscillates, and the scale reading for the extreme points of vibration is easily taken. The hours of observation are usually 1^h, 3^h, 9^h, and 21^h of Greenwich mean time. Remarking that the time of vibration of the magnet is about 20 seconds, and that the observer looks into the telescope about 40 seconds before the pre-arranged time, the manner of making the observation is generally similar to that already described for the upper declination magnet.

A thermometer, the bulb of which reaches considerably below the attached scale, is so planted in a nearly upright position on the outer magnet box that the bulb projects into the interior of the inner box containing the magnet. Readings of this thermometer are usually taken at 0^h, 1^h, 2^h, 3^h, 9^h, 21^h, 22^h, and 23^h. Its index error is insignificant.

The photographic record of the movements of the horizontal force magnet is made on the same revolving cylinder as is used for record of the motions of the lower declination magnet. And as described for that magnet, there is also attached to the carrier of the horizontal force magnet a concave mirror, 4 inches in diameter, reduced by a stop (on the introduction of the new photographic paper) to an effective diameter of about 1 inch. The arrangements as regards lamp, slit, and other parts are precisely similar to those for the lower declination magnet already described, and may be perfectly understood by reference to that description (pages *xii* and *xiii*), in which was incidentally included an explanation of some parts specially referring to register of horizontal force. The distance of the vertical slit from the concave mirror of the magnet is about 21 inches, and the distance of the axis of the registering cylinder from the concave mirror is 136·8 inches, the slit standing slightly out of the straight line joining the mirror and the registering cylinder. The same base line is used for measure of the horizontal force ordinates, and the register is similarly interrupted at each hour by the clock, and occasionally by the observer, for determination of time scale, the length of which is of course the same as that for declination.

The scale for measure of ordinates of the photographic curve is thus constructed. The distance from the concave mirror to the surface of the cylinder, in the actual path of the ray of light through the prism is (as for declination) practically the same as the horizontal distance of the centre of the cylinder from the mirror, or 136·8 inches. But, because of the reflexion at the concave mirror, the double of this measure, or 273·6 inches, is the distance that determines the extent of motion on the cylinder of the spot of light, which, in inches, for a change of 0·01 part of the whole horizontal force will therefore be 273·6 × tan. angle of torsion × 0·01. Taking for angle of torsion 42°. 0' the movement of the spot of light on the cylinder for a change of 0·01 of horizontal force is thus found to be 2·464 inches, and with this unit the pasteboard scale for measure of the curve ordinates for the year 1882 was prepared. The ordinates being measured for the times at which eye observations of the scale were made, combination of the measured ordinates with the observed scale readings converted into parts of the whole horizontal force, gives an apparent value of the base line for each observation. These being divided into groups, mean base line values are adopted, written on the sheets, and new base lines laid down, exactly in the same way as described for declination.

The indications of horizontal force are in a slight degree affected by the small changes of temperature to which the Magnetic Basement is subject. The temperature coefficient of the magnet was determined by artificially heating the Magnetic Basement to different temperatures, and observing the change of position of the magnet thereby produced. This process seems preferable to others in which was observed the effect which the magnet, when inclosed within a copper trough or box and artificially heated by hot water or hot air to different temperatures, produced on another suspended magnet, since the result obtained includes the entire effect of temperature upon all the various parts of the mounting of the magnet, as well as on the magnet itself. Referring to previous volumes for details, it is sufficient here to state that from a series of experiments made in the early part of the year 1868 on the principle mentioned, it appeared that when the marked end of the horizontal force magnet was to the west (its ordinary position) a change of 1° of temperature (Fahrenheit) produced a change of ·000174 of the whole horizontal force, a smaller number of observations made with the marked end of the magnet east indicating that a change of 1° of temperature produced a change of ·000187 of horizontal force, increase of temperature in both cases being accompanied by decrease of magnetic force. It is concluded that an increase of 1° of temperature produces a decrease of ·00018 of horizontal force.

On March 7 the cord attaching the single pulley to the small windlass broke: this was repaired on March 8, but further adjustment having become necessary on March 10, the results for March 8 and 9 have not been employed.

VERTICAL FORCE MAGNET.—The vertical force magnet, for measure of the variations of vertical magnetic force, is by Troughton and Simms. It is lozenge shaped, being broad at the centre and pointed at the ends, and is mounted on a solid brick pier capped with stone, situated in the western arm of the basement, its position being nearly symmetrical with that of the horizontal force magnet in the eastern arm. The supporting frame consists of two pillars, connected at their bases, on whose tops are the agate planes upon which rest the extreme parts of the continuous steel knife edge, attached to the magnet carrier by clamps and pinching screws. The knife edge, eight inches long, passes through an aperture in the magnet. The axis of the magnet is approximately transverse to the magnetic meridian, its marked end being east; its axis of vibration is thus nearly north and south magnetic. The magnet carrier is of iron; at its southern end there is fixed a small plane mirror for use in eye observations, whose plane makes with the axis of the magnet an angle of 52¾° nearly. A telescope fixed to the west side of the brick pier supporting the theodolite of the upper declination magnet is directed to the mirror, for observation by reflexion of the divisions of a vertical opal glass scale fixed to the pier that carries the telescope, very near to the telescope itself. The numbers of this fixed scale increase downwards, so that when the magnet is placed in its usual position with the marked end east, increasing readings of the scale, as seen in the telescope, denote increasing vertical force.

The magnet is placed excentrically between the bearing parts of its knife edge, nearer to the southern side, leaving a space of about four inches in the northern part of the iron frame, in which the concave mirror used for the photographic register is planted. Two screw stalks, carrying adjustible screw weights, are fixed to the magnet carrier, near its northern side; one stalk is horizontal, and a change in the position of the weight affects the position of equilibrium of the magnet; the other stalk is vertical, and change in the position of its weight affects the delicacy of the balance, and so varies the magnitude of its change of position produced by a given change in the vertical force of terrestrial magnetism.

On 1882 August 16 the vertical force magnet was dismounted, in order that Messrs. Troughton and Simms might substitute for the mirror of 4 inches diameter a much lighter mirror of 1 inch diameter, and might lower the position of the knife-edge bar with respect to the magnet so as to permit of a diminution of the adjustible counterpoise weights which as well as the mirror appear to largely affect the temperature correction of this balance-magnet. The use of a smaller and much lighter mirror was rendered possible by the much greater sensitiveness of the new photographic paper introduced in 1882 June. The magnet was out of use until 1882 October 3, when it was remounted.

The whole is enclosed in a rectangular box, resting upon the pier before mentioned, and having apertures, covered with glass, opposite to the two mirrors carried by the magnet.

The time of vibration of the magnet in the vertical plane is observed usually about once in each week, or more often should it appear to be desirable. From observations made on 30 days between January 4 and June 20 the time of vibration was found to be 15s·223; from observations made on 14 days between June 21 and August 15, 18s·647; and from observations made on 16 days between October 3 and December 31, 13s·884. The increased value during the second period was in all probability due to the weight on the vertical stalk having been accidentally very slightly shifted in an examination of the magnet made on June 21. On remounting the instrument on October 3 the time of vibration was diminished.

The time of vibration of the magnet in the horizontal plane is determined by suspending the magnet with all its attached parts from a tripod stand, its broad side being in a plane parallel to the horizon, so that its moment of inertia is the same as when in observation. A telescope, with a wire in its focus, being directed to the plane mirror carried by the magnet, a scale of numbers is placed on the floor, at right angles to the long axis of the magnet, which scale, by reflexion, can be seen in the fixed telescope. The magnet is observed only when swinging through a small arc. Observations made in the way described on 1879 December 31 gave for the time of vibration of the magnet in the horizontal plane = 17s·255;

other observations, made on 1883 April 4, after alteration of the magnet by Messrs. Troughton and Simms in the manner above described, gave $17^s{\cdot}171$.

The length of the normal to the fixed vertical scale that meets the face of the plane mirror is 186·07 inches, and $30^{div}{\cdot}85$ of the scale correspond to 12 inches. Consequently the angle which one division of the scale subtends, as seen from the mirror, is 7′. 11″·2, or the angular movement of the normal to the mirror, corresponding to a change of one division of scale reading, is 3′. 35″·6.

But the angular movement of the normal to the mirror is not the same as the angular movement of the magnet, but is less in the proportion of unity to the cosine of the angle which the normal to the mirror makes with the magnet, or in the proportion of unity to the sine of the angle which the plane of the mirror makes with the magnet. This angle, as already stated, is 52¾°, therefore dividing the result just obtained, 3′. 35″·6, by Sin. 52¾°, the angular motion of the magnet corresponding to a change of one division of scale reading is found to be 4′. 30″·9.

The variation of vertical force, in terms of the whole vertical force, producing angular motion of the magnet corresponding to change of one division of scale reading = cotan. dip × $\left(\frac{T}{T'}\right)^2$ × value of one division in terms of radius, in which T' is the time of vibration of the magnet in the horizontal plane, and T that in the vertical plane. From January 4 to June 20, assuming $T' = 17^s{\cdot}255$, $T = 15^s{\cdot}223$, and dip = 67°. 34¼′, the change of vertical force corresponding to change of one division of scale reading was found to be 0·000696; from June 21 to August 15, with the same value for T', and assuming $T = 18^s{\cdot}647$, and dip = 67°. 33½′, it was found to be 0·000464; from October 3 to December 31 with $T' = 17^s{\cdot}171$, $T = 13^s{\cdot}884$, and dip = 67°. 34¾′, it was found to be 0·000829. These values have been severally used during the periods mentioned for conversion of the observed scale readings into parts of the whole vertical force.

The method of observing with the vertical force magnet is precisely similar to that described for the horizontal force magnet, remarking the time of vertical vibration (see page *xx*), and the hours of observation are the same. The wire in the fixed telescope is here horizontal, and as the magnet oscillates the divisions of the scale are seen to pass upwards and downwards in the field of view.

In the same way as described for the horizontal force magnet a thermometer is provided whose bulb projects into the interior of the magnet box. Readings are taken usually at 0^h, 1^h, 2^h, 3^h, 9^h, 21^h, 22^h, and 23^h. Its index error is insignificant.

The photographic register of the movements of the vertical force magnet is made on a cylinder of the same size as that used for declination and horizontal force, driven also by chronometer movement. The cylinder is here placed vertical instead of horizontal, and opportunity is taken to register on the same cylinder the variations of the barometer. The slit is horizontal, and other arrangements are generally similar to those already described for declination and horizontal force. The concave mirror carried by the magnet is 4 inches in diameter (1 inch from October 3), and the slit is distant from it about 22 inches, being placed a little out of the straight line joining the mirror and the registering cylinder. There is a slight deviation in the further optical arrangements. Instead of a reflecting prism (as for declination and horizontal force) the converging horizontal beam from the concave mirror falls on a system of plano-convex cylindrical lenses, placed in front of the cylinder, with their axes parallel to that of the cylinder. The trace is made on the western side of the cylinder, the position of the magnet being so adjusted that the spot of light shall fall also on the lower part of the sheet. A base line is photographed, and the record is interrupted at each hour by the clock, and occasionally by the observer, for establishment of time scale, in the same way as for the other magnets. The length of the time scale is the same as that for the other magnetic registers.

The scale for measure of ordinates of the photographic curve is determined as follows:—The distance from the concave mirror to the surface of the registering cylinder is 100·2 inches. But the double of this measure, or 200·4 inches, is the distance that determines the extent of motion on the cylinder of the spot of light, which, in inches, for a change of 0·01 part of the whole vertical force, will therefore be $= 200{\cdot}4 \times \tan.\ \text{dip} \times \left(\frac{T}{T'}\right)^2 \times 0{\cdot}01$. Using the values of T, T′, and of dip, before given (page *xxi*), the movement of the spot of light on the cylinder for a change of 0·01 of vertical force is thus found to be, for the period January 4 to June 20, 3·779 inches, for the period June 21 to August 15, 5·666 inches, and from October 3 to December 31, 3·175 inches, and with these units the scales for measure of the curve ordinates were constructed. Base line values are then determined, and written on the sheets, exactly in the same way as was described for horizontal force.

In regard to the temperature correction of the vertical force magnet, it is only necessary here to say that, according to a series of experiments made at the same time as, and in a similar manner to those for the horizontal force magnet (page *xviii*), it appeared that an increase of 1° of temperature (Fahrenheit) produced an apparent increase of ·000880 of the whole vertical force. This is an amount of change not only much larger than has ever before been found, but it is also one which does not follow the usual law of increase of temperature producing loss of magnetic power. Yet since the effect produced is that due to the action of temperature on the various parts of the mounting of the magnet as well as on the magnet itself, the result should be superior to those found by action on the magnet alone, as in all former experiments. There would appear, therefore, to be no doubt of its accuracy in the actual case.

After the substitution of a small mirror for the large photographic mirror hitherto used (see page *xx*) other observations made 1882 October for determination of the temperature correction in the new condition of the magnet gave for an increase of 1° of temperature an apparent increase 0·00020 of vertical force. The value of the coefficient is thus greatly reduced, although still not following the ordinary law of increase of temperature producing loss of magnetic power. In practice a nearly uniform temperature is as far as possible maintained.

DIP INSTRUMENT.—The instrument with which the observations of magnetic dip have been made during the year 1882 is that which is known as Airy's instrument. It is mounted on a stout block of wood in the Magnet Office No. 7. The plan of the instrument was arranged by Sir G. B. Airy so that the points of the needles should be viewed by microscopes, and if necessary observed whilst the needles were in a state of vibration, that there should be power of employing needles of different lengths, and that the field of view of each microscope should be illuminated from the side opposite to the observer, in such way that the needle point should form a dark image in the bright field.

The instrument is adapted to the observation of needles of 9 inches, 6 inches, and 3 inches in length. The main portion of the instrument, that in which the needle under observation is placed, consists of a square box made of gun metal (carefully selected to ensure freedom from iron), with back and front of glass. Six microscopes, so planted as to command the points of the three different lengths of needles, are attached to a horizontal axis which allows them to be turned round in the vertical plane so as to follow the points of the needles in the different positions which in observation they take up. The object glasses and field glasses of the microscopes are within the front glass plate, their eye glasses being outside, and turning with them on the same axis. Upon the plane side of each field glass (the side next the object glass and on which the image of the needle point is formed) a scale is etched. And on the inner side of the front glass plate is etched the graduated circle, divided to 10′, and read by two verniers to 10″. The verniers (thin plates of metal, with notches instead of lines, being thus adapted to transmitted light) are carried by the horizontal axis, inside of the front glass plate, their reading lenses, attached to the same axis, being outside. Proper clamp with slow motion is provided. The microscopes and verniers are illuminated by one gas lamp, the light from which falling on eight corresponding prisms is thereby directed to each separate microscope and vernier. The prisms are carried behind the back glass plate on a circular frame in such way that, on reversion of the instrument in azimuth, the whole set of prisms can at one motion of the frame be shifted so as to bring each one again opposite to its proper microscope or vernier.

The whole of the apparatus is planted upon a circular horizontal plate, admitting of rotation in azimuth: a graduated circle near the circumference of the plate is read by two fixed verniers.

A brass zenith point needle, having points corresponding in position to the three different lengths of dip needles, is used to determine the zenith point for each particular length of needle.

The instrument carries two levels, one parallel to the plane of the vertical circle, the other at right angles to that plane, by means of which the instrument is from time to time adjusted in level. The readings of the first-mentioned level are also regularly employed to correct the apparent value of dip for any small outstanding error of level: the correction seldom exceeds a very few seconds.

The needles in regular use are of the ordinary construction, they are two 9-inch needles, B_1 and B_2, two 6-inch needles, C_1 and C_2, and two 3-inch needles, D_1 and D_2.

Until 1882 March 29 the Naylor equatoreal occupied the same position in the South Ground as since 1879 October. Its proximity to the Dip and Deflexion instruments has, however, been found (*see* Introduction, 1879, p. *vi.*) to exercise no appreciable influence on the indications of these instruments. On 1882 March 29 it was moved away a considerable distance, quite out of range of any sensible disturbing action.

DEFLEXION INSTRUMENT.—The observations of deflexion of a magnet in combination with observations of vibration of the deflecting magnet, for determination of the absolute intensity of magnetism, are made with a unifilar instrument, which, with the exception of some slight modification of the mechanical arrangements, is similar to those issued from the Kew Observatory. It is mounted on a block of wood in the Magnet Office No. 7, on the south side of the Dip instrument.

The deflected magnet, whose use is merely to ascertain the proportion which the power of the deflecting magnet at a given distance bears to the power of terrestrial magnetism, is 3 inches long, and carries a small plane mirror, to which is directed a telescope fixed to and rotating with the frame that carries also the suspension piece of the deflected magnet: a scale fixed to the telescope is seen by reflexion at the plane mirror. The deflecting magnet is a hollow cylinder 4 inches long, containing in its internal tube a collimator, by means of which in another apparatus its time of vibration is observed. In observations of deflexion the deflecting magnet is placed on the transverse deflection rod, carried by the rotating frame, at the distances 1·0 foot and 1·3 foot of the engraved scale from the deflected magnet, and with one end towards the deflected magnet. Observations are made at the two distances mentioned, with the deflecting magnet both east and west of the deflected magnet, and also with its poles in reversed positions. The fixed horizontal circle is 10 inches in diameter: it is graduated to 10′, and read by two verniers to 10″.

It will be convenient in this case to include with the description of the instrument an account of the method of reduction employed, in which the Kew precepts and generally the Kew notation are followed. Previous to the establishment of the instrument at the Royal Observatory the values of the various instrumental constants, as determined at the Kew Observatory, were kindly communicated by Professor Balfour Stewart, and have been since used in the reduction of all observations made with the instrument at Greenwich.

The instrumental constants as thus furnished are as follows:—

The increase in the magnetic moment of the deflecting magnet produced by the inducing action of a magnetic force equal to unity of the English system of absolute measurement $= \mu = 0{\cdot}00015587$.

The correction for decrease of the magnetic moment of the deflecting magnet required in order to reduce to the temperature 35° Fahrenheit $= q = 0{\cdot}00013126\,(t - 35) + 0{\cdot}000000259\,(t - 35)^2$: t representing the temperature at which the observation is made.

Moment of inertia of the deflecting magnet $= K$. At temperature 30°, log. $K = 0{\cdot}66643$; at temperature 90° $= 0{\cdot}66679$.

The distance on the deflection rod from 1ft·0 east to 1ft·0 west of the engraved scale, at temperature 62°, is too long by 0·0084 inch, and the distance from 1ft·3 east to 1ft·3 west is too long by 0·0053 inch.

The adopted value of K was confirmed in the year 1878 by a new and entirely independent determination made at the Royal Observatory, giving log. K at temperature 30° = 0·66727.

If, in the deflection observation, r = apparent distance of centre of deflecting magnet from deflected magnet, corrected for scale error and temperature (taking expansion of scale for 1° = ·00001), and u = observed angle of deflexion, then putting $A_1 = \frac{1}{2}\, r^3 \sin. u \left\{1 + \frac{2\mu}{r^3} + q\right\}$, in which r = 1·0 foot; and A_2 = corresponding expression for r = 1·3 foot; $P = \frac{A_1 - A_2}{A_1 - \frac{A_2}{(1{\cdot}3)^2}}$; but this is not convenient for logarithmic computation, especially as the logarithms of A_1 and A_2 are, in the calculation, first obtained. The difference between A_1 and A_2 being small, P may be taken equal to $(\text{Log. } A_1 - \text{Log. } A_2)\, \frac{1{\cdot}69}{(1{\cdot}69 - 1)\text{ modulus}} = (\text{Log. } A_1 - \text{Log. } A_2) \times 5{\cdot}64$. A mean value of P is adopted from various observations; then m being the magnetic moment of the deflecting magnet, and X the Horizontal component of the Earth's magnetic force, $\frac{m}{X} = A_1 \times \left(1 - \frac{P}{1}\right)$ from observation at distance 1·0 foot, or $= A_2 \times \left(1 - \frac{P}{1{\cdot}69}\right)$ from that at distance 1·3 foot. The mean of these is adopted for the true value of $\frac{m}{X}$.

For determination, from the observed vibrations, of the value of mX, let T_1 = time of vibration of the deflecting magnet corrected for rate and arc of vibration, then $T^2 = T_1^2 \left\{ 1 + \frac{H}{F} + \mu \frac{X}{m} - q \right\}$, in which $\frac{H}{F}$ is the ratio of the torsion force of the suspension thread of the deflecting magnet to the earth's directive force. And $mX = \frac{\pi^2 K}{T^2}$. The adopted time of vibration is the mean of 100 vibrations observed immediately before, and 100 observed immediately after the observations of deflexion.

From the combination of the values of $\frac{m}{X}$ and mX, m and X are immediately found. The computation is made with reference to English measure, taking as units of length and weight the foot and grain, but it is desirable to express X also in metric measure. If the English foot be supposed equal to α times the millimètre and the grain equal to β times the milligramme, then for reduction to metric measure $\frac{m}{X}$ and mX must be multiplied by α^3 and $\alpha^2\beta$ respectively, or X must be multiplied by $\sqrt{\frac{\beta}{\alpha}}$. Taking the mètre as equal to 39·37079 inches, and the gramme as equal to 15·43249 grains, the factor by which X is to be multiplied in order to obtain X in metric measure is $0{\cdot}46108 = \frac{1}{2{\cdot}1689}$. The values of X in metric measure thus derived from those in English measure are given in the proper table. Values of X in terms of the centimètre and gramme, known as the C.G.S. unit (centimètre-gramme-second unit), are readily obtained by dividing those referred to the millimètre and milligramme by 10.

EARTH CURRENT APPARATUS.—For observation of the spontaneous galvanic currents which in some measure are almost always discoverable in the earth, and which are occasionally very powerful, two insulated wires having earth connexions at Angerstein Wharf (on the bank of the River Thames near Charlton) and Lady Well for one circuit; and at the Morden College end of the Blackheath Tunnel and the North Kent East Junction of the South-Eastern Railway for the other circuit, have been employed. The connecting wires pass from the Royal Observatory to the Greenwich Railway Station and thence, by kind permission of the Directors of the South-Eastern Railway Company, along the lines of the South-Eastern Railway to the respective earths, in each case a copper plate. The direct distance between the earth plates of the Angerstein Wharf—Lady Well circuit is 3 miles, and the azimuth of the line, reckoning from magnetic north towards east, 50°; in the Blackheath—North Kent East circuit the direct distance is $2\frac{1}{2}$ miles, and the azimuth, from magnetic north towards west, 46°. The actual lengths of wire in the circuitous courses which the wires necessarily take in order to reach the Observatory registering apparatus are about $7\frac{1}{2}$ miles and 5 miles respectively. The identity of the four branches is tested from time to time as appears necessary.

In each circuit at the Royal Observatory there is placed a horizontal galvanometer, having its magnet suspended by a hair. Each galvanometer coil contains 150 turns of No. 29 copper wire, or the double coil of each instrument consists of 300 turns of wire. They are placed on opposite sides of the registering cylinder, which is of course horizontal. One galvanometer stands towards one end of the cylinder, and the other towards the other end, and each carries, on a light stalk extending downwards from its magnet, a small plane mirror. Immediately above the cylinder are placed two long reflecting prisms which, except that they are each but half the length of the cylinder, and are placed end to end, are generally similar to those used for magnetic declination and horizontal force, the front convex surface facing opposite ways, each one towards the mirror of its respective galvanometer. In each case the light of a gas lamp, passing through a vertical slit and a vertical cylindrical lens, falls upon the galvanometer mirror, which reflects the converging beam to the convex surface of the reflecting prism, by whose action it is made to form on the paper on the cylinder a small spot of light; thus all the azimuthal motions of the galvanometer magnet are registered. The extent of trace for each galvanometer is thus confined to half the length of the cylinder, which is of the same size as those used for the magnetic registers. The arrangements for turning the cylinder, automatically determining the time scale, and forming a base line are similar to those which have been before described. When the traces on the paper are developed the parts of the registers which appear in juxtaposition correspond, as for declination and horizontal force, to the same Greenwich time, and the scale of time is of the same length as for the magnetic registers.

§ 5. *Magnetic Reductions.*

The results given in the Magnetic Section refer to the astronomical day.

Before proceeding to discuss the photographic records of magnetic declination, horizontal force, and vertical force, they were divided into two groups, one including all days on which the traces showed no particular disturbance, and which therefore were suitable for the determination of diurnal inequality; the other comprising days of unusual and violent disturbance, when the traces were so irregular that it appeared impossible to treat them except by the exhibition of every motion of each magnet through the day. Following the principle of separation hitherto adopted, there are 15 days in the year 1882 which have been classed as days of great disturbance. These are April 16, 17, 19, 20, June 24, August 4, October 2, 5,

November 12, 13, 17, 18, 19, 20, and 21. There was lesser disturbance on 13 days, viz.: January 19, February 1, 20, June 14, July 16, 30, 31, September 11, November 11, 14, 25, December 20 and 21.

Separating the days of great disturbance, to be treated of hereafter, the photographic sheets for the remaining quiet days, including those of lesser disturbance, were thus treated. Through each photographic trace a pencil line was drawn representing the general form of the curve, without its petty irregularities. The ordinates of these pencil curves were then measured, with the proper pasteboard scales, at every hour, the measures being entered in a form having double argument, the vertical argument ranging through the 24 hours of the astronomical day, and the horizontal argument through the days of a calendar month, the means of the numbers standing in the vertical columns giving the mean daily value of the element, and the means of the numbers in the horizontal columns the mean monthly value at each hour of the day. Tables I. to III. contain the results for declination, Tables IV. to VIII. those for horizontal force, with corresponding tables of temperature, and Tables IX. to XIII. those for vertical force, with corresponding tables of temperature. Table XIV. gives the mean diurnal inequalities for declination, horizontal force, and vertical force for the year.

The temperature of the horizontal and vertical force magnets was maintained so nearly uniform through each day that the determination of the diurnal inequalities of horizontal and vertical force should possess great exactitude, although in regard to vertical force the magnitude of the temperature co-efficient, during the early portion of the year, introduces an element of some uncertainty. It was not possible under the circumstances to maintain similar uniformity of temperature through the seasons, a point however of less importance. Following the principle adopted for many years, the results are given uncorrected for temperature, but accompanied by corresponding tables of temperature. It is deemed best that in the yearly volumes the results should be thus exhibited, as more easily admitting of independent examination. When, as is done from time to time, the results for series of years are collected for general discussion, the temperature corrections are duly taken into account.

The variations of declination are given in the sexagesimal division of the circle, and those of horizontal and vertical force in parts of the whole horizontal and vertical forces respectively. The results contained in Tables III., VIII., XIII., and XIV. have been also expressed in terms of Gauss's absolute unit, as referred to the metrical system of the millimètre-milligramme-second.

The factors for conversion from the former to the latter system of measures are as follows:—

For variation of declination, expressed in minutes, the factor is

$$\text{H. F. metrical} \times \sin 1' = 1{\cdot}804 \times \sin 1' = 0{\cdot}0005248.$$

For horizontal force

$$\text{Variation of H. F. metrical} = \frac{\text{H. F. metrical}}{\text{Former H. F.}} \times \text{former variation} = 1{\cdot}804 \times \text{former variation,}$$

the former H. F. being = 1.

For vertical force

$$\text{Variation of V. F. metrical} = \frac{\text{V. F. metrical}}{\text{Former V. F.}} \times \text{former variation.}$$

The former V. F. = 1, but the V. F. metrical = H. F. metrical × tan dip, hence taking dip = 67°. 34′,

$$\begin{aligned}\text{Variation of V. F. metrical} &= 1{\cdot}804 \times \tan 67^{\circ}.34' \times \text{former variation} \\ &= 1{\cdot}3696 \times \text{former variation.}\end{aligned}$$

The measures as referred to the millimètre-milligramme-second are convertible into measures on the centimètre-gramme-second (C. G. S.) system by dividing by 10.

Tables XV. and XVI., now given for the first time, exhibit respectively the diurnal range of declination and horizontal force on each separate day, as determined from the 24 hourly ordinates of each element measured from the photographic register (as explained on page *xxiii*), and the monthly means of these numbers. In these tables the results for horizontal force are *corrected for temperature*. The monthly means for declination are such as, in previous volumes, have been given in the final column of Table III.; the daily values have not before been given.

In the Tables of magnetic dip, the result of each separate observation of dip with each of the six needles in ordinary use is given, and also the concluded monthly and yearly values for each needle.

The results of the observations for absolute measure of horizontal force require no special remark, the method of reduction and all necessary explanation having been given with the description of the instrument.

No numerical discussion of earth current records is contained in the present volume.

In the treatment of disturbed days it has been the custom in previous years to measure out for each element all salient points of the curves and to print the numerical values. But in the present volume it has been considered preferable to give instead reduced copies of the actual photographic curves (reproduced by photo-lithography from full-sized tracings of the original photographs), adding thereto copies of the corresponding earth current curves. The registers thus exhibited are those for the days of great and of lesser disturbance mentioned on pages *xxvii* and *xxviii*. A few other days in November have been added in order to complete the series for the period of visibility of the great November sunspot, which appeared on the eastern limb of the Sun on November 11, and disappeared at the western limb on November 25.

The plates are preceded by a brief description of *all* significant magnetic motions (superposed on the ordinary diurnal movement) recorded throughout the year. These, in combination with the plates, give very complete information on magnetic disturbances during the year 1882, affording thereby, it is hoped, facilities for making comparison with solar phenomena.

Referring now again to the plates, it may be remarked that on each day, with few exceptions, five distinct registers are given, viz.: declination, horizontal force, vertical force, and the two earth currents, all necessary information for proper understanding of the plates being given in the notes on page (xxviii). No attempt has been made to determine earth current scales in terms of any electrical unit, but it may be stated that the instrumental conditions are similar for the two circuits, excepting that the communicating wire of the E_1 circuit is longer than that of the E_2 circuit in the proportion of 3 to 2, and that the distances between the earth plates of the former and of the latter are in the proportion of 6 to 5.

The indications of horizontal and vertical force are given precisely as registered; they are therefore affected, slightly as compared with the amount of motion on disturbed days, by the small recorded changes of temperature of the magnets. The observed temperatures being inserted on the plates, reference to the temperature coefficients of the magnets, given at page *xix* for horizontal force, and pages *xxii* and *xxiii* for vertical force, will show the effect produced. Briefly, an increase of nearly 6° of temperature throws the horizontal force curve upward by 0·001 of the whole horizontal force; an increase of about 1° of temperature, Plates I. to VII., and an increase of 5° of temperature, Plates IX. to XXII., throws the vertical force curve downward by 0·001 of the whole vertical force.

The original photographs have been reduced in the proportion of 20 to 11 on the plates, and the corresponding scale values are :—

—	LENGTH IN INCHES				
	Of 1° of Declination throughout the Year.	Of 0·01 of Horizontal Force throughout the Year.	Of 0·01 of Vertical Force.		
			January 4 to June 20.	June 21 to August 15.	October 3 to December 31.
	in.	in.	in.	in.	in.
On the Photographs .	4·691	2·464	3·779	5·666	3·175
On the Plates .	2·580	1·355	2·078	3·116	1·746

But these scale values are not immediately comparable for the different elements, and it will therefore be desirable to refer them all to the same unit, say 0·01 of the horizontal force.

Taking 1° of Declination = ·0175 of Horizontal Force

and Vertical Force = Horizontal Force × tan. dip [dip = 67°. 34′]

we have the following equivalent scale values for the different elements, as applying to the plates :—

LENGTH OF UNIT, EQUIVALENT TO 0·01 OF HORIZONTAL FORCE.

For Declination Curve throughout the Year.	For Horizontal Force Curve throughout the Year.	For Vertical Force Curve. January 4 to June 20.	For Vertical Force Curve. June 21 to August 15.	For Vertical Force Curve. October 3 to December 31.
in.	in.	in.	in.	in.
1·47	1·36	0·86	1·29	0·72

It may be convenient to give also comparative scale values for the different systems of absolute measurement, viz. :—

Foot-grain-second, or	British unit, in terms of which Mean H. F. for 1882	= 3·913
Millimètre-milligramme-second, or	Metric unit, " " "	= 1·804
Centimètre-gramme-second, or	C. G. S. unit, " " "	= 0·1804

Dividing therefore the scale values last given by 3·913, 1·804, and 0·1804 respectively, the following comparative scale values for each of the elements on the plates as referred to 0·01 of these units respectively are found :—

UNIT.	LENGTH OF 0·01 OF UNIT. Declination throughout the Year.	Horizontal Force throughout the Year.	Vertical Force. January 4 to June 20.	Vertical Force. June 21 to August 15.	Vertical Force. October 3 to December 31.
	in.	in.	in.	in.	in.
British -	0·38	0·35	0·22	0·33	0·18
Metric -	0·82	0·75	0·48	0·71	0·40
C. G. S. -	8·2	7·5	4·8	7·1	4·0

Slight interruptions in the traces on the plates are due to various causes. In the originals there are breaks at each hour for time scale, so slight however that, in the copies, the traces could usually be made continuous without fear of error: in a few cases, however, this could not be done, as at 12^h on April 16, for declination. Further, to check the numeration of hours, the observer interrupts the register at definite times for about five minutes, usually at or near $2^h. 30^m$, $8^h. 30^m$, and $21^h. 30^m$, and at somewhat different times on Sundays. A weekly clearing of the gas pipes also causes a somewhat longer interruption, usually at about 22^h, as on August $4^d. 22^h$.

As regards longer interruptions, the register of declination was lost on account of defective photography from April $16^d. 23\frac{1}{2}^h$ to $17^d. 4^h$, and that of horizontal force from April $20^d. 0^h$ to 1^h, from April $21^d. 0^h$ to 3^h, and from November $16^d. 22\frac{1}{2}^h$ to $23\frac{1}{2}^h$: two small portions of vertical force register were similarly lost between November $17^d. 3\frac{1}{2}^h$ and 7^h. The vertical force register is also wanting from October $5^d. 22\frac{1}{2}^h$ to $6^d. 5^h$ on account of accidental interruption of the registration.

As respects earth currents, from July $31^d. 21^h$ to August $1^d. 0^h$ the E_1 circuit was interrupted, and from September $11^d. 15^h$ to 17^h the E_2 register was imperfect, owing to defect of instrumental adjustment.

From November $16^d. 22^h+$ to $17^d. 1^h$ nearly, and from November $17^d. 3\frac{1}{2}^h$ to 6^h during great magnetic disturbance, the earth current motions were so violent that the records could not be traced. In regard to other earth current omissions in November, it is to be remarked that the telegraphic lines were injured in the previous great gale of October 24, and were more or less defective during November. The registers were thus frequently vitiated on account of the defective insulation. Omissions from this cause occur on some part of every day from November 11 to 23.

On November 18, 19, and 21 portions of the E_1 trace are from some unknown cause temporarily displaced with reference to the instrumental zero.

It will be seen that when disturbance commences the first motion is frequently abrupt, and simultaneous for all elements. Instances of this occur at the following times:—April $16^d. 11^h. 30^m$, April $19^d. 15^h. 35^m$, June $14^d. 15^h. 5^m$, August $4^d. 3^h. 50^m$, September $11^d. 14^h. 50^m$, October $1^d. 21^h. 40^m$, November $16^d. 22^h. 15^m$, and November $25^d. 4^h. 30^m$. Simultaneous motions also occur on November $14^d. 20^h. 15^m$ and November $15^d. 20^h. 20^m$.

The original photographic records were first traced on thin paper, the separate records on each day being arranged one under another on the same sheet, and great attention being paid to accuracy as regards the scale of time. Each sheet containing the records for one or more days was then reduced by photo-lithography, in the proportion of 20 to 11, to bring it to a convenient size for insertion in the printed volume.

§ 6. *Meteorological Instruments.*

STANDARD BAROMETER.—The standard barometer, mounted in 1840 on the southern wall of the western arm of the upper magnet room, is Newman No. 64. Its tube is $0^{in}\cdot565$ in diameter, and the depression of the mercury due to capillary action is $0^{in}\cdot002$, but no correction is applied on this account. The cistern is of glass, and the graduated scale and attached rod are of brass; at its lower end the rod terminates in a point of ivory, which in observation is made just to meet the reflected image of the point as seen in the mercury. The scale is divided to $0^{in}\cdot05$, subdivided by vernier to $0^{in}\cdot002$.

The readings of this barometer until 1866 August 20 are considered to be coincident with those of the Royal Society's flint-glass standard barometer. It then became necessary to remove the sliding rod, for repair of its slow motion screw, which was completed on August 30. Before the removal of the rod the barometer had been compared with three other barometers, one of which, during repair of the rod, was used for the daily readings. After restoration of the rod comparison was again made with the same three barometers with the result that (all three auxiliary barometers giving accordant results) the readings of the standard, in its new state, required a correction of $-0^{in}\cdot006$, which correction has been applied to every observation, commencing on 1866 August 30.

An elaborate comparison of the standard barometers of the Greenwich and Kew Observatories, made, under the direction of the Kew Committee, by Mr. Whipple, Superintendent of the Kew Observatory, in the spring of the year 1877, showed that the difference between the two barometers (after applying to the Greenwich barometer readings the correction $-0^{in}\cdot006$) did not exceed $0^{in}\cdot001$. (*Proceedings of the Royal Society*, vol. 27, page 76.)

The height of the barometer cistern above the mean level of the sea is 159 feet, being $5^{ft}\ 2^{in}$ above Mr. Lloyd's reference mark in the then transit room, now the Astronomer Royal's official room (*Philosophical Transactions*, 1831).

The barometer is usually read at 21^h, 0^h, 3^h, 9^h (astronomical). Each reading is corrected by application of the index correction above mentioned, and reduced to the temperature 32° by means of Table II. of the "Report of the Committee of Physics" of the Royal Society. The readings thus found are used to determine the value of the instrumental base line on the photographic record.

PHOTOGRAPHIC BAROMETER.—The barometric record is made on the same cylinder as is used for magnetic vertical force, the register being arranged to fall on the upper half of the cylinder, on its eastern side. A syphon barometer fixed to the northern wall of the Magnetic Basement is employed, the bore of the upper and lower extremities of the tube being about 1·1 inch. A metallic float is partly supported by a counterpoise acting on a light lever, leaving a definite part of its weight to be supported by the mercury. The lever carries at its other end a vertical plate of blackened mica, having a small horizontal slit, whose distance from the fulcrum is about eight times that of the point of connexion with the float, and whose vertical movement is therefore about four times that of the ordinary barometric column. The light of a gas lamp, passing through this slit and falling on a cylindrical lens, forms a spot of light on the paper. The barometer can, by screw action, be raised or lowered so as to keep the photographic trace in a convenient part of the sheet. A base line is traced on the sheet, and the record is interrupted at each hour by the clock and occasionally by the observer in the same way as for the magnetic registers. The length of the time scale is also the same. Registration was interrupted from August 18 to 30, the time-piece which drives the registering cylinder having been removed by Messrs. E. Dent and Co. for cleaning and repair.

The barometric scale is determined by experimentally comparing the measured movement on the paper with the observed movement of the standard barometer; one inch of barometric movement is thus found = $4^{in.}\cdot39$ on the paper. Ordinates measured for the times of observation of the standard barometer, combined with the corrected readings of the standard barometer, give apparent values of the base line, from which mean values for each day are formed; these are written on the sheets and new base lines drawn, as for the magnetic registers.

As regards the effect of temperature, it will be understood from the construction of the apparatus that the photographic record is influenced only by the expansion of the column of mercury (about 4 inches in length) in the lower tube of the barometer, and from this circumstance, in combination with the near uniformity of temperature in the basement, no appreciable differential effect is produced on the photographic register.

DRY AND WET BULB THERMOMETERS.—The dry and wet bulb thermometers and maximum and minimum self-registering thermometers, both dry and wet, are mounted on a revolving frame planned by Sir G. B. Airy. A vertical axis fixed in the ground, in a position about 35 feet south of the south-west angle of the Magnetic Observatory, carries the frame, which consists of a horizontal board as base, of a vertical board projecting upwards from it connected with one edge of the horizontal board, and of two parallel inclined boards (separated about 3 inches) connected at the top with the vertical board and at the bottom with the other edge of the horizontal board: the outer inclined board is covered with zinc, and the air passes freely between all the boards. The dry and wet bulb thermometers are mounted near the centre of the vertical board, with their bulbs about 4 feet from the ground; the maximum and minimum thermometers for air temperature are placed towards one side of the vertical board, and those for evaporation temperature towards the other side, with their bulbs at about the same level as those of the dry and wet bulb thermometers. A small roof projecting from the frame protects the thermometers from rain. The frame is turned in azimuth as necessary to keep the inclined side always towards the sun.

The corrections to be applied to the thermometers in ordinary use (except the earth thermometers) are determined usually once each year for the whole extent of scale actually employed, by comparison with the standard thermometer, No. 515, kindly supplied to the Royal Observatory by the Kew Committee of the Royal Society.

The dry and wet bulb thermometers are Negretti and Zambra, Nos. 45354 and 45355 respectively. Until January 14 no correction was applied. From January 15 a correction of $-0^{\circ}\cdot1$ was applied to the readings of both thermometers.

The self-registering thermometers for temperature of air and evaporation are all by Negretti and Zambra. The maximum thermometers are on Negretti and Zambra's principle, the minimum thermometers are of Rutherford's construction. To the readings of No. 8527, for maximum temperature of the air has been applied a correction of $-0^{\circ}\cdot9$; to those of No. 4386, for minimum temperature of the air, until January 14 no correction was applied: from January 15 a correction of $-0^{\circ}\cdot2$ was applied. The readings of No. 44285 for maximum temperature of evaporation required a correction of $-0^{\circ}\cdot4$, and the readings of No. 3627 for minimum temperature of evaporation a correction of $+1^{\circ}\cdot2$.

The dry and wet bulb thermometers are usually read at 21^h, 0^h, 3^h, 9^h (astronomical). Readings of the maximum and minimum thermometers are usually taken at 21^h and 9^h. Those of the dry and wet bulb thermometers are employed to correct the indications of the photographic dry and wet bulb thermometers.

PHOTOGRAPHIC DRY AND WET BULB THERMOMETERS.—About 28 feet south-south-east of the south-east angle of the Magnetic Observatory, and about 25 feet east-north-east of the stand carrying the thermometers for eye-observation already described, is an open shed, 10 ft. 6 in. square, standing upon posts 8 feet high, under which are placed the photographic thermometers, the dry-bulb towards the east and the wet-bulb towards the west. Their bulbs are 8 inches in length and 0·4 inch internal bore, and their centres are about 4 feet above the ground. A registering cylinder of ebonite, 10 inches long and 19 inches in circumference, is placed with its axis vertical between the stems of the two thermometers. The registers are made simultaneously on opposite sides of the cylinder, and to avoid any accidental overlapping of the two registers the cylinder is made to revolve once in about 52 hours. The thermometer frames are covered by metal plates having longitudinal slits, so that light can pass through the slit only above the surface of the mercury. At each degree a fine cross wire is placed, thicker at the decades of degrees, and also at 32°, 52°, and 72°. A gas lamp is placed about 9 inches from each thermometer (east of the dry-bulb and west of the wet-bulb), and in each case the light, condensed by a cylindrical lens with axis vertical, shines through the tube above the mercury, and forms a well-defined line of light upon the paper. As the cylinder revolves horizontally under the light passing through the thermometer tube, the paper thus receives a broad sheet of photographic trace, whose breadth, in the direction of the axis of the cylinder, varies with the varying height of the mercury in the thermometer tube. When the sheet is developed the whole of that part of the paper which in each case passed the slit above the mercury will show photographic trace, with thin white lines corresponding to the degrees, the lower part of the paper remaining white; thus the boundary of the photographic trace indicates the varying temperature. The time scale is determined by interruption of the traces made by the observer at registered times, usually three times a day. The length of 24 hours on each of the thermometer traces is about 9 inches. Registration was interrupted from May 4 to 10, the timepiece which drives the registering cylinder having been removed by Messrs. E. Dent and Co. for repair.

RADIATION THERMOMETERS.—From 1880 January 31 to 1882 March 4 the radiation thermometers were exposed on the grass south of the magnetic offices, in what is known as the South Ground. On March 4 they were removed to the Magnet Ground, to the position (a little south of the Magnet House) which they had occupied before removal to the South Ground. The thermometer for solar radiation is a self-registering mercurial maximum thermometer by Negretti and Zambra, No. 38592; its bulb is blackened, and the thermometer is enclosed in a glass sphere from which the air has been exhausted. The thermometer for radiation to the sky is a self-registering spirit minimum thermometer of Rutherford's construction, by Horne and Thornthwaite, No. 3120. The thermometers are laid on short grass; they require no correction for index error.

EARTH THERMOMETERS.—These thermometers were made by Adie, of Edinburgh, under the superintendence of Professor J. D. Forbes. They are placed at the north-west corner of the photographic thermometer shed.

The thermometers are four in number, placed in one hole in the ground, the diameter of which in its upper half is 1 foot and in its lower half about 6 inches, each thermometer being attached in its whole length to a slender piece of wood. The thermometer No. 1 was dropped into the hole to such a depth that the centre of its bulb was 24 French feet (25·6 English feet) below the surface, then dry sand was poured in till the hole was filled to nearly half its height. Then No. 2 was dropped in till the centre of its bulb was 12 French feet below the surface; Nos. 3 and 4 till the centres of their bulbs were respectively 6 and 3 French feet below the surface; and the hole was then completely filled with dry sand. The upper parts of the tubes carrying the scales were left projecting above the surface; No. 1 by 27·5 inches, No. 2 by 28·0 inches, No. 3 by 30·0 inches, and No. 4 by 32·0 inches. Of these lengths, 8·5, 10·0, 11·0, and 14·5 inches respectively are in each case tube with narrow bore. The length of 1° on the scales is 1·9 inch, 1·1 inch, 0·9 inch, and 0·5 inch in each case respectively. The ranges of the scales are for No. 1, 46°·0 to 55°·5; No. 2, 43°·0 to 58°·0; No. 3, 44°·0 to 62°·0; and for No. 4, 37°·0 to 68°·0.

The bulbs of the thermometers are cylindrical, 10 or 12 inches long, and 2 or 3 inches in diameter. The bore of the principal part of each tube, from the bulb to the graduated scale, is very small; in that part to which the scale is attached it is larger; the fluid in the tubes is alcohol tinged red; the scales are of opal glass.

In consequence of the ranges of scale having in previous years been found insufficient, fluid has at times been removed from or added to the thermometers as necessary, proper corresponding alteration being made in the positions of the attached scales. Information in regard to these changes will be found in previous Introductions.

The parts of the tubes above the ground are protected by a small wooden hut fixed to the ground; the sides of the hut are perforated with numerous holes, and it has a double roof; in the north face is a plate of glass, through which the readings are taken. Within the hut are two small thermometers, one, No. 5, with bulb one inch in the ground, another, No. 6, whose bulb is freely exposed in the centre of the hut.

These thermometers are read every day at noon, and the readings are given without correction. The index errors of Nos. 1, 2, 3, and 4 are unknown; No. 5 appears to read too high by 0°·2, and No. 6 by 0°·4.

OSLER'S ANEMOMETER. — This self-registering anemometer, devised by A. Follett Osler, is fixed above the north-western turret of the ancient part of the Observatory. For direction of the wind a large vane, from which a vertical shaft proceeds down to the registering table within the turret, gives motion, by a pinion fixed at its lower end, to a rack-work carrying a pencil. A collar on the vane shaft bears upon anti-friction rollers, running in a cup of oil, rendering the vane very sensitive to changes of direction in light winds. The pencil marks a paper fixed to a board moved horizontally and uniformly by a clock, in a direction transverse to that of the motion of the pencil. The paper carries lines corresponding to the positions of N., E., S., and W. of the vane, with transversal hour-lines. The vane is 60 feet above the adjacent ground, and 215 feet above the mean level of the sea. A fixed mark on the north-eastern turret, in a known azimuth, as determined by celestial observation, is used for examining at any time the position of the direction plate over the registering table, to which reference is made by means of a direction pointer when adjusting a new sheet on the travelling board.

For the pressure of the wind the construction is as follows. At a distance of 2 feet below the vane there is placed a circular pressure plate having an area of $1\frac{1}{3}$ square feet, or 192 square inches, which, moving with the vane, and being thereby kept directed towards the wind, acts against a combination of springs in such way that, with a light wind, slender springs are first brought into action, but, as the wind increases, stiffer springs come into play. For a detailed account of the arrangement adopted the reader is referred to the Introduction for the year 1866. [Until 1866 the pressure plate was a square plate, 1 foot square, for which in that year a circular plate, having an area of 2 square feet, was substituted and employed until the spring of the year 1880, when the present circular plate, having an area of $1\frac{1}{3}$ square feet, was introduced.] A short flexible chain, fixed to a cross bar in connexion with the pressure plate, passing over a pulley in the upper part of the shaft, is then attached to a copper wire running down the centre of the shaft to the registering table, just before reaching which the wire communicates with a short length of silk cord, which, led round a pulley, gives horizontal motion to the arm carrying the pressure pencil. In 1882 September a flexible brass chain was substituted for the connecting copper wire, an alteration which has greatly increased the delicacy of movement of the pressure pencil, every small movement of the pressure plate being now registered. The scale for pressure, in lbs. on the square foot, is experimentally determined from time to time as appears necessary; the pressure pencil is brought to zero by a light spiral spring.

A rain gauge of peculiar construction forms part of the apparatus: this is described under the heading "Rain Gauges."

A new sheet of paper is applied to the instrument every day at noon. The scale of time is equal in length to that of the magnetic registers.

ROBINSON'S ANEMOMETER.—This instrument, mounted above the small building on the roof of the Octagon Room, is constructed on the principle described by the late Dr. Robinson in the *Transactions of the Royal Irish Academy*, Vol. XXII. The revolving hemispherical cups are 56 feet above the adjacent ground, and 211 feet above the mean level of the sea. The motion is given by the pressure of the wind on four hemispherical cups, each 5 inches in diameter, the centre of each cup being 15 inches distant from the vertical axis of rotation. The foot of the axis is a hollow flat cone bearing upon a sharp cone, which rises up from the base of a cup of oil. An endless screw acts on a train of wheels furnished with indices for reading off the amount of motion of the air in miles, and a pinion on the axis of one of the wheels draws upwards a rack, to which is attached a rod passing down to the pencil, which marks the paper placed on the vertical revolving cylinder in the chamber below. A motion of the pencil upwards through a space of one inch represents horizontal motion of the air through 100 miles.

The cylinder is driven by a clock in the usual way, and makes one revolution in 24 hours. A new sheet of paper is applied every day at noon. The scale of time is equal in length to that of Osler's Anemometer and the magnetic registers.

It is assumed, in accordance with the experiments made by Dr. Robinson, that the horizontal motion of the air is three times the space described by the centres of the cups. To verify this conclusion experiments were made in the year 1860 in Greenwich Park with the anemometer then in use, not the same as that now employed. The instrument was fixed to the end of a horizontal arm, which was made to revolve round a vertical axis. For more detailed account of these experiments see the Introduction for 1880. With the arm revolving in the direction N., E., S., W., opposite to the direction of rotation of the cups, for movement of the instrument through one mile 1·15 was registered; with the arm revolving in the direction N., W., S., E., in the same direction as the rotation of the cups, 0·97 was registered. This was considered to confirm sufficiently the accuracy of the assumption.

Rain Gauges.—During the year 1882 eight rain-gauges were employed, placed at different elevations above the ground, complete information in regard to which will be found at page (lxxiii) of the Meteorological Section.

The gauge No. 1 forms part of the Osler Anemometer apparatus, and is self-registering, the record being made on the sheet on which the direction and pressure of the wind are recorded. The receiving surface is a rectangular opening 10 × 20 inches, equal to 200 square inches. The collected water passes into a vessel suspended by spiral springs, which lengthen as the water accumulates, until 0·25 inch is collected, the water then discharges itself by means of the following modification of the syphon. A vertical copper tube, open at both ends, is fixed in the receiver, with one end just projecting below the bottom. Over this tube there is loosely placed, in the receiver, a larger tube, closed at the top. The accumulating water, having risen to the top of the inner tube, begins to flow off into a small tumbling bucket, fixed in a globe placed underneath, and carried by the receiver. When full the bucket falls over, throwing the water into a small exit pipe at the lower part of the globe—the only outlet. The water filling the bore of the pipe creates a partial vacuum in the globe sufficient to cause the longer leg of the syphon to act, and the whole remaining contents of the receiver then run off, through the globe, to a waste pipe. The spiral springs at the same time shorten, and raise the receiver. The gradual descent of the water vessel as the rain falls, and the immediate ascent on discharge of the water, act upon a pencil, and cause a corresponding trace to be made on the paper fixed to the moving board of the anemometer. The rain scale on the paper was determined experimentally by passing a known quantity of water through the receiver. The continuous record thus gives complete information on the rate of the fall of rain.

Gauge No. 2 is a ten-inch circular gauge, placed close to gauge No. 1, its receiving surface being precisely at the same level. The gauge is read daily.

Gauges Nos. 3, 4, and 5 are eight-inch circular gauges, placed respectively on the roof of the Octagon Room, over the roof of the Magnetic Observatory, and on the roof of the Photographic Thermometer Shed. All are read daily.

Gauges Nos. 6, 7, and 8 are also eight-inch circular gauges, placed on the ground south of the Magnetic Observatory; No. 6 is the old daily gauge, No. 7 the old monthly gauge, and No. 8 an additional gauge brought into use in July 1881, as a check on the readings of Nos. 6 and 7, the monthly amounts collected by these gauges showing occasionally greater differences than seemed proper. All three gauges have been read daily since the beginning of July 1881.

The gauges are also read at midnight on the last day of each calendar month.

ELECTROMETER.—The electricity of the atmosphere is collected by means of a Thomson self-recording electrometer, constructed by Mr. White of Glasgow.

For a very full description of the principle of the electrometer reference may be made to Sir William Thomson's "Report on Electrometers and Electrostatic Measurements," contained in the *British Association Report* for the year 1867. It will be sufficient here to give a general description of the instrument which, with its registering apparatus, is planted in the Upper Magnet Room on the slate slab which carries the suspension pulleys of the Horizontal Force Magnet. A thin flat needle of aluminium, carrying immediately above it a small light mirror, is suspended, on the bifilar principle, by two silk fibres from an insulated support within a large Leyden jar. A little strong sulphuric acid is placed in the bottom of the jar, and from the lower side of the needle depends a platinum wire, kept stretched by a weight, which connects the needle with the sulphuric acid, that is with the inner coating of the jar. A positive charge of electricity being given to the needle and jar, this charge is easily maintained at a constant potential by means of a small electric machine or replenisher forming part of the instrument, and by which the charge can be either increased or decreased at pleasure. A gauge is provided for the purpose of indicating at any moment the amount of charge. The needle hangs within four insulated quadrants, which may be supposed to be formed by cutting a circular flat brass box into quarters, and then slightly separating them. The opposite quadrants are placed in metallic connexion.

The electricity of the atmosphere is collected by means of Sir William Thomson's water-dropping apparatus. For this purpose a rectangular cistern of copper, capable of holding above 30 gallons of water, is placed near the ceiling on the west side of the south arm of the Upper Magnet Room. The cistern rests on four pillars of glass, each one encircled and nearly completely enclosed by a glass vessel containing sulphuric acid. A pipe passing out from the cistern, through the south face of the building, extends about six feet into the atmosphere, the nozzle from which the water flows being about ten feet above the ground; the water passing out through a very small hole, and breaking almost immediately into drops, the cistern is brought to the same electrical potential as that point of the atmosphere, which potential is, by means of a connecting wire, communicated to one of the pairs of electrometer quadrants, the other pair being connected to earth. The varying atmospheric potential thus influences the motions of the included needle, causing it to be deflected from zero in one direction or the other, according as the atmospheric potential is greater or less than that of the earth, that is according as it is positive or negative as respects that of the earth.

The small mirror carried by the needle is used for the purpose of obtaining photographic record of its motions. The light of a gas-lamp, falling through a slit upon the mirror, is thence reflected, and by means of a plano-convex cylindrical lens is brought to a focus at the surface of a horizontal cylinder of ebonite, nearly 7 inches long and 16 inches in circumference, which is turned by clock-work. A second fixed mirror, by means of the same gas-lamp, causes a reference line to be traced round the cylinder. The actual zero is found by cutting off the cistern communication, and placing the pairs of quadrants in metallic connexion with each other and with earth. The break of register at each hour is made by the driving-clock of the electrometer cylinder itself. Other photographic arrangements are generally similar to those which have been described for other instruments.

The scale of time is equal in length to that of the magnetic registers.

Inconvenience is sometimes caused by cobwebs making connexion between the cistern or its pipe and the walls of the building, and in winter, interruptions occasionally occur owing to the freezing of the water in the exit pipe.

SUNSHINE INSTRUMENT.—This instrument, contrived by Mr. J. F. Campbell, and kindly given by him to the Royal Observatory, consists of a very accurately formed sphere of glass, nearly 4 inches in diameter, supported concentrically within a well turned hemispherical metal bowl in such a manner that the image of the sun, formed when the sun shines, falls always on the concave surface of the bowl. A strip of blackened millboard being fixed in the bowl, the sun, when shining, burns away the surface at the points at which the image successively falls, by which means the record of periods of sunshine is obtained. The strip is removed after sunset, and a new one fixed ready for the following day. The place of the meridian is marked on the strip before removing it from the bowl. A series of time scales, suitable for different periods of the year, having been prepared, the proper scale is selected and placed against the record, which is then easily transferred to a sheet of paper specially ruled with equal vertical spaces to represent hours, each sheet containing the record for one calendar month. The daily sums, and sums during each hour (reckoning from apparent noon) through the month are thus readily formed. The recorded durations are to be understood as indicating the amount of *bright* sunshine, no register being obtained when the sun shines faintly through fog or cloud, neither is any register usually obtained when the sun's altitude is less than 5°. The instrument is placed on a table upon the platform above the Magnetic Observatory.

OZONOMETER.—This apparatus is fixed on the south-west corner of the roof of the Photographic Thermometer shed, at a height of about 10 feet from the ground. The box in which the papers are exposed is of wood: it is about 8 inches square, blackened inside, and so constructed that there is free circulation of air through the box, without exposure of the paper to light. The papers exposed at 21^h, 3^h, and 9^h are collected respectively at 3^h, 9^h, and 21^h, and the degree of tint produced is compared with a scale of graduated tints, numbered from 0 to 10. The value of ozone for the civil day is determined by taking the degree of tint obtained at each hour of collection as proportional to the period of exposure. Thus to form the values for any given civil day, three-fourths of the value registered at 21^h, the values registered at 3^h and 9^h, and one-fourth of that registered at the following 21^h, are added together, the resulting sum (which appears in the tables of "Daily Results of the Meteorological Observations") being taken as the value referring to the civil day.

The means of the 21ʰ, 3ʰ, and 9ʰ values, as observed, are also given for each month in the foot notes.

§ 7. *Meteorological Reductions.*

The results given in the Meteorological section refer in general to the civil day.

All results in regard to atmospheric pressure, temperature of air and of evaporation and deductions therefrom, and atmospheric electricity, are derived from the photographic records, excepting that the maximum and minimum values of air temperature are those given by eye-observation of the ordinary maximum and minimum thermometers at 9ʰ and 21ʰ, referring, however, to the photographic register when necessary to obtain the values corresponding to the civil day from midnight to midnight. The hourly readings of the photographic traces for the elements mentioned are entered into a form having double argument, the horizontal argument ranging through the 24 hours of the civil day, and the vertical argument through the days of a calendar month. It should be mentioned that before measuring out the electrometer ordinates, a pencil line was first drawn through the trace to represent the general form of the curve in the way described for the magnetic registers (page *xxviii*), excepting that no day has been omitted on account of unusual electrical disturbance, as it has been found difficult to decide on any limit of disturbance beyond which it would seem proper, as regards determination of diurnal inequality, to reject the results. The ordinates of the pencil curve, drawn as described, were measured by a scale of inches, calling the zero 10·00 to avoid negative values: the scale is thus arbitrary. Numbers greater than 10·00 indicate positive potential. Then, for all the photographic elements, the means of the numbers standing in the vertical columns of the monthly forms, into which the values are entered, give the mean monthly photographic values for each hour of the day, the means of the numbers in the horizontal columns giving the mean daily value.

To correct the photographic values of barometer and dry and wet bulb thermometer for small instrumental error, the means of the photographic readings at 21ʰ, 0ʰ, 3ʰ, and 9ʰ in each month are compared with the corresponding corrected mean readings of the standard barometer and standard dry and wet bulb thermometers, as given by eye-observation. A correction applicable to the photographic reading at each of these hours is thus obtained, and, by interpolation, corrections for the intermediate hours are found. The mean of the twenty-four hourly corrections in each month is adopted as the correction applicable to each mean daily value in the month. Thus mean hourly and mean daily values of the several elements are obtained for each month. The process of correction is equivalent to giving photographic indications in terms of corrected standard barometer, and in terms of the standard dry and wet bulb thermometers exposed on the free stand.

f 2

The mean daily temperature of the dew-point and degree of humidity are deduced from the mean daily temperatures of the air and evaporation by use of Glaisher's *Hygrometrical Tables*. The factors by which the dew-point given in these tables is calculated were found by Mr. Glaisher from the comparison of a great number of dew-point determinations obtained by use of Daniell's hygrometer, with simultaneous observations of dry and wet bulb thermometers, combining observations made at the Royal Observatory, Greenwich, with others made in India and at Toronto. The factors are given in the following table.

TABLE OF FACTORS by which the DIFFERENCE between the READINGS of the DRY-BULB and WET-BULB THERMOMETERS is to be MULTIPLIED in order to PRODUCE the CORRESPONDING DIFFERENCE between the DRY-BULB TEMPERATURE and that of the DEW-POINT.

Reading of Dry-bulb Thermometer.	Factor.	Reading of Dry-bulb Thermometer.	Factor.	Reading of Dry-bulb Thermometer.	Factor.	Reading of Dry-bulb Thermometer.	Factor.
10°	8·78	33°	3·01	56°	1·94	79°	1·69
11	8·78	34	2·77	57	1·92	80	1·68
12	8·78	35	2·60	58	1·90	81	1·68
13	8·77	36	2·50	59	1·89	82	1·67
14	8·76	37	2·42	60	1·88	83	1·67
15	8·75	38	2·36	61	1·87	84	1·66
16	8·70	39	2·32	62	1·86	85	1·65
17	8·62	40	2·29	63	1·85	86	1·65
18	8·50	41	2·26	64	1·83	87	1·64
19	8·34	42	2·23	65	1·82	88	1·64
20	8·14	43	2·20	66	1·81	89	1·63
21	7·88	44	2·18	67	1·80	90	1·63
22	7·60	45	2·16	68	1·79	91	1·62
23	7·28	46	2·14	69	1·78	92	1·62
24	6·92	47	2·12	70	1·77	93	1·61
25	6·53	48	2·10	71	1·76	94	1·60
26	6·08	49	2·08	72	1·75	95	1·60
27	5·61	50	2·06	73	1·74	96	1·59
28	5·12	51	2·04	74	1·73	97	1·59
29	4·63	52	2·02	75	1·72	98	1·58
30	4·15	53	2·00	76	1·71	99	1·58
31	3·70	54	1·98	77	1·70	100	1·57
32	3·32	55	1·96	78	1·69		

In the same way the mean hourly values of the dew-point and degree of humidity in each month (pages (lix) and (lx)) have been calculated from the corresponding mean hourly values of air and evaporation temperatures (pages (lviii) and (lix)).

The excess of the mean temperature of the air on each day above the average of 20 years, given in the "Daily Results," is found by comparing the numbers contained in column 6 with a table of average daily temperatures found by smoothing the accidental irregularities of the numbers given in Table LXXVII. of the "Reduction of Greenwich Meteorological Observations, 1847–1873," which are similarly deduced from photographic records. The smoothed numbers are given in the following table.

ADOPTED VALUES of MEAN TEMPERATURE of the AIR, deduced from TWENTY-FOUR HOURLY READINGS on each Day, for every Day of the Year, as obtained from the PHOTOGRAPHIC RECORDS for the Period 1849–1868.

Day of the Month.	January.	February.	March.	April.	May.	June.	July.	August.	September.	October.	November.	December.
1	38·1	40·5	40·3	45·3	48·7	57·5	61·6	62·6	60·1	54·7	47·0	41·5
2	37·9	40·6	40·4	45·7	48·9	57·7	61·5	62·7	60·0	54·4	46·7	41·8
3	37·8	40·7	40·3	46·1	49·1	57·9	61·4	62·7	59·8	54·0	46·4	42·1
4	37·7	40·7	40·5	46·4	49·4	58·1	61·4	62·7	59·7	53·7	46·0	42·4
5	37·6	40·6	40·5	46·6	49·7	58·2	61·5	62·7	59·5	53·4	45·6	42·6
6	37·6	40·4	40·5	46·7	50·0	58·3	61·7	62·7	59·3	53·0	45·2	42·7
7	37·6	40·2	40·6	46·8	50·3	58·4	61·9	62·7	59·0	52·7	44·7	42·8
8	37·7	39·9	40·6	46·8	50·6	58·5	62·2	62·7	58·8	52·5	44·3	42·8
9	37·7	39·6	40·7	46·9	50·8	58·5	62·5	62·7	58·5	52·3	43·8	42·8
10	37·8	39·3	40·7	46·9	51·1	58·6	62·7	62·7	58·3	52·1	43·4	42·7
11	37·9	39·1	40·8	47·0	51·4	58·7	62·9	62·7	58·1	51·9	43·0	42·5
12	38·1	38·9	40·8	47·1	51·8	58·8	63·1	62·6	58·0	51·7	42·6	42·2
13	38·2	38·8	40·9	47·2	52·1	58·9	63·3	62·5	57·8	51·6	42·3	41·8
14	38·3	38·7	41·0	47·4	52·5	59·1	63·4	62·4	57·6	51·4	42·0	41·5
15	38·4	38·7	41·1	47·5	52·9	59·3	63·4	62·3	57·4	51·3	41·8	41·1
16	38·5	38·8	41·2	47·6	53·3	59·5	63·5	62·1	57·3	51·2	41·6	40·8
17	38·6	38·9	41·3	47·8	53·7	59·7	63·5	61·9	57·1	51·1	41·5	40·5
18	38·8	39·0	41·4	47·9	54·1	59·9	63·4	61·8	56·9	51·0	41·5	40·2
19	38·9	39·2	41·4	48·0	54·4	60·2	63·3	61·6	56·8	50·8	41·4	40·0
20	39·1	39·3	41·5	48·1	54·7	60·5	63·2	61·4	56·6	50·6	41·3	39·8
21	39·3	39·5	41·6	48·2	55·0	60·8	63·0	61·3	56·4	50·4	41·2	39·6
22	39·5	39·6	41·7	48·2	55·3	61·1	62·9	61·3	56·2	50·1	41·1	39·4
23	39·6	39·7	41·8	48·3	55·5	61·4	62·8	61·2	56·1	49·7	41·0	39·3
24	39·7	39·8	42·0	48·3	55·7	61·7	62·7	61·1	55·9	49·4	41·0	39·3
25	39·8	39·9	42·3	48·4	55·9	61·9	62·7	61·0	55·8	49·1	40·9	39·2
26	39·9	40·0	42·6	48·4	56·1	62·0	62·7	60·9	55·7	48·8	40·8	39·1
27	40·0	40·1	43·0	48·4	56·3	62·0	62·6	60·8	55·5	48·5	40·8	39·0
28	40·1	40·2	43·4	48·5	56·5	61·9	62·6	60·7	55·4	48·2	40·9	38·8
29	40·2		43·8	48·5	56·8	61·8	62·6	60·6	55·2	47·9	41·0	38·7
30	40·3		44·3	48·6	57·0	61·7	62·6	60·4	54·9	47·6	41·2	38·5
31	40·4		44·8		57·3		62·6	60·3		47·3		38·3
Means	38·7	39·7	41·5	47·5	53·1	59·8	62·6	61·9	57·5	51·0	42·7	40·8

The mean of the twelve monthly values is 49°·7.

The daily register of rain contained in column 18 is that recorded by the gauge No. 6, whose receiving surface is 5 inches above the ground. This gauge is usually read at 21ʰ and 9ʰ. The continuous record of Osler's self-registering gauge shows whether the amounts measured at 21ʰ are to be placed to the same, or to the preceding civil day; and in cases in which rain fell both before and after midnight, also gives the means of ascertaining the proper proportion of the 21ʰ amount which should be placed to each civil day. The number of days of rain given in the foot notes, and in the abstract tables, pages (lvii) and (lxxiii), is formed from the records of this gauge. In this numeration only those days are counted on which the fall amounted to or exceeded 0ⁱⁿ·005.

The indications of electricity are derived from Thomson's Electrometer. On some days, not necessary to be specified, during interruption or failure of photographic registration, the results depend on eye observations.

No particular explanation of the anemometric results seems necessary. It may be understood generally that the greatest pressures usually occur in gusts of short duration.

The mean amount of cloud given in a foot note on the right-hand page, and in the abstract table, page (lvii), is the mean found from observations made usually at 21^h, 0^h, 3^h, and 9^h, of each day.

For understanding the divisions of time under the headings "Clouds and Weather" and "Electricity," the following remarks are necessary:—In regard to Clouds and Weather, the day is divided by columns into two parts (from midnight to noon, and from noon to midnight), and each of these parts is subdivided into two or three parts by colons (:). Thus, when there is a single colon in the first column, it denotes that the indications before it apply (roughly) to the interval from midnight to 6 A.M., and those following it to the interval from 6 A.M. to noon. When there are two colons in the first column, it is to be understood that the twelve hours are divided into three nearly equal parts of four hours each. And similarly for the second column. In regard to Electricity the results are included in one column; in this case the colons divide the whole period of 24 hours (midnight to midnight).

The notation employed for Clouds and Weather is as follows, it being understood that for clouds Howard's Nomenclature is used. The figure denotes the proportion of sky covered by cloud, an overcast sky being represented by 10.

a	denotes	*aurora borealis*	h	denotes	*haze*
ci	...	*cirrus*	slt-h	...	*slight haze*
ci-cu	...	*cirro-cumulus*	hl	...	*hail*
ci-s	...	*cirro-stratus*	l	...	*lightning*
cu	...	*cumulus*	li-cl	...	*light clouds*
cu-s	...	*cumulo-stratus*	lu-co	...	*lunar corona*
d	...	*dew*	lu-ha	...	*lunar halo*
hy-d	...	*heavy dew*	m	...	*mist*
f	...	*fog*	slt-m	...	*slight mist*
slt-f	...	*slight fog*	n	...	*nimbus*
tk-f	...	*thick fog*	p-cl	...	*partially cloudy*
fr	...	*frost*	r	...	*rain*
ho-fr	...	*hoar frost*	c-r	...	*continued rain*
g	...	*gale*	fr-r	...	*frozen rain*
hy-g	...	*heavy gale*	fq-r	...	*frequent rain*
glm	...	*gloom*	hy-r	...	*heavy rain*
gt-glm	...	*great gloom*	c-hy-r	...	*continued heavy rain*

m-r	denotes *misty rain*	sc	denotes *scud*
fq-m-r	... *frequent misty rain*	li-sc	... *light scud*
oc-m-r	... *occasional misty rain*	sl	... *sleet*
oc-r	... *occasional rain*	sn	... *snow*
sh-r	... *shower of rain*	oc-sn	... *occasional snow*
shs-r	... *showers of rain*	slt-sn	... *slight snow*
slt-r	... *slight rain*	so-ha	... *solar halo*
oc-slt-r	... *occasional slight rain*	sq	... *squall*
th-r	... *thin rain*	sqs	... *squalls*
fq-th-r	... *frequent thin rain*	fq-sqs	... *frequent squalls*
oc-th-r	... *occasional thin rain*	hy-sqs	... *heavy squalls*
hy-sh	... *heavy shower*	fq-hy-sqs	... *frequent heavy squalls*
slt-sh	... *slight shower*	oc-sqs	... *occasional squalls*
fq-shs	... *frequent showers*	t	... *thunder*
hy-shs	... *heavy showers*	t-sm	... *thunder storm*
fq-hy-shs	... *frequent heavy showers*	th-cl	... *thin clouds*
oc-hy-shs	... *occasional heavy showers*	v	... *variable*
li-shs	... *light showers*	vv	... *very variable*
oc-shs	... *occasional showers*	w	... *wind*
s	... *stratus*	st-w	... *strong wind*

The following is the notation employed for Electricity:—

N	denotes *negative*	w	denotes *weak*
P	... *positive*	s	... *strong*
m	... *moderate*	v	... *variable*

The duplication of the letter denotes intensity of the modification described, thus, s s, is very strong; v v, very variable. 0 indicates no electricity, and a dash "—" accidental failure of the apparatus.

The remaining columns in the tables of "Daily Results" seem to require no special remark; all necessary explanation regarding the results therein contained will be found in the notes at the foot of the left-hand page, or in the descriptions of the several instruments given in § 6.

In regard to the comparisons of the extremes and means, &c. of meteorological elements with average values, contained in the foot notes, it may be mentioned that the photographic barometric results are compared with the corresponding barometric results, 1854–1873, and the photographic thermometric results and deductions therefrom with the corresponding thermometric results, 1849–1868 (see "Reduction of Greenwich Meteorological Observations 1847-1873"). Other deductions, from eye observations, are compared with averages for the period 1841-1881.

The tables of Meteorological Abstracts following the tables of "Daily Results require no special explanation.

It may be pointed out that the monthly means for barometer and temperature of air and evaporation contained in the tables referring to diurnal inequality, pages (lviii) and (lix), do not in some cases agree with the true monthly means given in the daily results, pages (xxx) to (lii), and in the table on page (lvii), in consequence of occasional interruption of the photographic register, at which times daily values to complete the daily results could be supplied from the eye observations, as mentioned in the foot notes, but hourly values, for the diurnal inequality tables, could not be so supplied. In such cases however the means given with these tables are the proper means to be used in connexion with the numbers standing immediately above them, for formation of the actual diurnal inequality.

In preparing the table of "Abstract of the Changes of the Direction of the Wind" it was formerly the practice to consider all turnings of the vane, but in the formation of the table contained in the present volume, page (lxvi), those turnings which are evidently of an accidental nature, though still included in the body of the table, have been placed in brackets and omitted in the formation of the resulting value for the whole year.

In regard to electricity, in addition to giving the hourly values in each month, including all available days, the days in each month have been in this year further divided into two groups, one containing all days on which the rainfall amounted to or exceeded $0^{in}\cdot020$, the other including only days on which no rainfall was recorded, the values of daily rainfall given in column 18 of the "Daily Results" being adopted in selecting the days. These additional tables are given on pages (lxxi) and (lxxii) respectively.

In regard to the observations of Luminous Meteors it is simply necessary to say that in general only special meteor showers are watched for, such as those of August and November. The observers of meteors in the year 1882 were Mr. Ellis, Mr. Nash, Mr. Greengrass, Mr. Hugo, Mr. McClellan, and Mr. Finch; their observations are distinguished by the initials E, N, G, H, M, and F respectively.

Royal Observatory, Greenwich,
1884 April 17.

W. H. M. CHRISTIE.

ROYAL OBSERVATORY, GREENWICH.

RESULTS

OF

MAGNETICAL OBSERVATIONS.

1882.

ROYAL OBSERVATORY, GREENWICH.

REDUCTION

OF THE

MAGNETIC OBSERVATIONS

(EXCLUDING THE DAYS OF GREAT MAGNETIC DISTURBANCE).

1882.

TABLE I.—MEAN MAGNETIC DECLINATION WEST FOR EACH ASTRONOMICAL DAY.

(Each result is the mean of 24 hourly ordinates from the photographic register.)

1882.

Days of the Month.	January.	February.	March.	April.	May.	June.	July.	August.	September.	October.	November.	December.
	18°	18°	18°	18°	18°	18°	18°	18°	18°	18°	18°	18°
	′	′	′	′	′	′	′	′	′	′	′	′
1	25·4	26·1	25·2	24·1	22·4	22·5	21·2	22·1	21·2	21·1	20·7	18·9
2	24·7	25·1	24·9	24·1	22·8	22·9	22·1	21·9	20·4	..	19·8	19·4
3	25·7	25·6	24·6	24·2	23·9	22·2	21·7	22·4	20·3	21·5	20·2	18·9
4	24·5	25·8	25·5	24·0	23·1	22·6	22·0	..	21·0	19·6	20·6	18·6
5	24·5	25·8	24·5	23·7	23·0	22·6	22·3	21·4	21·0	..	19·0	19·4
6	24·2	23·7	24·4	23·7	23·0	22·6	22·2	20·7	20·8	21·2	20·1	19·6
7	25·5	25·3	24·0	23·6	22·1	22·9	22·7	22·0	21·7	20·5	21·1	19·7
8	23·8	24·8	24·1	24·0	22·9	22·9	23·2	21·3	21·0	20·0	19·6	19·5
9	25·1	26·0	24·3	23·9	23·4	22·4	21·9	21·6	20·2	20·3	20·4	20·5
10	24·8	24·8	23·5	24·1	24·3	22·2	22·0	21·2	21·4	20·4	20·4	20·8
11	24·3	23·0	23·3	23·2	24·9	22·9	22·0	20·7	18·8	20·5	21·1	21·0
12	24·3	24·4	24·0	23·7	23·8	23·4	21·8	22·9	20·9	20·3	..	19·9
13	25·2	24·9	24·1	23·7	23·6	21·4	21·6	20·0	20·4	20·1	..	19·1
14	23·7	25·3	24·3	24·7	23·7	23·3	21·1	21·1	20·5	19·9	22·3	19·0
15	25·0	25·4	23·9	24·4	23·7	23·4	21·1	21·3	20·5	21·5	20·8	18·5
16	24·9	25·2	24·3	..	22·9	22·1	22·0	21·6	20·1	21·0	20·4	19·3
17	25·0	24·7	24·2	..	23·4	22·0	22·5	21·5	19·7	21·8	..	19·1
18	25·3	25·6	24·5	23·6	23·5	21·7	21·7	20·9	20·1	21·2	..	19·0
19	22·8	26·7	25·7	..	23·0	21·9	22·1	21·6	19·4	21·0	..	19·7
20	24·3	24·3	24·9	..	24·5	21·7	22·7	22·2	19·9	20·8	..	18·9
21	25·0	25·2	25·1	23·3	21·8	22·6	21·9	20·9	20·0	21·2	..	20·1
22	24·2	25·1	24·6	22·2	24·2	22·2	21·5	22·1	19·8	21·2	19·6	19·5
23	24·6	25·3	24·2	23·2	24·1	22·4	22·6	21·9	20·3	22·0	19·2	19·6
24	24·9	25·4	24·1	22·3	23·8	..	22·1	21·8	20·8	24·0	19·2	19·7
25	24·8	25·1	23·9	22·2	22·4	21·7	22·1	20·4	19·9	21·1	18·6	19·0
26	25·1	25·1	22·9	23·0	24·1	22·3	22·0	22·1	19·7	21·5	19·9	17·9
27	24·4	25·5	23·5	23·4	23·2	22·9	21·7	21·3	19·3	20·9	20·1	18·0
28	24·7	25·3	24·0	21·4	24·1	21·2	21·7	21·5	19·8	20·8	19·8	17·9
29	24·2		24·2	21·6	23·6	21·9	21·4	22·1	19·9	21·3	20·1	18·3
30	25·2		24·3	22·5	23·2	22·5	23·6	22·7	20·0	20·5	19·8	18·6
31	24·6		23·9		23·4		21·9	22·4		20·7		18·3

TABLE II.—MONTHLY MEANS OF MAGNETIC DECLINATION WEST AT EACH HOUR OF THE DAY.

1882.

Hour, Greenwich Mean Solar Time.	January.	February.	March.	April.	May.	June.	July.	August.	September.	October.	November.	December.
	18°	18°	18°	18°	18°	18°	18°	18°	18°	18°	18°	18°
h	′	′	′	′	′	′	′	′	′	′	′	′
0	27·2	28·8	28·6	29·2	29·5	26·6	26·4	26·7	25·6	26·0	23·3	21·6
1	28·0	29·7	30·6	30·8	30·8	27·8	27·9	28·2	26·8	26·7	23·8	22·1
2	27·5	29·7	30·7	30·7	30·7	28·0	27·7	28·1	26·1	25·8	23·3	21·8
3	26·6	28·4	29·2	28·7	29·7	27·3	26·8	26·7	24·8	24·5	22·2	21·1
4	26·0	26·8	27·0	26·8	28·0	26·0	25·3	24·7	22·8	22·5	21·4	20·4
5	25·4	25·7	25·2	25·2	26·2	24·7	23·8	23·0	21·3	21·4	20·9	20·0
6	25·1	25·2	24·4	23·6	24·5	23·7	22·9	21·7	20·4	20·7	20·2	19·0
7	24·8	24·7	23·6	22·5	23·3	22·7	22·2	21·1	19·4	19·7	19·4	18·5
8	23·8	24·0	23·0	22·1	22·6	22·4	21·8	20·7	18·7	19·0	18·8	17·7
9	22·9	23·5	22·6	22·4	22·1	22·1	21·6	20·6	18·8	18·7	17·9	17·1
10	22·3	23·3	22·5	22·1	22·0	21·8	21·3	20·4	18·6	18·8	17·9	17·4
11	22·1	23·5	22·4	21·9	21·8	21·8	21·1	20·1	18·5	19·0	18·4	17·4
12	22·4	23·6	22·5	21·8	21·5	21·6	20·6	20·0	18·7	19·0	18·8	17·3
13	22·9	23·8	22·7	22·0	21·4	21·3	20·2	20·1	19·1	19·3	19·2	17·9
14	23·6	24·1	22·9	21·7	21·0	20·8	20·2	19·7	19·2	19·7	19·5	18·4
15	24·1	24·1	22·9	21·0	20·7	20·8	20·1	19·6	19·0	20·0	19·8	18·5
16	24·3	23·9	22·9	21·3	20·5	20·2	19·9	19·4	19·1	20·1	19·9	18·7
17	24·5	24·3	23·2	21·5	19·9	19·3	19·3	19·2	19·1	20·1	19·5	19·0
18	24·5	24·4	23·0	21·0	19·3	18·4	18·5	18·6	18·4	20·1	19·5	19·2
19	24·4	24·6	22·1	19·8	18·8	18·1	18·5	17·7	16·9	19·5	19·6	19·1
20	24·1	24·0	21·0	18·7	19·0	18·2	18·7	17·7	16·3	18·4	19·0	19·4
21	24·2	23·7	21·1	19·8	20·3	19·0	19·4	18·9	17·2	18·7	18·8	19·2
22	25·1	24·9	22·9	22·3	23·0	21·0	20·6	21·2	19·5	21·1	19·9	19·7
23	26·2	27·0	25·7	26·1	26·5	23·8	23·3	24·0	22·8	24·0	21·7	20·6

TABLE III.

1882.

Month.	Mean Magnetic Declination in each Month. West.	Excess of Magnetic Declination above 17°, expressed as Westerly Force, in terms of Gauss's Metrical Unit.
	° ′	
January	18. 24·7	0·04445
February	18. 25·2	·04471
March	18. 24·5	·04424
April	18. 23·5	·04382
May	18. 23·5	·04382
June	18. 22·4	·04324
July	18. 22·0	·04303
August	18. 21·6	·04282
September	18. 20·3	·04214
October	18. 21·0	·04251
November	18. 20·1	·04204
December	18. 19·2	·04156
Mean	18. 22·3	0·04320

The unit adopted in column 3 is the Millimètre-Milligramme-Second Unit. To express the forces on the Centimètre-Gramme-Second (C.G.S.) system, the numbers must be divided by 10, equivalent to shifting the decimal point one step towards the left.

TABLE IV.—MEAN HORIZONTAL MAGNETIC FORCE (diminished by a Constant) FOR EACH ASTRONOMICAL DAY.

(Each result is the mean of 24 hourly ordinates from the photographic register, expressed in parts of the whole Horizontal Force, and is uncorrected for temperature.)

1882.

Days of the Month.	January.	February.	March.	April.	May.	June.	July.	August.	September.	October.	November.	December.
1	..	0·13818	0·13774	0·13636	0·13508	0·13537	0·13581	0·13431	0·13733	0·13722	0·13505	0·13437
2	..	·13869	·13788	·13653	·13437	·13521	·13563	·13485	·13658	..	·13533	·13506
3	0·13815	·13888	·13783	·13648	·13501	·13645	·13608	·13534	·13637	·13448	·13473	·13533
4	·13852	·13932	·13765	·13548	·13520	·13676	·13637	..	·13649	·13567	·13515	·13451
5	·13840	·13858	·13767	·13607	·13526	·13709	·13613	·13441	·13598	..	·13518	·13494
6	·13780	·13766	·13755	·13562	·13504	·13748	·13636	·13444	·13658	·13335	·13487	·13530
7	·13862	·13832	..	·13597	·13529	·13750	·13629	·13424	·13661	·13355	·13470	·13544
8	·13884	·13806	..	·13570	·13555	·13770	·13643	·13488	·13690	·13399	·13437	·13363
9	·13799	·13824	..	·13595	·13598	·13766	·13568	·13555	·13670	·13437	·13420	·13523
10	·13812	·13841	·13382	·13606	·13585	·13765	·13605	·13515	·13697	·13459	·13483	·13568
11	·13747	·13799	·13400	·13615	·13518	·13774	·13651	·13581	·13688	·13508	·13447	·13529
12	·13730	·13747	·13471	·13579	·13506	·13611	·13657	·13542	·13652	·13490	..	·13515
13	·13755	·13803	·13465	·13663	·13482	·13571	·13650	·13546	·13665	·13520	..	·13550
14	·13749	·13789	·13475	·13483	·13426	·13647	·13677	·13546	·13680	·13473	·13357	·13554
15	·13777	·13764	·13515	·13495	·13435	·13513	·13719	·13489	·13700	·13484	·13440	·13485
16	·13772	·13764	·13435	..	·13543	·13473	·13632	·13529	·13691	·13424	·13471	·13454
17	·13796	·13738	·13500	..	·13533	·13486	·13644	·13541	·13689	·13437	..	·13555
18	·13861	·13710	·13555	·13343	·13487	·13528	·13680	·13597	·13688	·13401	..	·13547
19	·13636	·13735	·13472	..	·13519	·13585	·13690	·13501	·13702	·13462	..	·13520
20	·13684	·13583	·13475	..	·13524	·13554	·13641	·13515	·13681	·13534	..	·13370
21	·13814	·13667	·13569	·13393	·13505	·13526	·13665	·13515	·13682	·13498	..	·13451
22	·13828	·13660	·13688	·13384	·13464	·13550	·13716	·13533	·13662	·13355	·13277	·13499
23	·13847	·13727	·13699	·13441	·13467	·13578	·13681	·13651	·13681	·13465	·13424	·13529
24	·13863	·13732	·13640	·13450	·13504	..	·13728	·13665	·13727	·13422	·13414	·13596
25	·13900	·13781	·13675	·13520	·13586	·13460	·13573	·13672	·13594	·13364	·13370	·13636
26	·13942	·13789	·13666	·13561	·13556	·13493	·13558	·13654	·13633	·13440	·13406	·13651
27	·13907	·13775	·13640	·13544	·13523	·13477	·13572	·13645	·13620	·13461	·13355	·13630
28	·13945	·13772	·13658	·13504	·13492	·13533	·13618	·13657	·13662	·13361	·13406	·13557
29	·13939		·13651	·13518	·13414	·13493	·13628	·13649	·13694	·13429	·1350[illegible]	·13380
30	·13932		·13634	·13548	·13526	·13528	·13582	·13625	·13724	·13464	·13466	·13553
31	·13953		·13639		·13497		·13390	·13682		·13484		·13578

TABLE V.—MEANS of READINGS of the THERMOMETER placed within the box inclosing the HORIZONTAL FORCE MAGNET, for each Astronomical Day.

1882.

Days of the Month.	January.	February.	March.	April.	May.	June.	July.	August.	September.	October.	November.	December.
d	°	°	°	°	°	°	°	°	°	°	°	°
1	..	58·6	61·1	62·6	60·8	64·5	63·3	66·5	65·1	64·1	59·1	59·1
2	..	59·0	60·3	63·0	62·9	64·9	64·2	66·6	66·1	..	59·4	59·5
3	62·2	60·0	59·8	63·4	64·8	64·6	65·0	64·8	65·8	63·0	60·0	60·6
4	60·3	58·6	59·7	63·5	64·0	63·2	64·2	..	63·3	61·1	59·5	60·6
5	61·5	59·0	60·4	62·5	64·0	63·0	63·6	65·1	64·8	..	59·4	59·5
6	61·5	60·4	60·8	63·3	63·3	63·2	63·3	63·6	64·3	63·0	59·8	58·4
7	59·8	60·7	..	63·2	63·7	62·3	62·6	65·8	63·9	64·6	59·1	59·6
8	60·0	59·8	..	62·9	62·1	61·6	62·8	65·2	63·9	64·4	57·7	59·8
9	61·3	58·6	..	61·7	62·0	61·0	62·9	64·6	63·8	64·1	57·6	58·9
10	61·6	59·0	63·8	61·9	63·5	60·5	62·5	64·6	63·7	64·1	58·5	57·1
11	62·3	59·8	63·5	62·5	64·5	59·6	62·8	65·0	63·7	63·9	59·0	57·3
12	62·8	60·5	62·5	62·9	63·8	59·3	63·3	66·2	62·6	62·0	..	58·4
13	62·7	61·1	62·4	63·1	62·4	59·4	63·3	66·9	61·4	61·5	..	59·4
14	61·2	62·5	63·0	63·0	59·8	60·6	64·6	67·1	60·3	61·9	59·9	59·6
15	60·1	61·9	63·3	62·4	59·9	60·5	64·7	66·1	60·5	60·7	59·7	59·9
16	60·9	61·3	63·6	..	60·6	61·3	64·3	64·0	61·8	60·8	58·6	60·4
17	60·2	62·7	63·2	..	61·1	61·4	64·2	64·3	62·2	61·3	..	60·7
18	59·3	62·8	62·8	60·9	62·4	60·8	64·3	65·1	62·8	63·4	..	60·6
19	60·8	60·8	62·1	..	62·8	60·5	64·3	64·9	64·4	62·8	..	60·2
20	60·8	61·5	62·2	..	63·3	61·7	64·0	64·0	64·2	58·9	..	60·2
21	60·0	62·5	59·9	63·5	64·4	62·2	64·6	63·5	62·6	62·7	..	60·0
22	60·0	62·6	59·6	64·0	66·6	61·9	64·9	63·7	62·2	61·8	61·5	59·2
23	59·3	61·2	60·5	62·8	65·9	61·5	64·0	63·1	62·6	58·0	60·9	58·6
24	58·7	61·1	61·5	62·0	64·9	..	63·6	62·8	62·9	57·8	60·2	57·2
25	58·0	61·9	61·2	60·4	64·3	62·6	63·4	63·4	62·9	57·2	58·3	58·2
26	58·8	62·3	60·6	60·6	65·0	62·8	63·7	64·2	63·2	57·3	58·7	58·3
27	60·6	62·6	60·8	60·0	65·7	63·2	64·3	63·9	62·3	58·0	60·4	60·5
28	61·7	61·9	61·4	60·2	66·5	64·0	64·6	63·9	61·5	58·0	60·9	60·7
29	60·6		62·2	59·8	67·6	64·4	65·1	63·5	61·2	57·1	60·8	60·2
30	60·7		62·1	58·7	66·9	63·4	65·3	63·6	62·0	57·5	59·1	60·9
31	59·6		62·5		65·2		65·2	63·8		58·6		61·0

TABLE VI.—MONTHLY MEANS OF HORIZONTAL MAGNETIC FORCE (diminished by a Constant) AT EACH HOUR OF THE DAY.

(The results are expressed in parts of the whole Horizontal Force, and are uncorrected for temperature.)

1882.

Hour, Greenwich Mean Solar Time.	January.	February.	March.	April.	May.	June.	July.	August.	September.	October.	November.	December.
h												
0	0·13782	0·13711	0·13519	0·13417	0·13392	0·13482	0·13540	0·13444	0·13574	0·13372	0·13377	0·13485
1	·13809	·13734	·13562	·13470	·13449	·13508	·13571	·13505	·13627	·13403	·13402	·13510
2	·13819	·13755	·13587	·13517	·13402	·13561	·13625	·13554	·13664	·13431	·13419	·13523
3	·13824	·13775	·13598	·13550	·13523	·13611	·13676	·13590	·13687	·13443	·13433	·13543
4	·13830	·13780	·13613	·13570	·13542	·13654	·13700	·13615	·13700	·13445	·13449	·13549
5	·13829	·13780	·13622	·13591	·13573	·13682	·13717	·13625	·13715	·13464	·13471	·13546
6	·13829	·13790	·13618	·13620	·13603	·13716	·13730	·13632	·13727	·13485	·13468	·13534
7	·13831	·13791	·13617	·13618	·13614	·13728	·13728	·13632	·13730	·13494	·13473	·13540
8	·13827	·13802	·13627	·13612	·13609	·13707	·13711	·13628	·13735	·13496	·13471	·13535
9	·13823	·13793	·13636	·13608	·13596	·13679	·13693	·13623	·13734	·13487	·13463	·13544
10	·13827	·13794	·13644	·13613	·13571	·13658	·13674	·13618	·13727	·13503	·13466	·13542
11	·13827	·13806	·13641	·13617	·13555	·13643	·13662	·13618	·13722	·13494	·13470	·13536
12	·13827	·13804	·13634	·13591	·13557	·13632	·13649	·13608	·13721	·13495	·13464	·13531
13	·13822	·13799	·13626	·13579	·13567	·13627	·13641	·13593	·13716	·13496	·13452	·13515
14	·13827	·13796	·13624	·13571	·13534	·13617	·13638	·13587	·13714	·13487	·13446	·13510
15	·13833	·13800	·13622	·13565	·13550	·13613	·13642	·13586	·13722	·13482	·13443	·13526
16	·13846	·13808	·13626	·13538	·13544	·13617	·13635	·13583	·13719	·13492	·13467	·13545
17	·13863	·13807	·13629	·13560	·13528	·13603	·13618	·13565	·13712	·13497	·13484	·13559
18	·13867	·13814	·13643	·13547	·13500	·13564	·13593	·13541	·13688	·13491	·13470	·13568
19	·13858	·13811	·13641	·13524	·13460	·13524	·13567	·13507	·13643	·13467	·13467	·13566
20	·13856	·13793	·13609	·13479	·13399	·13492	·13542	·13439	·13589	·13422	·13440	·13543
21	·13828	·13735	·13553	·13419	·13355	·13457	·13514	·13410	·13538	·13375	·13401	·13512
22	·13803	·13694	·13514	·13383	·13327	·13446	·13406	·13394	·13505	·13349	·13367	·13495
23	·13794	·13693	·13510	·13401	·13350	·13463	·13501	·13416	·13525	·13355	·13365	·13487

TABLE VII.—MONTHLY MEANS of READINGS of the THERMOMETER placed within the box inclosing the HORIZONTAL FORCE MAGNET, at each of the ordinary Hours of Observation.

1882.

Hour, Greenwich Mean Solar Time.	January.	February.	March.	April.	May.	June.	July.	August.	September.	October.	November.	December.
h	°	°	°	°	°	°	°	°	°	°	°	°
0	60·5	60·7	61·4	61·9	63·6	62·0	63·8	64·6	63·0	60·9	59·4	59·3
1	60·6	60·8	61·5	62·1	64·0	62·1	63·9	64·8	63·1	61·1	59·6	59·6
2	60·7	60·9	61·6	62·3	64·3	62·3	64·1	64·9	63·3	61·3	59·8	59·7
3	60·8	61·1	61·9	62·4	64·5	62·4	64·2	65·0	63·4	61·4	59·9	59·8
9	61·0	61·4	62·8	63·2	64·4	62·6	64·6	65·4	63·7	61·7	60·0	59·9
21	60·4	60·7	61·5	61·7	62·7	61·7	63·7	64·4	62·9	60·6	59·2	59·4
22	60·4	60·7	61·4	61·6	63·0	61·7	63·7	64·4	62·9	60·6	59·2	59·4
23	60·3	60·7	61·3	61·6	63·2	61·8	63·8	64·4	62·9	60·6	59·2	59·4

TABLE VIII.

1882.

Month.	Mean Horizontal Magnetic Force in each Month, uncorrected for Temperature. Expressed in parts of the whole Horizontal Force (diminished by a Constant).	Expressed in terms of Gauss's Metrical Unit (diminished by a Constant).	Mean Temperature.
January	0·13828	0·24946	60°·6
February	·13778	·24856	60·9
March, 1 to 6	·13772	·24845	60·3
March, 10 to 31	·13559	·24460	62·0
April	·13541	·24428	62·1
May	·13509	·24370	63·7
June	·13595	·24525	62·1
July	·13628	·24585	64·0
August	·13556	·24455	64·7
September	·13672	·24664	63·1
October	·13455	·24273	61·0
November	·13443	·24251	59·5
December	·13532	·24412	59·6

The unit adopted in column 3 is the Millimètre-Milligramme-Second Unit. The value of the whole Horizontal Force in terms of this unit is 1·80 nearly. To express the forces on the Centimètre-Gramme-Second (C.G.S.) system, the numbers must be divided by 10, equivalent to shifting the decimal point one step towards the left.

On March 7 the cord which sustains the suspension skein gave way, thus breaking the continuity of the observations.

TABLE IX.—MEAN VERTICAL MAGNETIC FORCE (diminished by a Constant) FOR EACH ASTRONOMICAL DAY.

(Each result is the mean of 24 hourly ordinates from the photographic register, expressed in parts of the whole Vertical Force, and is uncorrected for temperature.)

1882.

Days of the Month.	January.	February.	March.	April.	May.	June.	July.	August.	September.	October.	November.	December.
d												
1	..	0·03168	0·03402	0·03673	0·03356	0·03270	0·01943	0·02216	..	..	0·05250	0·05233
2	..	·03201	·03311	·03675	·03561	·03305	·02016	·02223	..	..	·05250	·05227
3	..	·03279	·03297	·03753	·03820	·03321	·02100	·01997	..	0·05288	·05272	·05257
4	0·03341	·03120	·03259	·03796	·03771	·03166	·01990	..	..	·05285	·05260	·05271
5	·03445	·03145	·03309	·03694	·03784	·03127	·01915	·02034	..	..	·05257	·05238
6	·03432	·03313	·03379	·03770	·03695	·03108	·01841	·02054	..	·05390	·05264	·05210
7	·03253	·03361	·03483	·03769	·03718	·03034	·01887	[illegible]	..	[illegible]	·05263	·05213
8	·03252	·03274	·03605	·03738	·03523	·02938	·01823	·01993	..	·05352	·05222	·05208
9	·03388	·03145	·03652	·03557	·03555	·02854	·01833	·01927	..	·05333	·05220	·05241
10	·03412	·03198	·03692	·03524	·03629	·02724	·01815	·01921	..	·05332	·05212	·05183

TABLE IX.—MEAN VERTICAL MAGNETIC FORCE (diminished by a Constant) FOR EACH ASTRONOMICAL DAY—*concluded.*

1882.

Days of the Month.	January.	February.	March.	April.	May.	June.	July.	August.	September.	October.	November.	December.
11	0·03527	0·03313	0·03714	0·03601	0·03757	0·02648	0·01835	0·01927	..	0·05347	0·05223	0·05172
12	·03611	·03396	·03580	·03635	·03743	·02573	·01894	·02143	..	·05314	..	·05206
13	·03541	·03432	·03561	·03615	·03554	·02603	·01877	·02158	..	·05298	..	·05228
14	·03385	·03573	·03653	·03661	·03360	·02717	·01999	·02183	..	·05304	·05268	·05238
15	·03262	·03485	·03666	·03575	·03379	·02725	·02013	·02046	..	·05287	·05244	·05244
16	·03377	·03440	·03755	..	·03363	·02841	·01938	..	..	·05260	·05210	·05267
17	·03299	·03593	·03643	..	·03437	·02804	·01964	..	..	·05270	..	·05265
18	·03173	·03576	·03552	·03528	·03512	·02733	·01981	..	..	·05321	..	·05259
19	·03407	·03372	·03475	..	·03535	·02771	·01950	..	..	·05307	..	·05270
20	·03433	·03420	·03575	..	·03605	·02877	·01929	..	..	·05228	..	·05252
21	·03363	·03553	·03347	·03737	·03718	·01842	·01984	..	..	·05315	..	·05281
22	·03342	·03609	·03233	·03783	·03966	·01796	·02009	..	..	·05295	·05318	·05258
23	·03255	·03445	·03296	·03607	·03887	·01730	·01896	..	..	·05203	·05328	·05235
24	·03195	·03415	·03419	·03579	·03837	..	·01885	..	..	·05198	·05313	·05186
25	·03083	·03490	·03440	·03429	·03727	·01891	·01867	..	..	·05202	·05290	·05203
26	·03158	·03473	·03300	·03374	·03805	·01868	·01872	..	..	·05189	·05258	·05247
27	·03366	·03549	·03378	·03256	·03866	·01922	·01960	..	..	·05186	·05283	·05269
28	·03487	·03495	·03428	·03284	·03932	·02011	·01963	..	..	·05216	·05273	·05288
29	·03378		·03504	·03203	·04107	·02035	·02044	..	..	·05213	·05248	·05292
30	·03389		·03514	·03170	·04009	·01933	·02060	..	..	·05211	·05237	·05313
31	·03281		..		..		·02069	..		·05237		·05320

TABLE X.—MEANS of READINGS of the THERMOMETER placed within the box inclosing the VERTICAL FORCE MAGNET, for each Astronomical Day.

1882.

Days of the Month.	January.	February.	March.	April.	May.	June.	July.	August.	September.	October.	November.	December.
	°	°	°	°	°	°	°	°	°	°	°	°
1	..	58·1	60·8	62·8	60·6	64·0	62·7	65·8	..	..	60·1	59·1
2	..	58·2	60·1	63·0	62·3	64·5	63·6	66·0	..	..	60·3	59·4
3	..	59·2	59·7	63·5	64·1	64·3	64·3	64·3	..	63·3	60·5	60·5
4	59·1	57·7	59·4	63·6	63·6	62·6	63·4	..	..	61·5	59·9	60·6
5	59·8	57·9	60·1	62·8	63·7	62·6	62·8	64·4	..	..	59·9	59·3
6	59·6	59·5	60·6	63·5	63·2	62·5	62·5	64·8	..	63·2	60·2	58·3
7	58·0	60·3	61·9	63·3	63·4	61·8	62·0	64·9	..	64·5	59·4	59·5
8	58·2	59·3	63·0	62·9	62·0	61·0	62·1	64·3	..	64·4	58·2	59·8
9	59·5	58·2	63·4	61·5	62·0	60·3	62·0	63·7	..	64·0	58·2	58·8
10	60·0	58·7	63·7	61·4	63·3	59·8	61·9	63·8	..	63·8	58·7	56·7
11	60·7	59·8	63·7	62·1	64·3	59·5	62·1	64·3	..	63·7	59·7	56·9
12	61·5	60·4	62·5	62·6	63·9	58·7	62·5	65·5	..	61·9	..	58·5
13	61·2	61·0	62·4	62·5	62·6	59·1	62·7	65·9	..	61·7	..	59·8
14	59·6	62·3	63·0	62·7	60·1	60·3	63·8	66·0	..	61·9	59·3	59·9
15	58·4	61·5	63·4	62·0	60·1	60·3	64·1	65·0	..	60·6	59·2	59·5
16	59·4	60·9	63·8	..	60·5	60·9	63·6	..	..	60·7	58·6	59·7
17	58·9	62·7	63·1	..	61·2	61·0	63·5	..	..	60·9	..	59·9
18	57·9	62·1	62·1	61·0	62·4	60·4	63·6	..	..	63·0	..	60·0
19	60·2	60·3	61·4	..	62·7	60·1	63·5	..	..	62·5	..	59·9
20	60·5	60·7	62·2	..	63·0	61·1	63·4	..	..	59·1	..	60·2
21	59·8	62·1	59·9	63·4	64·2	62·0	64·0	..	..	62·7	..	59·9
22	59·7	62·4	59·6	63·6	66·2	61·3	64·2	..	..	61·7	61·9	59·3
23	58·8	61·0	60·4	62·6	65·5	61·0	63·4	..	..	58·4	61·5	58·6
24	58·1	60·9	61·3	61·8	64·7	..	62·9	..	..	58·2	60·8	57·3
25	56·9	61·6	61·1	60·1	64·0	62·1	62·9	..	..	57·8	58·9	58·6
26	58·0	61·6	60·3	60·3	64·6	62·2	63·2	..	..	57·9	59·1	60·3
27	60·1	62·3	60·7	59·5	65·3	62·6	63·7	..	..	58·7	60·3	61·0
28	61·2	61·7	61·4	60·1	66·0	63·4	64·0	..	..	58·9	60·6	61·0
29	60·4		62·3	59·2	67·3	63·6	64·6	..	..	58·1	60·8	60·6
30	60·3		62·3	58·3	66·4	62·7	64·7	..	..	58·6	59·3	60·9
31	59·2		..		..		64·8	..		59·7		60·7

TABLE XI.—MONTHLY MEANS OF VERTICAL MAGNETIC FORCE (diminished by a Constant) AT EACH HOUR OF THE DAY.
(*The results are expressed in parts of the whole Vertical Force, and are uncorrected for temperature.*)

1882.

Hour, Greenwich Mean Solar Time.	January.	February.	March.	April.	May.	June.	July.	August.	September.	October.	November.	December.
h												
0	0·03330	0·03338	0·03388	0·03503	0·03611	0·02541	0·01854	0·02001	..	0·05259	0·05250	0·05233
1	·03348	·03360	·03415	·03538	·03665	·02566	·01885	·02032	..	·05275	·05261	·05244
2	·03369	·03387	·03446	·03573	·03712	·02590	·01915	·02070	..	·05291	·05275	·05255
3	·03378	·03414	·03476	·03604	·03743	·02609	·01939	·02101	..	·05303	·05287	·05262
4	·03386	·03438	·03516	·03631	·03776	·02633	·01966	·02124	..	·05310	·05288	·05262
5	·03392	·03447	·03546	·03656	·03801	·02648	·01986	·02141	..	·05305	·05283	·05259
6	·03400	·03454	·03563	·03673	·03815	·02656	·01999	·02146	..	·05300	·05285	·05261
7	·03400	·03455	·03570	·03678	·03811	·02664	·02006	·02140	..	·05299	·05286	·05260
8	·03395	·03449	·03568	·03677	·03795	·02661	·02008	·02134	..	·05293	·05280	·05258
9	·03384	·03429	·03555	·03669	·03769	·02652	·02002	·02129	..	·05289	·05273	·05256
10	·03375	·03415	·03540	·03649	·03750	·02641	·01995	·02118	..	·05286	·05265	·05251
11	·03369	·03411	·03536	·03633	·03728	·02631	·01988	·02111	..	·05278	·05259	·05244
12	·03366	·03407	·03529	·03618	·03705	·02619	·01977	·02096	..	·05275	·05250	·05239
13	·03354	·03390	·03504	·03596	·03672	·02604	·01965	·02078	..	·05272	·05243	·05237
14	·03345	·03374	·03484	·03569	·03643	·02593	·01952	·02060	..	·05268	·05244	·05238
15	·03334	·03364	·03468	·03552	·03624	·02581	·01940	·02051	..	·05269	·05249	·05239
16	·03325	·03353	·03458	·03534	·03607	·02575	·01934	·02041	..	·05268	·05247	·05237
17	·03318	·03345	·03442	·03520	·03595	·02565	·01926	·02031	..	·05263	·05245	·05234
18	·03313	·03339	·03433	·03514	·03588	·02554	·01913	·02021	..	·05261	·05243	·05233
19	·03314	·03346	·03441	·03513	·03589	·02544	·01897	·02007	..	·05265	·05243	·05233
20	·03314	·03348	·03434	·03503	·03596	·02535	·01885	·01996	..	·05266	·05246	·05233
21	·03308	·03347	·03423	·03487	·03600	·02520	·01873	·01981	..	·05257	·05243	·05231
22	·03309	·03340	·03408	·03476	·03604	·02508	·01863	·01971	..	·05247	·05236	·05231
23	·03307	·03335	·03391	·03465	·03606	·02501	·01856	·01969	..	·05243	·05236	·05233

TABLE XII.—MONTHLY MEANS of READINGS of the THERMOMETER placed within the box inclosing the VERTICAL FORCE MAGNET, at each of the ordinary Hours of Observation.

1882.

Hour, Greenwich Mean Solar Time.	January.	February.	March.	April.	May.	June.	July.	August.	September.	October.	November.	December.
h	°	°	°	°	°	°	°	°	°	°	°	°
0	59·4	60·3	61·4	61·9	63·4	61·3	63·2	64·9	..	61·1	59·8	59·4
1	59·6	60·5	61·6	62·2	63·8	61·7	63·4	65·2	..	61·4	60·1	59·6
2	59·7	60·6	61·7	62·2	63·9	61·8	63·5	65·2	..	61·5	60·1	59·7
3	59·7	60·8	62·0	62·3	64·0	61·9	63·6	65·2	..	61·6	60·2	59·7
9	59·7	60·8	62·5	62·8	63·9	62·0	63·9	65·5	..	61·7	60·1	59·8
21	59·2	60·2	61·4	61·4	62·7	61·2	62·9	64·3	..	60·5	59·4	59·3
22	59·2	60·2	61·3	61·3	62·9	61·2	62·9	64·4	..	60·6	59·3	59·3
23	59·2	60·2	61·3	61·4	63·1	61·2	63·0	64·5	..	60·6	59·4	59·3

TABLE XIII.

1882.

Month.	Mean Vertical Magnetic Force in each Month, uncorrected for Temperature.		Mean Temperature.
	Expressed in parts of the whole Vertical Force (diminished by a Constant).	Expressed in terms of Gauss's Metrical Unit (diminished by a Constant).	
			°
January	0·03351	0·14643	59·5
February	·03387	·14800	60·4
March	·03481	·15211	61·7
April	·03576	·15626	61·9
May	·03684	·16098	63·4
June, 1 to 20	·02906	·12698	61·2
June, 21 to 30	·01892	·08267	62·3
July	·01938	·08468	63·3
August	·02065	·09023	64·9
September	..	..	..
October	·05277	·23058	61·1
November	·05259	·22980	59·8
December	·05244	·22914	59·5

The unit adopted in column 3 is the Millimètre-Milligramme-Second Unit. The value of the whole Vertical Force in terms of this unit is 4·37 nearly. To express the forces on the Centimètre-Gramme-Second (C.G.S.) system, the numbers must be divided by 10, equivalent to shifting the decimal point one step towards the left.

On March 31, May 31, and June 21 changes were made in the adjustment of the magnet, by which the continuity of the observations became in each case broken. On August 16 the magnet was removed for attachment of a new and much smaller mirror; it was restored to its position on October 3.

TABLE XIV.—MEAN DIURNAL INEQUALITIES of DECLINATION, HORIZONTAL FORCE, and VERTICAL FORCE, for the Year 1882.

(Each result is the mean of the twelve monthly mean values: those for Horizontal Force and Vertical Force are not corrected for Temperature.)

January to December.

Hour, Greenwich Mean Solar Time.	Inequality of Declination.	Equivalent in terms of Gauss's Metrical Unit.	Inequality of Horizontal Force.	Equivalent in terms of Gauss's Metrical Unit.	Inequality of Vertical Force. (11 months.)	Equivalent in terms of Gauss's Metrical Unit. (11 months.)
h	′					
0	+ 4·31	+ 0·00226	− 0·00087	− 0·00157	− 0·00050	− 0·00218
1	+ 5·45	+ 286	− 49	− 88	− 24	− 105
2	+ 5·21	+ 273	− 16	− 29	+ 3	+ 13
3	+ 4·02	+ 211	+ 9	+ 16	+ 24	+ 105
4	+ 2·49	+ 131	+ 25	+ 45	+ 43	+ 188
5	+ 1·25	+ 66	+ 39	+ 70	+ 56	+ 245
6	+ 0·30	+ 16	+ 51	+ 92	+ 64	+ 280
7	− 0·49	− 26	+ 53	+ 99	+ 65	+ 284
8	− 1·10	− 58	+ 52	+ 94	+ 60	+ 262
9	− 1·46	− 77	+ 45	+ 81	+ 50	+ 218
10	− 1·62	− 85	+ 41	+ 74	+ 39	+ 170
11	− 1·65	− 87	+ 37	+ 67	+ 30	+ 131
12	− 1·67	− 88	+ 31	+ 56	+ 21	+ 92
13	− 1·48	− 78	+ 25	+ 45	+ 6	+ 26
14	− 1·42	− 75	+ 20	+ 36	− 8	− 35
15	− 1·43	− 75	+ 20	+ 36	− 17	− 74
16	− 1·47	− 77	+ 25	+ 45	− 25	− 109
17	− 1·57	− 82	+ 24	+ 43	− 33	− 144
18	− 1·91	− 100	+ 13	+ 23	− 40	− 175
19	− 2·39	− 125	− 9	− 16	− 42	− 184
20	− 2·78	− 146	− 43	− 78	− 45	− 197
21	− 2·29	− 120	− 87	− 157	− 53	− 232
22	− 0·55	− 29	− 114	− 206	− 60	− 262
23	+ 1·99	+ 104	− 106	− 191	− 65	− 284

Hour, Greenwich Mean Solar Time.	Mean Readings of Thermometers. Horizontal Force.	Vertical Force. (11 months.)
h	°	°
0	61·76	61·49
1	61·94	61·73
2	62·09	61·81
3	62·23	61·91
9	62·57	62·05
21	61·56	61·13
22	61·57	61·15
23	61·60	61·21

The unit adopted in columns 3, 5, and 7 is the Millimètre-Milligramme-Second Unit. To express the inequalities on the Centimètre-Gramme-Second (C.G.S.) system, the numbers must be divided by 10, equivalent to shifting the decimal point one step towards the left.

TABLE XV.—DIURNAL RANGE of DECLINATION and HORIZONTAL FORCE, as deduced from the TWENTY-FOUR HOURLY MEASURES of ORDINATES of the PHOTOGRAPHIC REGISTER on each DAY.

(The Declination is expressed in minutes of arc: for Horizontal Force the unit is ·0001 of the whole Horizontal Force. The results for Horizontal Force are corrected for temperature.)

1882.

Day of Month.	January.		February.		March.		April.		May.		June.		July.		August.		September.		October.		November.		December.	
	Dec.	H.F.	Dec.	H.F.	Dec.	H.F.	Dec.	H.F.	Dec.	H.F.	Dec.	H.F.	Dec.	H.F.	Dec.	H.F.	Dec.	H.F.	Dec.	H.F.	Dec.	H.F.	Dec.	H.F.
d	′		′		′		′		′		′		′		′		′		′		′		′	
1	4·0	..	14·2	23	7·0	17	16·8	25	17·2	50	14·0	31	11·5	31	13·8	39	12·2	25	11·5	20	7·3	22	10·0	16
2	4·7	..	9·9	30	8·7	15	12·9	29	13·1	46	12·0	20	11·2	42	12·4	39	12·8	27	..	..	8·8	20	4·2	10
3	7·2	26	6·3	12	11·4	17	15·6	26	10·1	35	14·3	21	13·7	28	11·5	31	13·7	26	8·6	32	7·4	20	5·8	12
4	6·9	8	3·9	16	13·3	14	20·2	45	12·7	28	12·6	27	8·8	30	..	..	7·4	27	11·0	28	5·1	21	7·7	18
5	5·4	12	11·2	32	11·2	28	13·0	33	13·2	34	13·1	31	10·8	33	8·8	40	20·4	31	..	..	8·1	23	5·3	12
6	3·7	7	15·9	27	8·9	27	12·8	24	13·9	34	9·9	31	11·4	28	9·8	26	9·5	37	14·1	27	5·4	20	4·8	10
7	4·8	11	7·6	19	9·9	..	11·3	36	16·8	33	10·5	24	12·2	30	6·0	25	10·3	24	9·9	21	8·0	18	5·3	16
8	10·2	15	11·9	23	15·5	..	12·5	27	13·7	24	7·0	27	7·0	39	7·2	26	12·0	24	10·1	19	7·9	16	4·8	18
9	5·3	8	10·8	33	11·8	..	13·2	25	10·3	26	8·7	35	12·0	26	5·2	25	9·7	23	10·8	32	10·8	25	9·8	18
10	4·2	12	8·8	21	11·3	16	12·4	19	14·9	33	9·0	28	8·5	21	16·1	30	7·3	25	14·8	23	6·1	16	3·5	22
11	7·5	21	7·2	18	8·1	14	13·7	33	13·9	46	12·4	32	11·8	24	13·5	31	13·5	61	12·8	23	8·6	38	9·5	26
12	7·9	13	11·9	17	10·0	12	13·0	24	12·2	31	8·0	40	10·5	32	18·8	45	10·8	36	11·0	21	..	..	5·9	15
13	6·5	19	8·3	19	7·4	13	13·9	62	13·1	71	12·9	30	12·0	22	12·0	32	14·9	47	10·7	23	..	..	4·5	14
14	12·4	18	6·2	21	10·9	15	16·0	43	18·7	46	6·6	39	9·9	26	16·3	40	13·8	32	8·9	27	9·4	33	4·5	11
15	10·5	13	6·6	20	10·1	24	14·1	47	13·2	23	11·2	53	12·6	20	12·1	32	12·5	31	12·8	30	6·0	23	8·3	38
16	5·6	14	9·5	25	11·5	21	..	..	14·9	31	12·4	45	15·9	67	14·2	34	10·9	30	10·5	27	5·0	23	8·7	31
17	6·2	12	9·9	26	11·1	21	..	..	16·3	37	15·0	40	12·1	34	10·1	33	10·5	26	9·7	27	..	..	5·4	10
18	3·1	10	7·1	20	11·5	15	17·6	51	13·6	38	8·8	35	7·7	36	11·2	32	8·9	17	7·8	20	..	..	6·6	18
19	19·5	50	8·9	26	11·6	33	..	..	13·0	45	13·8	40	8·7	23	12·3	30	10·5	27	10·4	18	..	..	4·7	16
20	6·5	20	14·4	36	10·9	26	..	..	16·5	30	17·3	40	11·0	29	9·2	29	9·8	27	10·1	31	..	..	23·0	39
21	7·9	32	7·5	19	15·4	32	13·4	49	16·9	43	13·3	49	11·0	36	10·9	52	7·7	22	8·3	14	..	..	12·7	24
22	8·8	21	10·5	25	10·7	28	10·9	35	15·5	24	5·1	41	9·9	33	9·3	28	9·4	19	15·7	30	6·0	12	8·7	19
23	8·7	14	7·5	24	12·5	30	12·7	26	11·4	33	10·7	27	11·5	20	9·3	30	12·4	18	9·8	17	9·7	28	7·8	16
24	8·8	15	10·3	21	12·0	33	11·5	37	12·4	33	..	..	8·8	14	11·0	21	12·1	50	12·1	29	7·6	11	5·2	25
25	7·4	11	8·5	16	9·8	20	11·2	28	13·8	34	8·5	26	10·5	26	14·3	40	15·5	28	11·6	24	13·0	22	5·5	21
26	5·0	13	5·9	17	9·5	24	9·7	26	10·5	35	11·8	41	9·3	16	10·5	40	8·5	29	6·5	15	8·0	29	6·3	15
27	9·9	14	6·6	11	10·9	37	8·5	24	17·5	51	11·6	47	8·2	16	14·6	43	10·4	31	9·4	23	4·8	19	6·0	15
28	5·5	23	9·9	15	12·4	39	17·1	36	14·0	46	11·6	37	10·3	18	12·7	37	11·6	32	19·1	28	7·1	18	10·0	11
29	10·5	16			14·4	32	14·8	35	10·7	49	11·0	27	13·0	21	11·6	29	12·7	29	10·4	24	3·8	19	8·9	16
30	6·6	12			13·6	29	17·9	31	11·3	44	9·7	31	12·3	46	10·1	24	13·6	26	6·1	25	12·5	14	7·4	18
31	6·6	17			11·7	27			14·1	41			24·0	83	12·5	24			7·0	21			8·5	14

TABLE XVI.—MONTHLY MEAN DIURNAL RANGE of DECLINATION and HORIZONTAL FORCE, as deduced from the numbers contained in Table XV.

(The Declination is expressed in minutes of arc: for Horizontal Force the unit is ·00001 of the whole Horizontal Force. The results for Horizontal Force are corrected for temperature.)

1882.

Month.	Declination.	Horizontal Force.
	′	
January	7·3	164
February	9·2	219
March	11·1	235
April	13·7	336
May	13·9	385
June	11·1	343
July	11·2	307
August	11·6	329
September	11·5	296
October	10·7	242
November	7·7	213
December	7·4	182
Means	10·5	271

ROYAL OBSERVATORY, GREENWICH.

RESULTS

OF

OBSERVATIONS

OF THE

MAGNETIC DIP.

1882.

RESULTS of OBSERVATIONS of MAGNETIC DIP, on each Day of Observation.

Day and Approximate Hour, 1881.		Needle.	Length of Needle.	Magnetic Dip.	Observer.
	d h			° ′ ″	
January	5. 2	C 2	6 inches	67. 34. 36	N
	10. 2	D 1	3 ,,	67. 34. 47	N
	13. 2	C 1	6 ,,	67. 34. 12	N
	17. 1	B 1	9 ,,	67. 34. 47	N
	17. 2	D 2	3 ,,	67. 34. 52	N
	20. 0	B 2	9 ,,	67. 35. 7	N
	20. 2	C 1	6 ,,	67. 34. 43	N
	27. 1	B 1	9 ,,	67. 34. 33	N
	27. 2	D 1	3 ,,	67. 33. 45	N
February	3. 2	D 2	3 ,,	67. 34. 44	N
	9. 1	C 2	6 ,,	67. 34. 44	N
	9. 2	D 1	3 ,,	67. 35. 10	N
	10. 2	B 2	9 ,,	67. 35. 1	N
	14. 1	C 1	6 ,,	67. 34. 47	N
	14. 2	C 2	6 ,,	67. 34. 28	N
	22. 1	B 1	9 ,,	67. 34. 18	N
	23. 0	B 2	9 ,,	67. 33. 49	N
	23. 2	D 2	3 ,,	67. 34. 14	N
	28. 1	C 1	6 ,,	67. 34. 9	N
March	2. 1	B 1	9 ,,	67. 33. 25	N
	2. 2	B 2	9 ,,	67. 33. 57	N
	3. 1	C 1	6 ,,	67. 34. 49	N
	3. 2	C 2	6 ,,	67. 33. 48	N
	9. 1	D 1	3 ,,	67. 34. 27	N
	9. 2	D 2	3 ,,	67. 34. 42	N
	14. 2	C 2	6 ,,	67. 33. 53	N
	23. 1	D 1	3 ,,	67. 34. 35	N
	28. 2	D 2	3 ,,	67. 35. 16	N
	29. 1	B 1	9 ,,	67. 32. 55	N
	30. 1	B 2	9 ,,	67. 32. 3	N
	30. 2	C 1	6 ,,	67. 34. 33	N
April	4. 2	D 1	3 ,,	67. 33. 27	N
	6. 1	B 2	9 ,,	67. 32. 18	N
	6. 2	D 2	3 ,,	67. 33. 7	N
	12. 1	B 1	9 ,,	67. 32. 23	N
	14. 0	C 1	6 ,,	67. 38. 21	N
	25. 0	C 2	6 ,,	67. 36. 27	N
	25. 2	D 2	3 ,,	67. 35. 42	N
	26. 0	B 1	9 ,,	67. 33. 40	N
	27. 23	B 2	9 ,,	67. 33. 56	N
	28. 1	D 1	3 ,,	67. 36. 26	N
	28. 2	C 1	6 ,,	67. 36. 43	N
May	5. 2	C 2	6 ,,	67. 33. 48	N
	9. 2	C 1	6 ,,	67. 34. 51	N
	10. 0	B 1	9 ,,	67. 33. 19	N
	10. 2	B 2	9 ,,	67. 31. 4	N
	12. 2	D 2	3 ,,	67. 33. 47	N
	19. 2	B 2	9 ,,	67. 33. 0	N
	23. 0	C 2	6 ,,	67. 33. 59	N
	23. 2	D 1	3 ,,	67. 34. 47	N
	26. 2	D 2	3 ,,	67. 34. 58	N
	30. 23	B 1	9 ,,	67. 33. 35	N
	31. 2	C 1	6 ,,	67. 33. 19	N
June	7. 2	C 2	6 inches	67. 35. 11	N
	14. 2	C 1	6 ,,	67. 31. 55	N
	16. 1	B 1	9 ,,	67. 35. 2	N
	16. 2	D 1	3 ,,	67. 33. 46	N
	21. 2	D 2	3 ,,	67. 34. 27	N
	22. 23	C 1	6 ,,	67. 34. 4	N
	23. 2	B 2	9 ,,	67. 31. 59	N
	26. 23	B 1	9 ,,	67. 34. 48	N
	27. 1	B 2	9 ,,	67. 34. 3	N
	27. 2	C 2	6 ,,	67. 35. 42	N
	28. 1	C 1	6 ,,	67. 36. 56	N
	29. 0	B 2	9 ,,	67. 33. 3	N
	30. 1	D 1	3 ,,	67. 35. 50	N
	30. 2	C 2	6 ,,	67. 35. 15	N
July	5. 2	D 1	3 ,,	67. 35. 2	N
	18. 1	D 2	3 ,,	67. 34. 5	N
	18. 2	D 1	3 ,,	67. 32. 57	N
	19. 0	B 1	9 ,,	67. 33. 38	N
	19. 1	B 2	9 ,,	67. 32. 49	N
	19. 2	C 1	6 ,,	67. 33. 15	N
	21. 2	C 2	6 ,,	67. 34. 37	N
	26. 2	C 1	6 ,,	67. 32. 56	N
	28. 0	B 2	9 ,,	67. 32. 29	N
	28. 2	D 2	3 ,,	67. 32. 52	N
	31. 2	C 2	6 ,,	67. 32. 37	N
August	4. 2	D 2	3 ,,	67. 33. 10	N
	9. 2	D 1	3 ,,	67. 33. 7	N
	9. 23	B 1	9 ,,	67. 33. 49	N
	10. 0	C 2	6 ,,	67. 35. 50	N
	18. 0	B 2	9 ,,	67. 32. 16	N
	21. 2	C 1	6 ,,	67. 34. 52	N
	21. 23	D 1	3 ,,	67. 34. 9	N
	22. 0	D 2	3 ,,	67. 33. 51	N
	22. 2	C 2	6 ,,	67. 32. 45	N
	23. 2	C 1	6 ,,	67. 33. 36	N
	24. 0	B 2	9 ,,	67. 31. 45	N
	25. 2	B 1	9 ,,	67. 31. 5	N
September	5. 1	D 1	3 ,,	67. 33. 14	N
	6. 1	C 2	6 ,,	67. 34. 27	N
	6. 2	D 2	3 ,,	67. 34. 5	N
	8. 0	D 1	3 ,,	67. 31. 19	N
	8. 1	B 1	9 ,,	67. 30. 35	N
	15. 1	B 1	9 ,,	67. 32. 8	N
	15. 2	D 2	3 ,,	67. 32. 18	N
	27. 1	B 2	9 ,,	67. 31. 40	N
	27. 2	C 2	6 ,,	67. 33. 7	N
	27. 23	D 1	3 ,,	67. 33. 52	N
	28. 1	D 2	3 ,,	67. 33. 42	N
	28. 2	C 1	6 ,,	67. 33. 34	N
	30. 1	B 1	9 ,,	67. 32. 37	N
October	7. 2	D 1	3 ,,	67. 35. 10	N
	13. 1	D 2	3 ,,	67. 34. 27	N
	20. 1	C 1	6 ,,	67. 33. 43	N

The initial N is that of Mr. Nash.

RESULTS of OBSERVATIONS of MAGNETIC DIP, on each Day of Observation—*concluded.*

Day and Approximate Hour, 1882.	Needle.	Length of Needle.	Magnetic Dip.	Observer.	Day and Approximate Hour, 1882.	Needle.	Length of Needle.	Magnetic Dip.	Observer.
d h			° ′ ″		d h			° ′ ″	
October 20. 2	D 1	3 inches	67. 32. 33	N	November 25. 1	B 2	9 inches	67. 35. 9	N
25. 0	B 1	9 "	67. 35. 56	N	28. 1	B 1	9 "	67. 35. 1	N
25. 2	B 2	9 "	67. 35. 41	N	30. 0	C 1	6 "	67. 33. 45	N
25. 3	D 1	3 "	67. 35. 43	N	30. 2	C 2	6 "	67. 33. 44	N
25. 23	C 2	6 "	67. 35. 22	N					
26. 1	D 2	3 "	67. 34. 55	N	December 4. 2	D 2	3 "	67. 35. 18	N
30. 23	B 2	9 "	67. 34. 5	N	13. 1	C 1	6 "	67. 34. 38	N
31. 1	B 1	9 "	67. 33. 12	N	13. 2	D 1	3 "	67. 32. 4	N
31. 2	C 2	6 "	67. 34. 28	N	16. 1	C 2	6 "	67. 35. 53	N
					19. 1	B 1	9 "	67. 34. 42	N
November 4. 1	D 1	3 "	67. 34. 58	N	20. 23	D 1	3 "	67. 35. 56	N
10. 2	C 1	6 "	67. 34. 34	N	21. 0	B 2	9 "	67. 36. 48	N
11. 1	D 2	3 "	67. 33. 4	N	28. 0	B 1	9 "	67. 34. 9	N
22. 1	C 2	6 "	67. 37. 13	N	29. 0	B 2	9 "	67. 34. 1	N
24. 1	B 1	9 "	67. 34. 6	N	29. 1	D 2	3 "	67. 34. 21	N
24. 2	D 2	3 "	67. 36. 14	N	29. 2	C 2	6 "	67. 35. 21	N

The initial N is that of Mr. Nash.

MONTHLY MEANS of MAGNETIC DIP.

Month, 1882.	B 1, 9-inch Needle.	Number of Observations.	B 2, 9-inch Needle.	Number of Observations.	C 1, 6-inch Needle.	Number of Observations.
	° ′ ″		° ′ ″		° ′ ″	
January	67. 34. 40	2	67. 35. 7	1	67. 34. 28	2
February	67. 34. 18	1	67. 34. 25	2	67. 34. 28	2
March	67. 33. 10	2	67. 33. 0	2	67. 34. 41	2
April	67. 33. 2	2	67. 33. 7	2	67. 37. 32	2
May	67. 33. 27	2	67. 32. 2	2	67. 34. 5	2
June	67. 34. 55	2	67. 33. 2	3	67. 34. 18	3
July	67. 33. 38	1	67. 32. 39	2	67. 33. 6	2
August	67. 32. 27	2	67. 32. 1	2	67. 34. 14	2
September	67. 31. 47	3	67. 31. 40	1	67. 33. 34	1
October	67. 34. 34	2	67. 34. 53	2	67. 33. 43	1
November	67. 34. 34	2	67. 35. 9	1	67. 34. 9	2
December	67. 34. 26	2	67. 35. 24	2	67. 34. 38	1
Means	67. 33. 38	Sum 23	67. 33. 27	Sum 22	67. 34. 28	Sum 22

Month, 1882.	C 2, 6-inch Needle.	Number of Observations.	D 1, 3-inch Needle.	Number of Observations.	D 2, 3-inch Needle.	Number of Observations.
	° ′ ″		° ′ ″		° ′ ″	
January	67. 34. 36	1	67. 34. 16	2	67. 34. 52	1
February	67. 34. 36	2	67. 35. 10	1	67. 34. 29	2
March	67. 33. 51	2	67. 34. 31	2	67. 34. 59	2
April	67. 36. 27	1	67. 34. 56	2	67. 34. 25	2
May	67. 33. 53	2	67. 34. 47	1	67. 34. 23	2
June	67. 35. 23	3	67. 34. 48	2	67. 34. 27	1
July	67. 33. 37	2	67. 33. 59	2	67. 33. 29	2
August	67. 34. 17	2	67. 33. 38	2	67. 33. 31	2
September	67. 33. 47	2	67. 32. 48	3	67. 33. 22	3
October	67. 34. 55	2	67. 34. 29	3	67. 34. 41	2
November	67. 35. 29	2	67. 34. 58	1	67. 34. 39	2
December	67. 35. 37	2	67. 34. 0	2	67. 34. 50	2
Means	67. 34. 40	Sum 23	67. 34. 13	Sum 23	67. 34. 16	Sum 23

For this table the monthly means have been formed without reference to the hour at which the observation was made on each day.
In combining the monthly results, to form the annual means, weights have been given proportional to the number of observations.

YEARLY MEANS of MAGNETIC DIP for each of the NEEDLES, and GENERAL MEAN for the Year 1882.

Lengths of the several Sets of Needles.	Needles.	Number of Observations with each Needle.	Mean Yearly Dip from Observations with each Needle.	Mean Yearly Dip from each Set of Needles.	Mean Yearly Dip from all the Sets of Needles.
			° ′ ″	° ′	° ′ ″
9-inch Needles	B 1	23	67. 33. 38	67. 33. 33	
	B 2	22	67. 33. 27		
6-inch Needles	C 1	22	67. 34. 28	67. 34. 34	67. 34. 7
	C 2	23	67. 34. 40		
3-inch Needles	D 1	23	67. 34. 13	67. 34. 14	
	D 2	23	67. 34. 16		

ROYAL OBSERVATORY, GREENWICH.

OBSERVATIONS

OF

DEFLEXION OF A MAGNET

FOR

ABSOLUTE MEASURE

OF

HORIZONTAL FORCE.

1882.

ABSTRACT of the OBSERVATIONS of DEFLEXION of a MAGNET for ABSOLUTE MEASURE of HORIZONTAL FORCE.

Month and Day, 1862.		Distances of Centres of Magnets.	Temperature.	Observed Deflexion.	Mean of the Times of Vibration of Deflecting Magnet.	Number of Vibrations.	Temperature.	Observer.
		ft.	°	° ′ ″				
January	24	1·0 1·3	41·8	10. 45. 26 4. 52. 51	5·644 5·644	100 100	41·8 43·2	N
February	24	1·0 1·3	48·5	10. 44. 14 4. 52. 22	5·652 5·652	100 100	48·8 51·0	N
March	24	1·0 1·3	52·8	10. 43. 17 4. 51. 55	5·654 5·654	100 100	52·8 54·1	N
April	26	1·0 1·3	52·6	10. 42. 45 4. 51. 35	5·645 5·648	100 100	54·1 54·3	N
May	30	1·0 1·3	73·1	10. 39. 43 4. 50. 20	5·665 5·660	100 100	75·4 72·9	N
June	29	1·0 1·3	68·0	10. 40. 47 4. 50. 48	5·660 5·657	100 100	68·4 69·9	N
July	27	1·0 1·3	75·1	10. 38. 44 4. 49. 49	5·656 5·661	100 100	77·9 75·3	N
August	24	1·0 1·3	65·6	10. 40. 3 4. 50. 24	5·653 5·662	100 100	67·0 65·5	N
September	29	1·0 1·3	59·2	10. 40. 25 4. 50. 35	5·658 5·659	100 100	59·1 59·5	N
October	27	1·0 1·3	50·5	10. 42. 5 4. 51. 22	5·658 5·654	100 100	50·2 51·0	N
November	29	1·0 1·3	44·5	10. 41. 22 4. 51. 32	5·653 5·654	100 100	43·3 45·3	N
December	22	1·0 1·3	45·9	10. 42. 19 4. 51. 33	5·655 5·652	100 100	47·1 46·7	N

The Deflecting Magnet is placed on the East side of the suspended Magnet, with its marked pole alternately E. and W., and on the West side with its marked pole also alternately E. and W.; the deflexion given in the table above is the mean of the four deflexions observed in those positions of the magnets.

The lengths of 1 foot and 1·3 foot correspond to 304·8 and 396·2 millimètres respectively.

The initial N is that of Mr. Nash.

In the following calculations every observation is reduced to the temperature 35°.

COMPUTATION of the VALUES of ABSOLUTE MEASURE of HORIZONTAL FORCE in the Year 1882.

Month and Day, 1882.		In English Measure.									In Metric Measure.
		Apparent Value of A_1.	Apparent Value of A_2.	Apparent Value of P.	Mean Value of P.	Log. $\frac{m}{X}$	Adopted Time of Vibration of Deflecting Magnet.	Log. $m X$	Value of m.	Value of X.	Value of X.
January	24	0·09342	0·09355	−0·00350		8·97212	5·6440	0·15644	0·3667	3·910	1·803
February	24	0·09335	0·09350	−0·00400		8·97184	5·6520	0·15573	0·3663	3·908	1·802
March	24	0·09328	0·09342	−0·00372		8·97151	5·6540	0·15565	0·3661	3·909	1·802
April	26	0·09320	0·09332	−0·00299		8·97107	5·6465	0·15687	0·3664	3·917	1·806
May	30	0·09310	0·09325	−0·00400		8·97068	5·6625	0·15578	0·3658	3·913	1·804
June	29	0·09317	0·09331	−0·00384		8·97099	5·6585	0·15606	0·3660	3·913	1·804
July	27	0·09299	0·09312	−0·00333	−0·00398	8·97011	5·6585	0·15658	0·3659	3·920	1·807
August	24	0·09303	0·09315	−0·00327		8·97027	5·6575	0·15601	0·3657	3·916	1·806
September	29	0·09297	0·09310	−0·00344		8·97003	5·6585	0·15559	0·3654	3·915	1·805
October	27	0·09308	0·09322	−0·00367		8·97054	5·6560	0·15536	0·3656	3·912	1·804
November	29	0·09288	0·09317	−0·00773		8·96997	5·6535	0·15532	0·3653	3·914	1·805
December	22	0·09304	0·09320	−0·00429		8·97040	5·6535	0·15531	0·3655	3·913	1·804
Means		..	..	..	..	..	..	..	..	3·913	1·804

The value of X in column 10 is referred to the unit Foot-Grain-Second, and that in column 11 to the unit Millimètre-Milligramme-Second. To obtain X in the Centimètre-Gramme-Second (C.G.S.) unit, the value given in column 11 must be divided by 10, equivalent to shifting the decimal point one step towards the left.

ROYAL OBSERVATORY, GREENWICH.

MAGNETIC DISTURBANCES

AND

EARTH CURRENTS.

1882.

MAGNETIC DISTURBANCES in DECLINATION, HORIZONTAL FORCE, and VERTICAL FORCE, and EARTH CURRENTS: recorded at the ROYAL OBSERVATORY, GREENWICH, in the Year 1882.

The following notes give a brief description of all magnetic movements (superposed on the ordinary diurnal movement) exceeding 5′ in Declination, 0·0015 in Horizontal Force, or 0·0005 in Vertical Force, as taken from the photographic records of the respective Magnetometers. The movements in Horizontal and Vertical Force are expressed in parts of the whole Horizontal and Vertical Force respectively. When any one of the three elements is not specifically mentioned it is to be understood that the movement, if any, was insignificant. Any failure or want of register is specially indicated.

The term "wave" is used to indicate a movement in one direction and return; "double wave" a movement in one direction and return with continuation in the opposite direction and return; "two successive waves" consecutive wave movements in the same direction; "fluctuations" a number of movements in both directions. The extent and direction of the movement are indicated in brackets, + denoting an increase and − a decrease of the magnetic element. In the case of fluctuations the sign ± denotes positive and negative movements of generally equal extent.

In all cases of magnetic movement for which there are earth-current photographs, the registers show corresponding earth currents, but it has not been thought necessary to refer to these in detail.

Magnetic movements which do not admit of brief description in this way are exhibited with their corresponding earth currents on accompanying plates.

The time is Greenwich Mean Solar Time (Astronomical Reckoning).

1882.

January 4. $10\frac{1}{2}^{h}$. to 14^{h}. Wave in Dec. (− 7′): fluctuations in H.F. (± ·001).

5. $0\frac{1}{2}^{h}$. to 4^{h}. Two successive waves in Dec. (each − 5′): in H.F. (− ·001 and − ·0015).

8. $9\frac{1}{2}^{h}$. to $10\frac{3}{4}^{h}$. Wave in Dec. (− 11′): in H.F. (+ ·002). Fluctuations in Dec. (± 2′) until $18\frac{1}{2}^{h}$.

11. 7^{h}. to 16^{h}. Long wave in Dec. (− 7′): in H.F. (− ·002): with superposed fluctuations, in Dec. (± 3′), in H.F. (± ·001).

12. Waves in Dec. at 5^{h}. (− 9′), and at 9^{h}. (− 12′). Fluctuations in H.F. $4\frac{1}{2}^{h}$. to 11^{h}. (− ·002 to + ·001).

13. 2^{h}. to 18^{h}. Fluctuations in Dec. (± 3′): in H.F. (± ·001).

14. 6^{h}. to 17^{h}. Fluctuations in Dec. (± 3′): in H.F. (± ·001): with wave in Dec. at 7^{h}. (− 11′), and wave in H.F. at 11^{h}. (+ ·003).

15. 2^{h}. to 14^{h}. Fluctuations in Dec. (± 3′): in H.F. (± ·001).

16. 5^{h}. to 12^{h}. Fluctuations in Dec. (± 3′): with wave in H.F. at 7^{h}. (+ ·002).

19. Disturbed day. See Plate I.

20. 13^{h}. Wave in H.F. (+ ·0025).

21. $9\frac{1}{2}^{h}$. Wave in Dec. (− 6′).

22. 5^{h}. to 10^{h}. Two successive waves in Dec. (each − 7′): fluctuations in H.F. (− ·001 to + ·002): in V.F. small.

23. 9^{h}. to 10^{h}. Double wave in Dec. (− 10′ to + 4′): in H.F. (− ·001 to + ·0005): in V.F. small.

24. $4\frac{1}{2}^{h}$. to $6\frac{1}{2}^{h}$. Wave in Dec. (− 11′). $1\frac{1}{2}^{h}$. to 6^{h}. Fluctuations in H.F. (± ·001): in V.F. small.

25. $8\frac{1}{2}^{h}$. to $13\frac{1}{2}^{h}$. Fluctuations in Dec. (± 5′): in H.F. (± ·001): in V.F. small.

27. 7^{h}. Wave in Dec. (− 5′): in H.F. (− ·002). 11^{h}. to $13\frac{1}{2}^{h}$. Flat wave in Dec. (− 8′): in H.F. (+ ·001).

29. 9^{h}. to 17^{h}. Fluctuations in Dec. (± 6′): 8^{h}. to 12^{h}. in H.F. (± ·001).

31. $12\frac{1}{2}^{h}$. to 16^{h}. Fluctuations in Dec. (± 3′): in H.F. (− ·001 to + ·0015).

February 1. Disturbed day. See Plate I.

2. 7^{h}. Wave in Dec. (− 15′): in H.F. (+ ·005): in V.F. small. 13^{h}. to 18^{h}. Fluctuations in Dec. (± 5′): in H.F. (± ·001).

5. Waves in Dec., $5\frac{1}{2}^{h}$. to 7^{h}. (− 8′), 12^{h}. to 13^{h}. (+ 8′). Two successive waves in H.F. 10^{h}. to $13\frac{1}{2}^{h}$. (+ ·004 and + ·006): wave in H.F. 17^{h}. to $18\frac{1}{2}^{h}$. (+ ·004). Small fluctuations generally from February 5. 0^{h}. to February 6. $1\frac{1}{2}^{h}$. in Dec., H.F., and V.F.

6. 5^{h}. to 13^{h}. Fluctuations in Dec. (± 10′): in H.F. (± ·003): in V.F. (± ·0003).

8. Fluctuations throughout in Dec. (± 5′): in H.F. (± ·0015): in V.F. small.

9. $11\frac{1}{2}^{h}$. Sharp double wave in Dec. (+ 9′ to − 4′): in H.F. (− ·0035 to − ·0015): in V.F. small. Small fluctuations generally throughout the day.

17. 12^{h}. to 17^{h}. Fluctuations in Dec. (± 3′): in H.F. (± ·001): in V.F. small.

20. Disturbed day. See Plate I.

1882.

February 22. $8\frac{1}{2}^h$. Wave in Dec. (− 10′): in H.F. (− ·001).

23. 12^h. to 15^h. Fluctuations in Dec. (± 4′): in H.F. (± ·001).

24. 8^h. Wave in Dec. (− 8′).

March 4. $1\frac{1}{2}^h$. to $3\frac{1}{2}^h$. Double wave in Dec. (+ 7′ to − 4′): in H.F. (+ ·0015 to − ·003): in V.F. small. 7^h. to 17^h. Fluctuations in Dec. (± 4′): in H.F. (± ·001).

5. 4^h. to 12^h. Fluctuations in Dec. (± 3′): in H.F. (± ·001), terminating with wave, steep at commencement, (+ ·003).

8. Fluctuations throughout in Dec. (± 7′): in H.F. (± ·002): in V.F. (± ·0004).

9. 4^h. to 11^h. Sharp wave in Dec. 4^h. to $5\frac{1}{4}^h$. (− 20′), followed by fluctuations (± 6′): fluctuations in H.F. (± ·0025): in V.F. small.

15. $8\frac{1}{4}^h$. to $9\frac{1}{4}^h$. Sharp wave in Dec. (− 12′): in H.F. (+ ·0035): in V.F. small.

17. $8\frac{1}{4}^h$. Wave in Dec (− 5′): in H.F. (− ·001): in V.F. small.

19. 5^h. to 7^h. and from 11^h. to 18^h. Fluctuations in Dec. (± 5′): in H.F. (± ·001): in V.F. small.

21. 2^h. to 15^h. Fluctuations in Dec. (± 5′): in H.F. (± ·002): in V.F. small.

23. 1^h. to 13^h. Fluctuations in Dec. (± 3′): in H.F. (± ·0015): in V.F. small.

26. 7^h. to 14^h. Fluctuations in Dec. (± 2′): in H.F. (± ·001): in V.F. small.

27. 9^h. to 10^h. Fluctuations in Dec. (± 2′): wave in H.F. (+ ·002).

28. 3^h. to 15^h. Fluctuations in Dec. (± 3′): in H.F. (± ·001): in V.F. (± ·0002).

April 1. $8\frac{1}{2}^h$. to 13^h. Fluctuations in Dec. (± 4′): in H.F. (± ·001).

2. 13^h. to 14^h. Wave in Dec. (+ 9′): in H.F. (+ ·001).

4. $2\frac{1}{2}^h$. to $11\frac{1}{2}^h$. Sharp fluctuations in Dec. (± 7′): in H.F. (± ·003): in V.F. (± ·0005). $17\frac{1}{2}^h$. to 19^h. Wave in Dec. (+ 16′): in H.F. (− ·003): in V.F. (− ·0003).

5. 7^h. to 18^h. Fluctuations in Dec. (± 5′): in H.F. (± ·001).

6. 4^h. to 17^h. Fluctuations in Dec. (± 5′): in H.F. (± ·0015): in V.F. (± ·0002).

7. 5^h. to 12^h. Fluctuations in Dec. (± 3′): in H.F. (± ·001).

8. 5^h. to 9^h. Fluctuations in Dec. (± 3′): in H.F. (± ·001).

13. 11^h. to 19^h. Fluctuations in Dec. (± 3′), with wave at commencement (− 10′), and wave at 16^h. (+ 10′): in H.F. fluctuations (± ·0015): in V.F. (± ·0003).

14. 0^h. to 13^h. Fluctuations in Dec. (± 3′) with wave at $6\frac{1}{4}^h$. (− 8′): in H.F. fluctuations (± ·0015): in V.F. small.

15. 11^h. to 16^h. Fluctuations in Dec. (± 3′): in H.F. (± ·001).

16. $1\frac{1}{2}^h$. to 7^h. Fluctuations in H.F. (± ·0015).

16. } 17. } Disturbed days. See Plate II.

18. $8\frac{1}{4}^h$. Sharp wave in Dec. (− 6′): in H.F. (+ ·0025): in V.F. small.

19. } 20. } Disturbed days. See Plate III.

23. [0^h. to $7\frac{1}{2}^h$. No register of Dec., H.F., or V.F.] $8\frac{1}{2}^h$. to 21^h. Fluctuations in Dec. (± 5′): in H.F. (± ·001): in V.F. (± ·0002).

28. 11^h. to 20^h. Fluctuations in Dec. (± 8′): in H.F. (± ·001): in V.F. (± ·0002).

29. $9\frac{3}{4}^h$. to $11\frac{1}{2}^h$. Sharp fluctuations in Dec. (− 7′ to + 12′): in H.F. (± ·0015): in V.F. (± ·0004).

30. $10\frac{1}{4}^h$. to 13^h. Fluctuations in Dec. (± 5′): waves in H.F. at $2\frac{1}{4}^h$. (− ·003) and at 11^h. (+ ·0035): in V.F. at $11\frac{1}{2}^h$. (− ·0003).

May 1. 6^h. to 18^h. Fluctuations in Dec. (± 7′): in H.F. (± ·0025): in V.F. (± ·0002).

2. 3^h. to 17^h. Fluctuations in Dec. (± 3′): in H.F. (± ·0015): in V.F. small.

3. $15\frac{1}{2}^h$. to 18^h. Wave in Dec. (+ 10′).

4. $8\frac{3}{4}^h$. Wave in Dec. (− 7′).

11. $13\frac{1}{2}^h$. Wave in Dec. (+ 6′): in H.F. (+ ·0025).

13. $4\frac{1}{2}^h$. to $11\frac{1}{4}^h$. Fluctuations in Dec. (± 7′): in H.F. (± ·002): in V.F. (± ·0002).

14. 8^h. to 12^h. Fluctuations in Dec. (± 7′). 8^h. to $9\frac{1}{2}^h$. Wave in H.F. (+ ·006) with superposed fluctuations (± ·0015), followed by fluctuations (± ·002), ending with sharp wave (− ·0045) at $11\frac{3}{4}^h$. $11\frac{3}{4}^h$. Wave in V.F. (− ·0025).

17. 9^h. to 17^h. Fluctuations in Dec. (± 4′). $3\frac{1}{2}^h$. to 14^h. Fluctuations in H.F. (± ·002).

1882.

May 21. $22\frac{1}{2}^{h}$. Wave in H.F. (— ·004).

22. $2\frac{1}{2}^{h}$. Wave in Dec. (+ 3′): in H.F. (+ ·003). Waves in Dec. at $8\frac{1}{2}^{h}$. and 13^{h}. (each — 6′). $6\frac{1}{2}^{h}$. to $9\frac{1}{2}^{h}$. Fluctuations in H.F. (± ·001).

27. 12^{h}. to 16^{h}. Double wave in Dec. (+ 6′ to — 14′). 6^{h}. to 14^{h}. Fluctuations in H.F. (± ·001).

28. 6^{h}. to 16^{h}. Fluctuations in Dec. (± 7′). 0^{h}. to 18^{h}. Fluctuations in H.F. (± ·0015): in V.F. (± ·0002).

29. $7\frac{1}{2}^{h}$. to 10^{h}. Fluctuations in Dec. (± 3′): in H.F. (± ·0015).

30. $9\frac{1}{2}^{h}$. to $10\frac{1}{2}^{h}$. Wave in Dec. (— 6′): fluctuations in H.F. (± ·001).

31. 10^{h}. to 17^{h}. Fluctuations in Dec. (± 3′). 4^{h}. to 13^{h}. Fluctuations in H.F. (± ·0015).

June 1. 4^{h}. to 16^{h}. Fluctuations in Dec. (± 3′): in H.F. (± ·001).

6. 5^{h}. to 12^{h}. Fluctuations in Dec. (± 3′). 3^{h}. to 12^{h}. Fluctuations in H.F. (± ·0015): in V.F. small.

7. $4\frac{1}{2}^{h}$. to 8^{h}. Fluctuations in H.F. (± ·001).

9. 3^{h}. to 11^{h}. Fluctuations in H.F. (± ·001).

12. 17^{h}. to $19\frac{1}{2}^{h}$. Wave in Dec. (+ 10′): in H.F. (— ·003).

14. Disturbed day. See Plate IV.

15. $1\frac{1}{2}^{h}$. to 6^{h}. Fluctuations in H.F. (± ·0015). $11\frac{3}{4}^{h}$. to 21^{h}. Fluctuations in Dec. (± 7′): in H.F. (± ·001): in V.F. (± ·0002).

16. 7^{h}. to 19^{h}. Fluctuations in Dec. (± 5′). 2^{h}. to 19^{h}. Fluctuations in H.F. (± ·001).

17. $10\frac{1}{2}^{h}$. to $11\frac{3}{4}^{h}$. Wave in Dec. (— 4′): in H.F. (+ ·0015).

19. $10\frac{1}{2}^{h}$. to 13^{h}. Fluctuations in Dec. (± 3′): in H.F. (± ·001): in V.F. small.

20. $4\frac{1}{2}^{h}$. to 5^{h}. Decrease of Dec. (8′): wave in H.F. (— ·003): in V.F. (— ·0002). 13^{h}. to 21^{h}. Fluctuations in Dec. (± 5′): in H.F. (± ·001).

21. 0^{h}. to 15^{h}. Fluctuations in Dec. (± 4′): in H.F. (± ·001): in V.F. (± ·0003).

22. Waves in Dec. at $6\frac{1}{2}^{h}$. (— 3′), and at $8\frac{3}{4}^{h}$. (— 5′). Fluctuations in H.F. 3^{h}. to 7^{h}. (± ·001).

23. 2^{h}. to 18^{h}. Fluctuations in H.F. (± ·001).

24. Disturbed day. See Plate IV.

25. 8^{h}. to 12^{h}. Fluctuations in Dec. (± 2′). 5^{h}. to 12^{h}. Fluctuations in H.F. (± ·001).

26. 1^{h}. to 19^{h}. Fluctuations in Dec. (± 3′): in H.F. (± ·001): in V.F. (± ·0002).

27. $6\frac{3}{4}^{h}$. to $7\frac{3}{4}^{h}$. Wave in Dec. (— 7′). $2\frac{1}{2}^{h}$. to $7\frac{3}{4}^{h}$. Fluctuations in H.F. (± ·0015).

July 2. 3^{h}. to 8^{h}. Fluctuations in H.F. (± ·002).

7. $0\frac{1}{2}^{h}$. to $6\frac{1}{2}^{h}$. Fluctuations in H.F. (± ·0015): in V.F. small.

12. 7^{h}. to $8\frac{1}{2}^{h}$. Wave in Dec. (— 6′): in H.F. (+ ·0015).

16. Disturbed day. See Plate V.

17. 1^{h}. to 15^{h}. Fluctuations in Dec. (± 2′): in H.F. (± ·0015): in V.F. (± ·0002).

18. 7^{h}. to 12^{h}. Fluctuations in Dec. (± 2′): in H.F. (± ·0015): in V.F. (± ·0002).

19. $17\frac{1}{4}^{h}$. to $19\frac{1}{4}^{h}$. Wave in H.F. (— ·002).

20. $16\frac{1}{4}^{h}$. to $18\frac{3}{4}^{h}$. Wave in Dec. (+ 6′).

22. 14^{h}. to 17^{h}. Fluctuations in Dec. (± 2′): in H.F. (± ·001).

30.
31. } Disturbed days. See Plates V., VI., and VII.
August 4.

5. $3\frac{1}{2}^{h}$. to $5\frac{3}{4}^{h}$. Fluctuations in Dec. (± 2′): in H.F. (± ·001): in V.F. (± ·0001).

9. $15\frac{1}{4}^{h}$. to $21\frac{1}{2}^{h}$. Fluctuations in Dec. (± 2′): in H.F. (± ·001).

10. $9\frac{1}{2}^{h}$. Wave in Dec. (— 6′): in H.F. (+ ·0035). $12\frac{1}{2}^{h}$. to $13\frac{1}{2}^{h}$. Sharp wave in Dec. (+ 20′): in V.F. (— ·0007). Small fluctuations generally at other times from 3^{h}. to 17^{h}.

11. 12^{h}. to 20^{h}. Fluctuations in Dec. (± 3′): in H.F. (± ·001).

12. 1^{h}. to 6^{h}. Fluctuations in Dec. (± 3′): in H.F. (± ·002).

13. 4^{h}. to $12\frac{1}{2}^{h}$. Fluctuations in Dec. (± 2′): in H.F. (± ·0015).

14. 2^{h}. to 12^{h}. Fluctuations in Dec. (± 2′): in H.F. (± ·001).

16. 5^{h}. to 20^{h}. Fluctuations in Dec. (± 3′): in H.F. (± ·0015), with wave at $3\frac{1}{4}^{h}$. (+ ·003). [No register of V.F.]

17. 10^{h}. to 16^{h}. Fluctuations in Dec. (± 2′): in H.F. (± ·001). [No register of V.F.]

20. $8\frac{1}{2}^{h}$. Wave in H.F. (+ ·0015). [No register of V.F.]

21. $6\frac{3}{4}^{h}$. to 19^{h}. Fluctuations in Dec. (± 4′): in H.F. (± ·0015), with wave at 11^{h}. (+ ·003). [No register of V.F.]

1882.

August 25. 7^{h}. to 13^{h}. Fluctuations in Dec. (± 5′): in H.F. (± ·001). [No register of V.F.]

28. 5^{h}. to 11^{h}. Fluctuations in Dec. (± 2′): in H.F. (± ·001). [No register of V.F.]

September 2. 5^{h}. to 13^{h}. Fluctuations in Dec. (± 3′): in H.F. (± ·001). [No register of V.F.]

3. 4^{h}. to 8^{h}. Fluctuations in Dec. (± 2′). $0\frac{1}{2}^{h}$. to 8^{h}. Fluctuations in H.F. (± ·001). [No register of V.F.]

5. 1^{h}. to 12^{h}. Fluctuations in Dec. (± 5′): in H.F. (± ·0015). Sharp wave in Dec. at $8\frac{1}{2}^{h}$. (− 17′). [No register of V.F.]

6. 5^{h}. to 10^{h}. Fluctuations in Dec. (± 4′): in H.F. (± ·001). [No register of V.F.]

11. Disturbed day. See Plate VIII.

12. 8^{h}. Wave in Dec. (− 6′): in H.F. (+ ·002): with fluctuations in Dec. (± 2′) until 17^{h}. [No register of V.F.]

13. $8\frac{1}{2}^{h}$. to 10^{h}. Wave in Dec. (+ 5′). 0^{h}. to 10^{h}. Fluctuations in H.F. (± ·001). [No register of V.F.]

14. 4^{h}. Wave in Dec. (− 5′): in H.F. (− ·0015). $7\frac{3}{4}^{h}$. to 10^{h}. Two successive waves in Dec. (− 10′ and − 4′): fluctuations in H.F. (± ·001). [No register of V.F.]

18. $6\frac{3}{4}^{h}$. to 8^{h}. Sharp wave in Dec. (− 8′). $6\frac{3}{4}^{h}$. to $8\frac{1}{2}^{h}$. Fluctuations in H.F. (± ·001). [No register of V.F.]

19. $3\frac{3}{4}^{h}$. Sharp wave in Dec. (− 3′): in H.F. (− ·0025). $8\frac{1}{2}^{h}$. to 11^{h}. Fluctuations in H.F. (± ·001). [No register of V.F.]

20. 9^{h}. to 14^{h}. Fluctuations in Dec. (± 5′): in H.F. (± ·0015). [No register of V.F.]

23. 10^{h}. to 11^{h}. Wave in H.F. (+ ·002). [No register of V.F.]

24. 15^{h}. to 21^{h}. Fluctuations in Dec. (± 2′): in H.F. (± ·001). [No register of V.F.]

25. $7\frac{1}{4}^{h}$. to $8\frac{1}{4}^{h}$. Sharp wave in Dec. (− 10′): in H.F. (− ·0025). 2^{h}. to 10^{h}. Fluctuations in Dec. (± 2′): in H.F. (± ·0015). [No register of V.F.]

26. 9^{h}. to 20^{h}. Fluctuations in Dec. (± 3′): in H.F. (± ·001). [No register of V.F.]

October 2. Disturbed day. See Plate IX.

4. 4^{h}. to 11^{h}. Fluctuations in Dec. (± 5′): in H.F. (± ·001), with sharp wave at 10^{h}. (+ ·004): in V.F. small.

5. Disturbed day. See Plate X.

8. $7\frac{1}{2}^{h}$. to 13^{h}. Fluctuations in Dec. (± 5′): in H.F. (± ·0005).

9. $7\frac{1}{2}^{h}$. to 14^{h}. Fluctuations in Dec. (± 5′): in H.F. (± ·0015).

10. $6\frac{1}{4}^{h}$. to $8\frac{1}{2}^{h}$. Wave in Dec. (− 20′). 5^{h}. to 8^{h}. Fluctuations in H.F. (± ·0015): in V.F. small.

11. 6^{h}. to $7\frac{3}{4}^{h}$. Wave in Dec. (− 7′): in H.F. (− ·0015). 0^{h}. to 3^{h}. and 10^{h}. to 13^{h}. Small fluctuations in Dec. and H.F.

14. 3^{h}. to 20^{h}. Fluctuations in Dec. (± 2′): in H.F. (± ·001).

17. $7\frac{1}{2}^{h}$. to 15^{h}. Fluctuations in Dec. (± 2′): in H.F. (± ·001).

22. 2^{h}. to 17^{h}. Fluctuations in Dec. (± 5′): in H.F. (± ·001): in V.F. small. 7^{h}. to 8^{h}. Double wave in Dec. (− 10′ to + 10′): in H.F. (+ ·004 to − ·002): in V.F. small.

24. 17^{h}. to $20\frac{1}{2}^{h}$. Wave in Dec. (+ 15′). $16\frac{1}{2}^{h}$. to $19\frac{1}{2}^{h}$. Fluctuations in H.F. (± ·002): in V.F. small.

25. $6\frac{3}{4}^{h}$. Wave in Dec. (− 8′): in H.F. (− ·002). 10^{h}. Wave in Dec. (+ 5′): in H.F. (+ ·003). $13\frac{1}{2}^{h}$. to 16^{h}. Fluctuations in Dec. (± 3′).

27. $8\frac{1}{2}^{h}$. to $18\frac{1}{2}^{h}$. Fluctuations in Dec. (± 7′): in H.F. (± ·0015): in V.F. small.

28. 2^{h}. to $17\frac{1}{2}^{h}$. Fluctuations in Dec. (± 5′): in H.F. (± ·002): in V.F. small. Waves in Dec. 4^{h}. to 5^{h}. (− 18′), and $7\frac{1}{2}^{h}$. to $8\frac{1}{2}^{h}$. (− 13′).

29. 4^{h}. to 14^{h}. Fluctuations in Dec. (± 5′): in H.F. (± ·001): in V.F. small.

November 2. $8\frac{1}{4}^{h}$. to 11^{h}. Wave in Dec. (− 9′), sharp at commencement. $12\frac{3}{4}^{h}$. Wave, very sharp at commencement, in Dec. (+ 5′): in H.F. (+ ·0045): in V.F. (+ ·0004): followed by small fluctuations until 18^{h}.

5. $7\frac{1}{2}^{h}$. to 16^{h}. Fluctuations in Dec. (± 3′): in H.F. (± ·0015): in V.F. small.

6. 5^{h}. to 14^{h}. Fluctuations in Dec. (± 2′): in H.F. (± ·001).

7. 1^{h}. to 13^{h}. Fluctuations in Dec. (± 3′): in H.F. (± ·001): in V.F. small.

9. 6^{h}. to 13^{h}. Fluctuations in Dec. (± 2′): in H.F. (± ·001).

10. $9\frac{1}{2}^{h}$. to 11^{h}. Wave in Dec. (− 4′).

11 to 26. Disturbed period. See Plates X. to XXI.

30. $9\frac{1}{4}^{h}$. to 11^{h}. Wave in Dec. (− 10′): in H.F. (+ ·0025).

December 1. 10^{h}. to 15^{h}. Four successive waves in Dec. (− 4′, − 10′, − 2′, and − 3′): fluctuations in H.F. (± ·0015): in V.F. small.

3. 5^{h}. to $9\frac{1}{2}^{h}$. Fluctuations in Dec. (± 3′): in H.F. (± ·001).

1882.

December

4. $11\frac{3}{4}^{h}$. to $12\frac{1}{2}^{h}$. Fluctuations in Dec. (± 4′): in H.F. (± ·002): in V.F. small.
5. 8^{h}. to 10^{h}. Fluctuations in Dec. (± 2′): in H.F. (± ·0005).
6. $8\frac{1}{4}^{h}$. Wave in Dec. (− 6′).
7. 8^{h}. to 10^{h}. Fluctuations in Dec. (± 2′). $8\frac{1}{2}^{h}$. to $9\frac{1}{2}^{h}$. Wave in H.F. (+ ·002).
8. 19^{h}. Wave in Dec. (+ 4′): in H.F. (+ ·0013).
9. 5^{h}. to 13^{h}. Fluctuations in Dec. (± 3′): in H.F. (± ·0015). Wave at $10\frac{1}{4}^{h}$. in Dec. (− 7′): in H.F. (+ ·0023).
11. $5\frac{1}{4}^{h}$. Wave in Dec. (− 7′): in H.F. (− ·0015). 7^{h}. to 14^{h}. Fluctuations in Dec. (± 3′): in H.F. (± ·001).
12. 1^{h}. to $7\frac{1}{2}^{h}$. Fluctuations in Dec. (± 2′): in H.F. (± ·0005).
15. $8\frac{1}{4}^{h}$. Change in Dec. (− 10′): in H.F. (− ·0015). $11\frac{3}{4}^{h}$. Wave, very sharp at commencement, in Dec. (+ 6′): in H.F. (+ ·004): in V.F. (+ ·0005): followed by fluctuations in Dec. (± 3′): in H.F. (± ·001): in V.F. (± ·0002) until 20^{h}.
16. 8^{h}. to 10^{h}. Wave in Dec. (− 25′). $7\frac{1}{2}^{h}$. to 9^{h}. Wave in H.F. (− ·005): in V.F. (+ ·0003).
18. 9^{h}. to 19^{h}. Fluctuations in Dec. (± 3′): in H.F. (± ·002): in V.F. small.

20.
21. } Disturbed days. See Plate XXII.

26. Waves in Dec. at $7\frac{1}{4}^{h}$. (− 7′), at $8\frac{1}{2}^{h}$. (− 8′), with small fluctuations until 18^{h}. Fluctuations in H.F. 7^{h}. to 13^{h}. (± ·001).
27. $8\frac{1}{2}^{h}$. to 16^{h}. Fluctuations in Dec. (± 5′): in H.F. (± ·0015): in V.F. small.
29. 6^{h}. to 12^{h}. Fluctuations in Dec. (± 5′). Waves in H.F. at $8\frac{1}{2}^{h}$. (+ ·0025), at $11\frac{3}{4}^{h}$. (+ ·0035).
30. $5\frac{1}{2}^{h}$. to $7\frac{1}{2}^{h}$. Wave in Dec. (− 13′), followed by fluctuations (± 2′) until 12^{h}. Fluctuations in H.F. $5\frac{1}{2}^{h}$. to 12^{h}. (± ·001).
31. 5^{h}. to 17^{h}. Fluctuations in Dec. (± 2′): in H.F. (± ·001).

EXPLANATION OF THE PLATES.

The magnetic motions figured on the Plates are—

(1.) Those for days of great disturbance—April 16, 17, 19, 20, June 24, August 4, October 2, 3, November 12, 13, 17, 18, 19, 20, 21.

(2.) Those for days of lesser disturbance—January 19, February 1, 20, June 14, July 16, 30, 31, September 11, November 11, 14, 25, December 20, 21.

(3.) Those for days required to complete the period of visibility of the great November sun-spot—November 15, 16, 22, 23, 24, 26.

The day is the astronomical day commencing at Greenwich mean noon.

The magnetic declination, horizontal force, and vertical force are indicated by the letters D., H., and V. respectively: the declination (west) is expressed in minutes of arc, and the horizontal and vertical forces in parts of the whole horizontal and vertical forces respectively, the corresponding scales being given on the sides of each diagram.

Downward motion indicates increase of declination and of horizontal and vertical force.

The earth current register E_1 is that of the line Angerstein Wharf—Lady Well, making an angle of 50° with the magnetic meridian, reckoning from north to east. The E_2 register is that of the line Blackheath—North Kent East, making an angle of 46° with the magnetic meridian, reckoning from north to west. Zero E_1 and Zero E_2 indicate the respective instrumental zeros.

Downward motion of earth current register indicates in the E_1 circuit the passage of a current, corresponding to that from the copper pole of a battery, in the direction Angerstein Wharf to Lady Well (N.E. to S.W.), and in the E_2 circuit to the passage of a similar current in the direction Blackheath to North Kent East (S.E. to N.W.)

An arrow (↓) indicates that the register was out of range of registration in the direction of the arrow-head. Other causes of interruption are stated in the Introduction. From November 16^{d}. $22\frac{1}{2}^{h}$. to 17^{d}. 1^{h}. and from November 17^{d}. $17\frac{1}{2}^{h}$. to $23\frac{1}{2}^{h}$. the vertical force magnet was in vibration, presumably through rapid magnetic disturbances.

The temperatures given in small figures on the Diagrams represent those of the horizontal and vertical force magnets at the corresponding hours of observation, usually 0^{h}, 1^{h}, 2^{h}, 3^{h}, 9^{h}, 21^{h}, 22^{h}, 23^{h}.

Until June 14 there were no available earth current registers, and on September 11 and October 2 there were no registers of magnetic vertical force, the magnet being away for alteration.

Magnetic Disturbances and Earth Currents recorded at the Royal Observatory Greenwich, 1882.

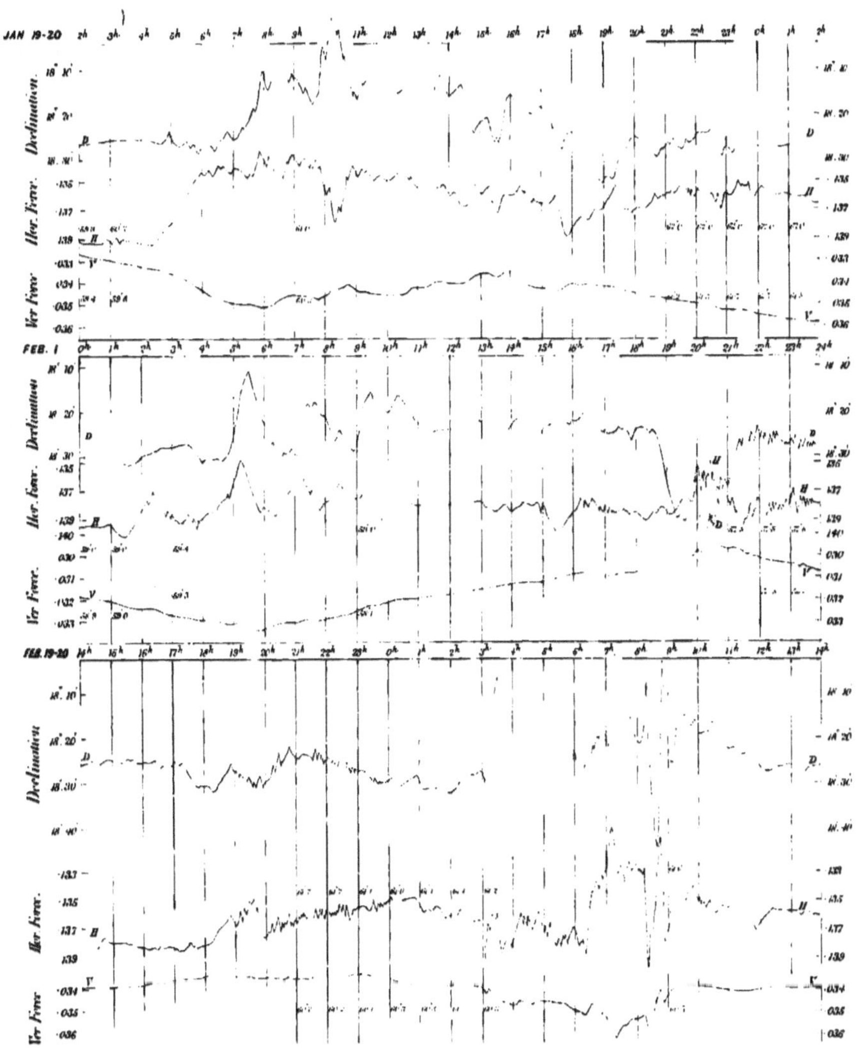

Magnetic Disturbances and Earth Currents recorded at the Royal Observatory Greenwich, 1882.

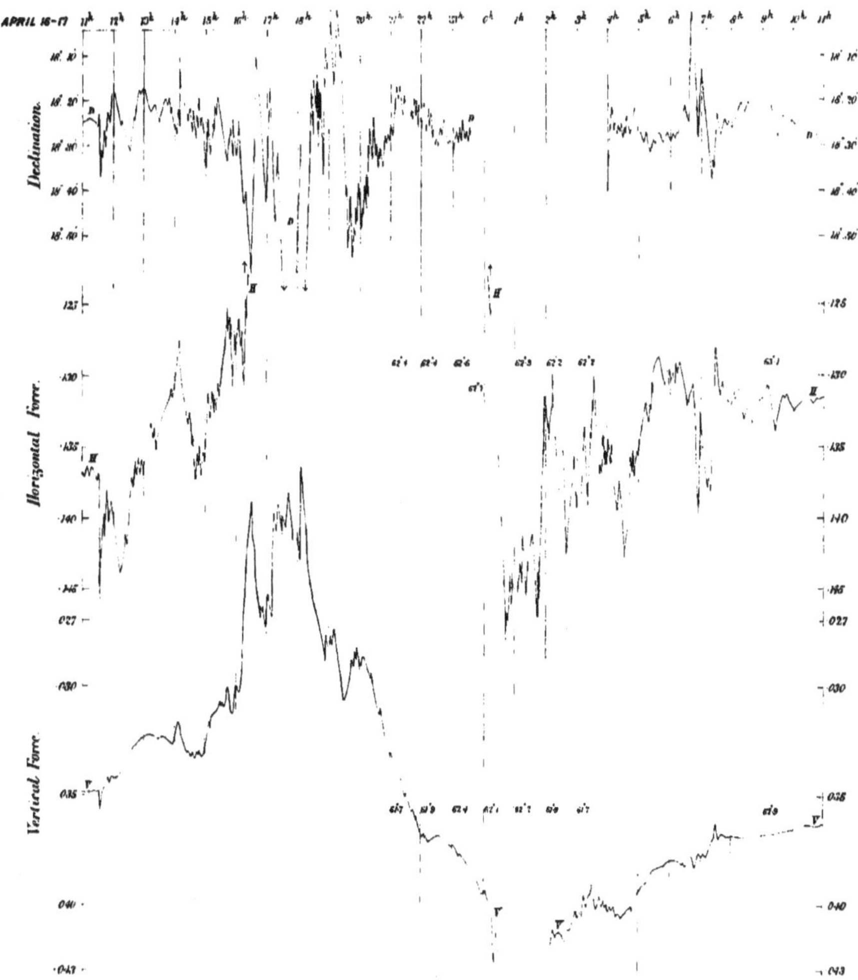

Plate III.

Magnetic Disturbances and Earth Currents recorded at the Royal Observatory Greenwich, 1882.

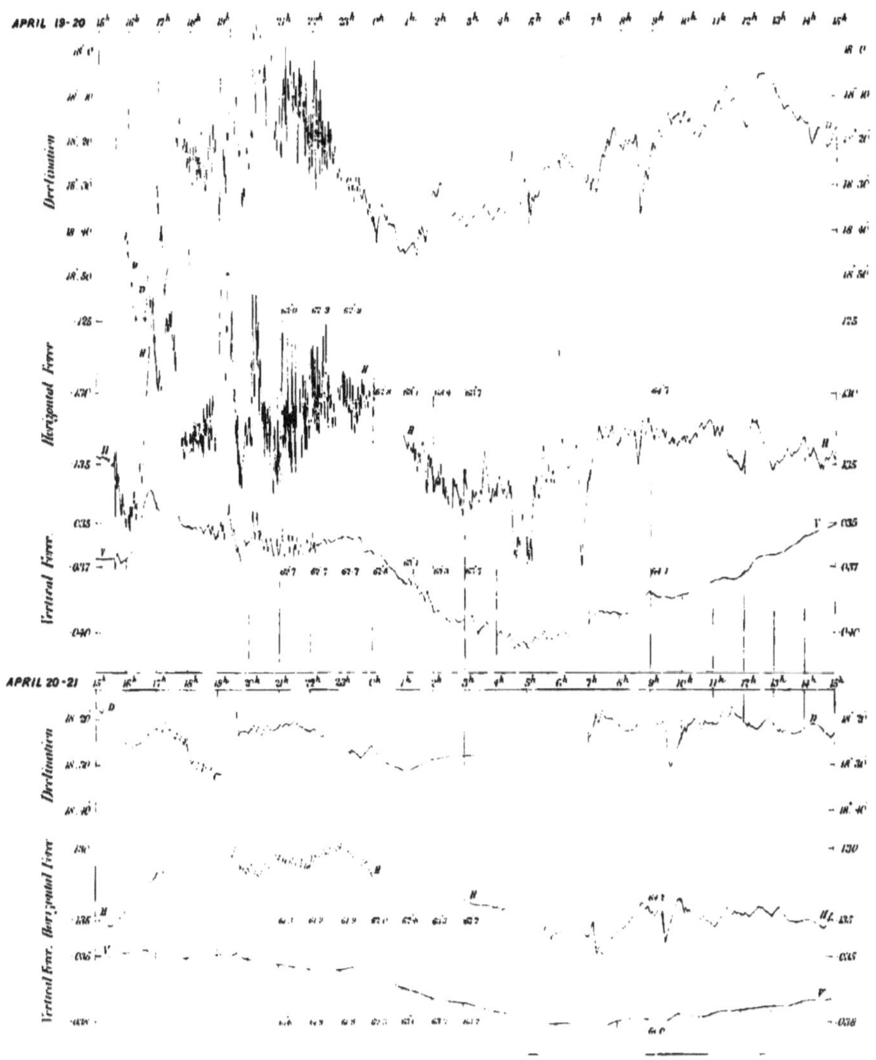

Dangerfield, Lith 22 Bedford St Covent Garden

Magnetic Disturbances and Earth Currents recorded at the Royal Observatory Greenwich, 1882.

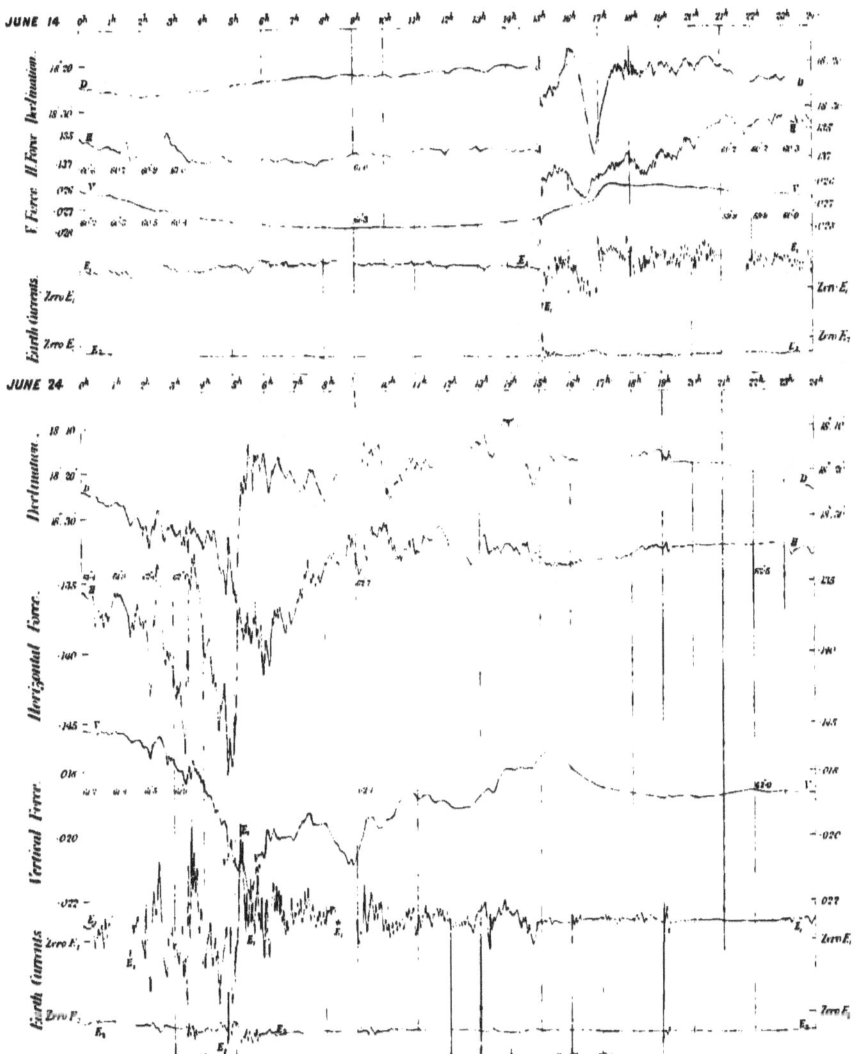

Magnetic Disturbances and Earth Currents recorded at the Royal Observatory Greenwich, 1882.

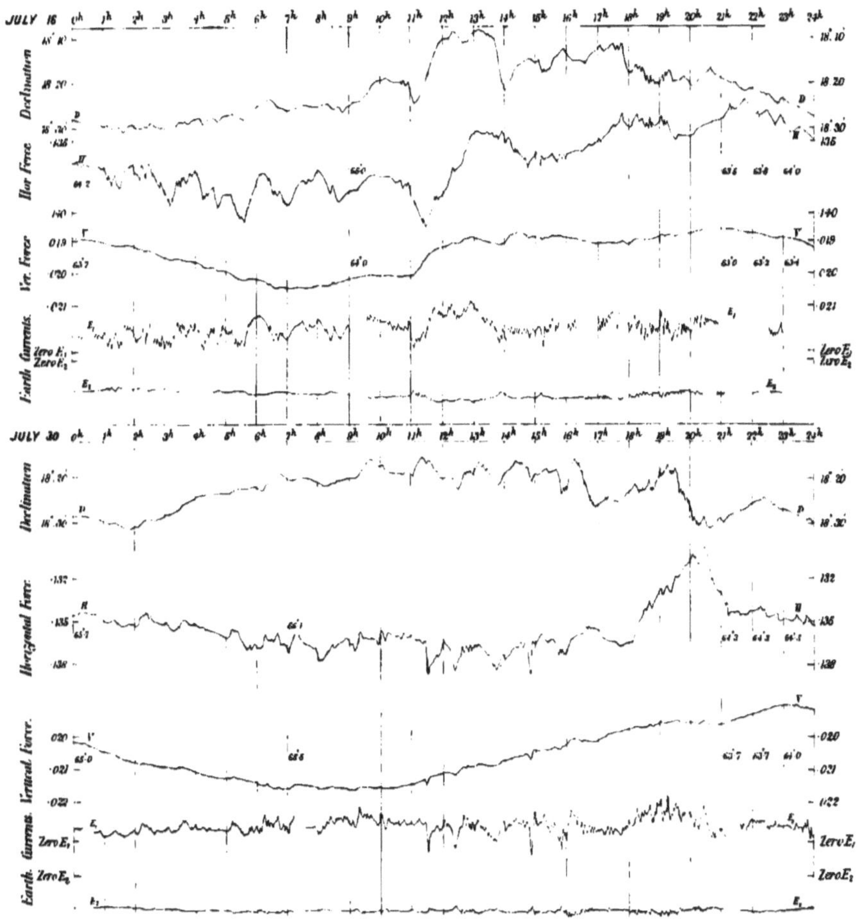

Magnetic Disturbances and Earth Currents recorded at the Royal Observatory Greenwich, 1882.

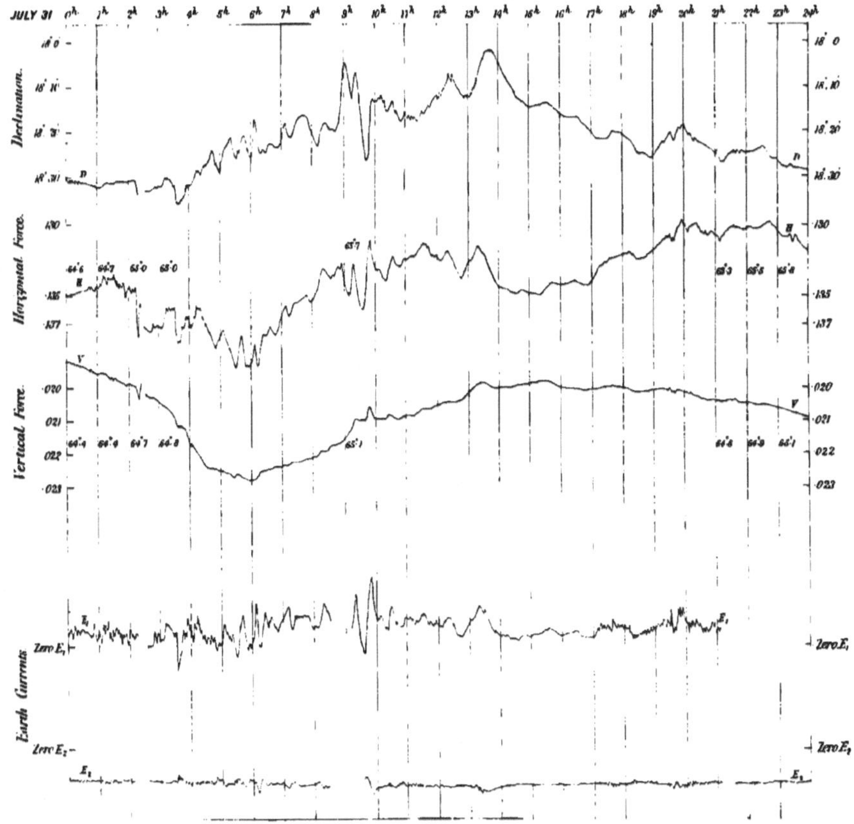

Dangerfield Lith 22 Bedford St Covent Garden

Magnetic Disturbances and Earth Currents recorded at the Royal Observatory Greenwich, 1882.

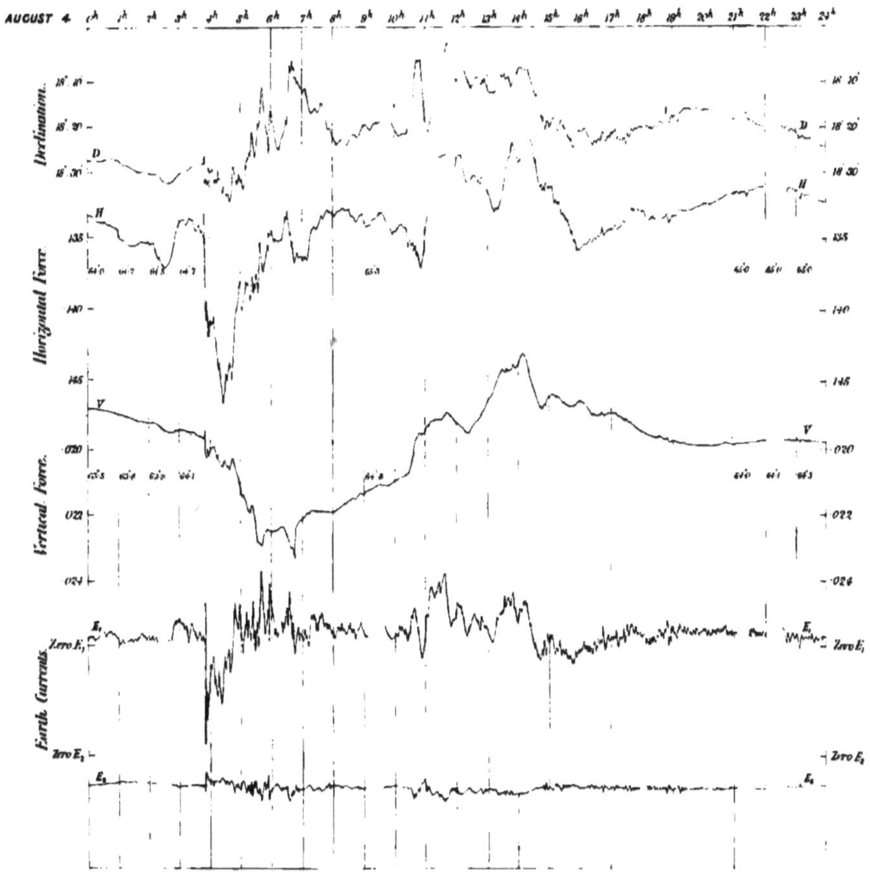

Magnetic Disturbances and Earth Currents recorded at the Royal Observatory Greenwich, 1882.

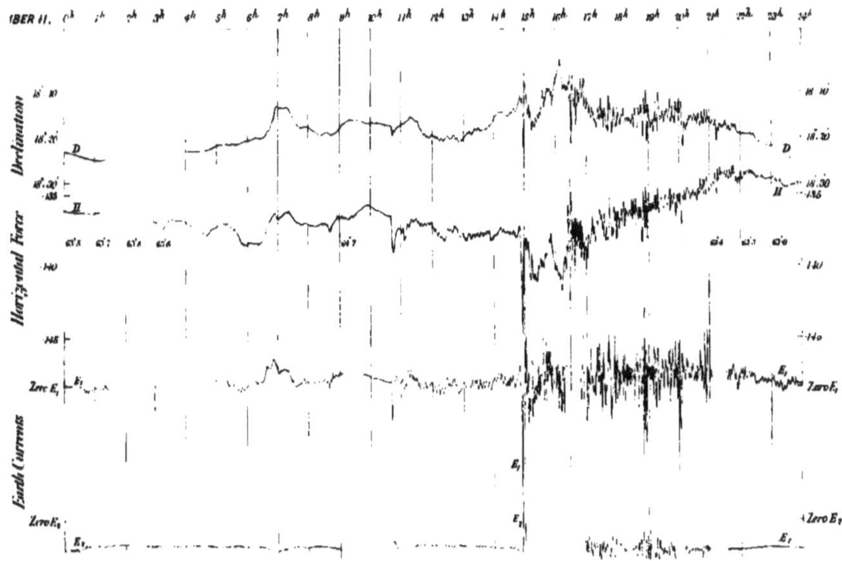

Magnetic Disturbances and Earth Currents recorded at the Royal Observatory Greenwich, 1882.

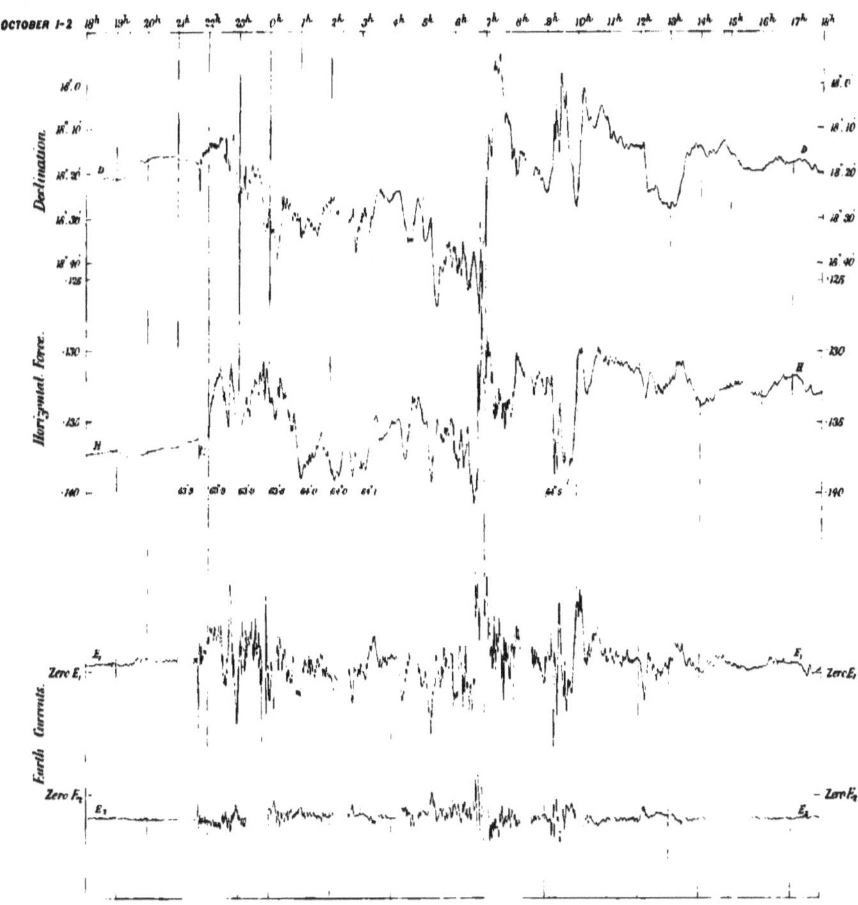

DANCERFIELD, LITH 22 BEDFORD ST COVENT GARDEN

Magnetic Disturbances and Earth Currents recorded at the Royal Observatory Greenwich, 1882.

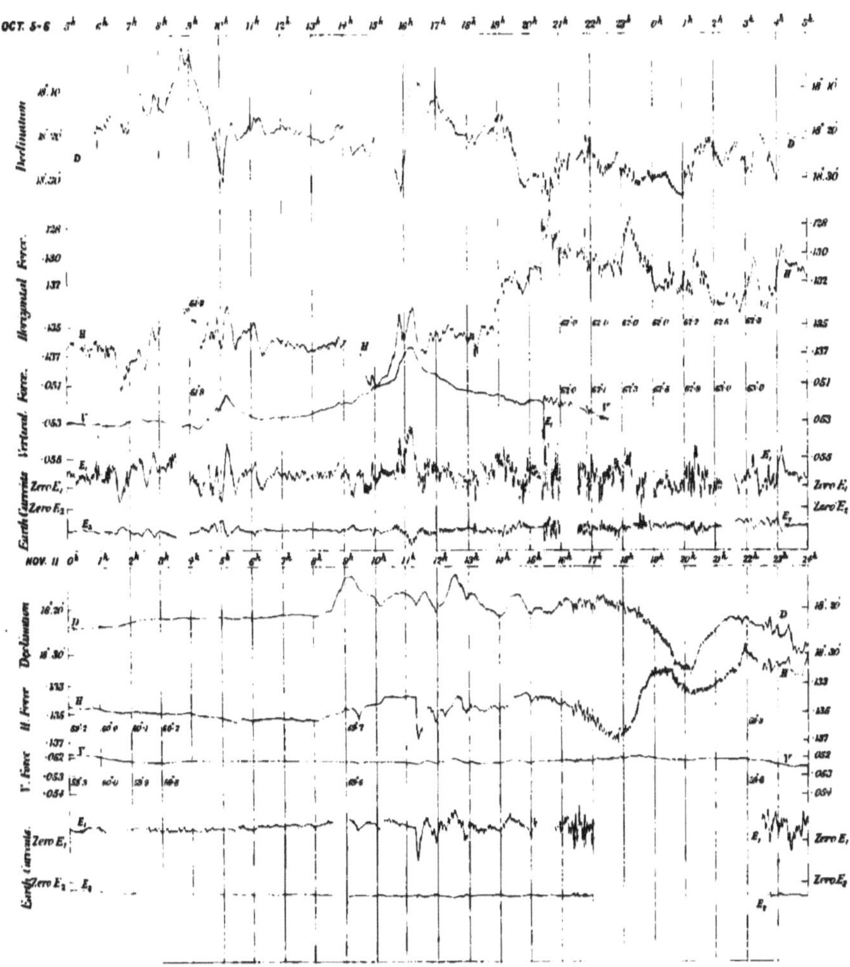

Magnetic Disturbances and Earth Currents recorded at the Royal Observatory Greenwich, 1882.

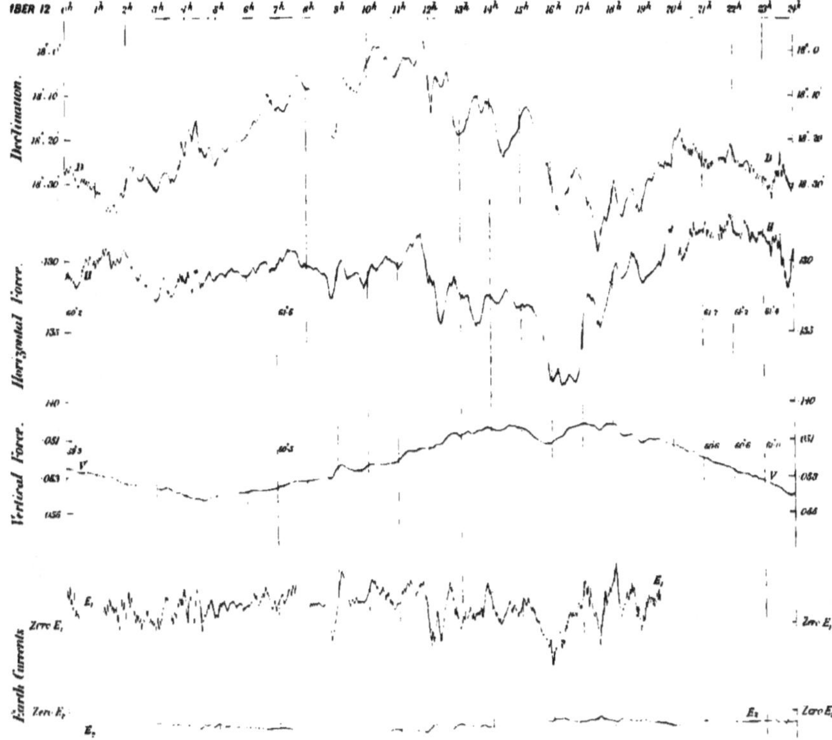

Magnetic Disturbances and Earth Currents recorded at the Royal Observatory Greenwich, 188?.

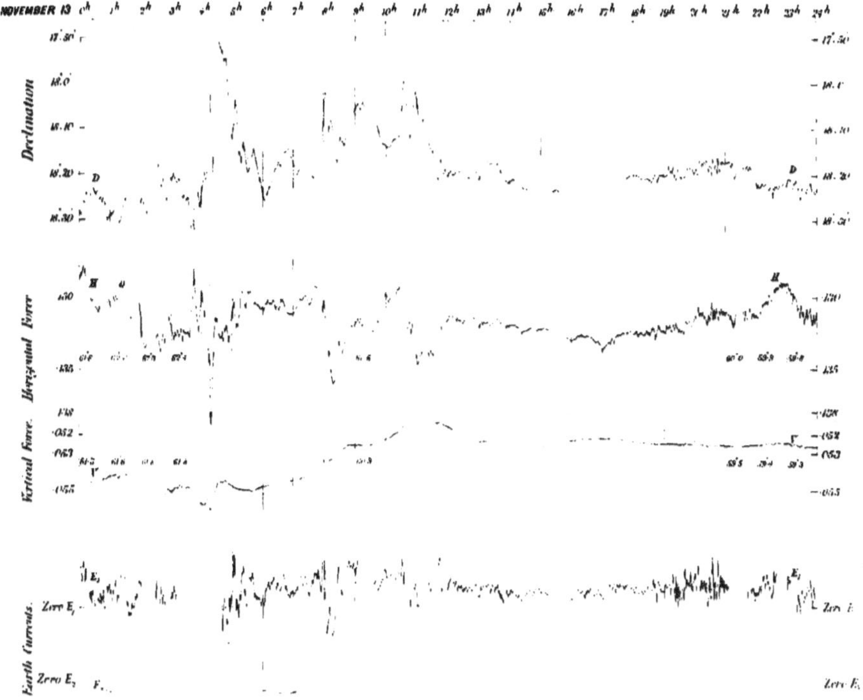

Plate XIII.

Magnetic Disturbances and Earth Currents recorded at the Royal Observatory Greenwich, 1882.

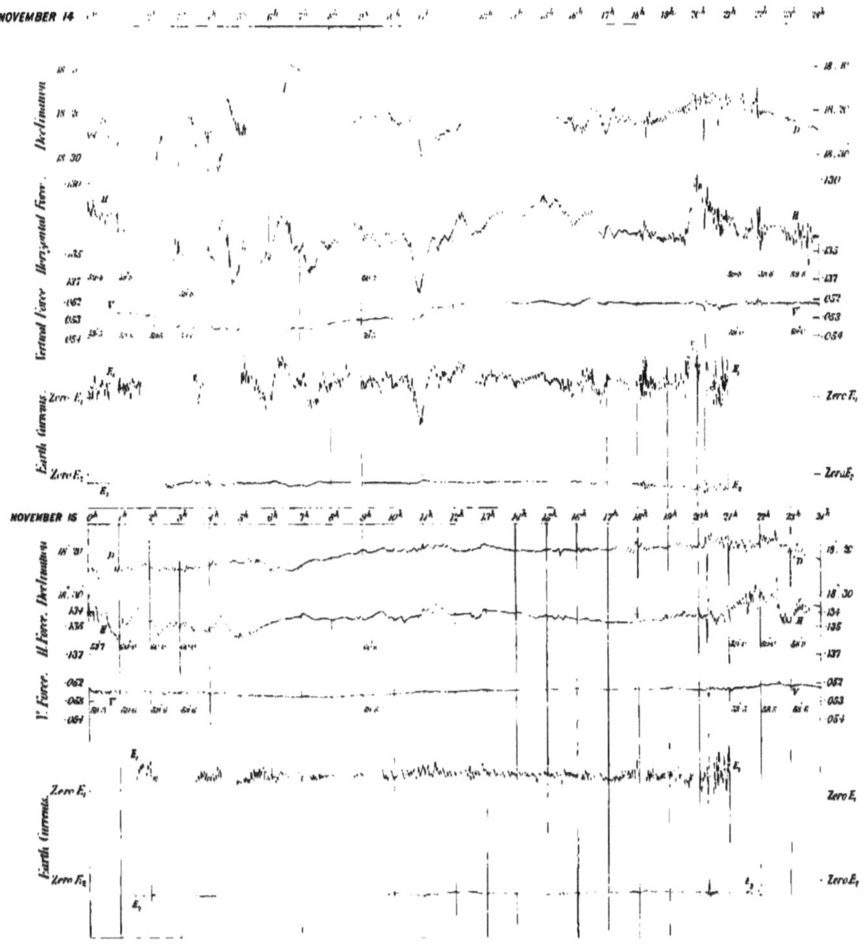

Magnetic Disturbances and Earth Currents recorded at the Royal Observatory Greenwich, 1882.

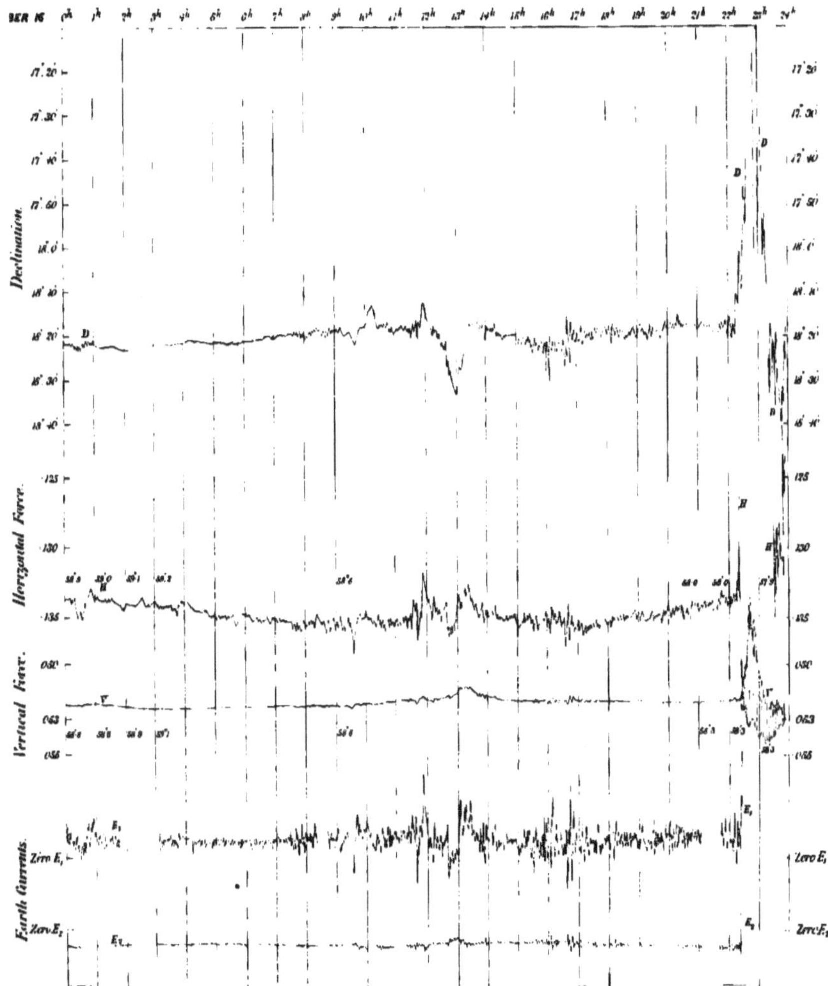

Magnetic Disturbances and Earth Currents recorded at the Royal Observatory Greenwich, 1882.

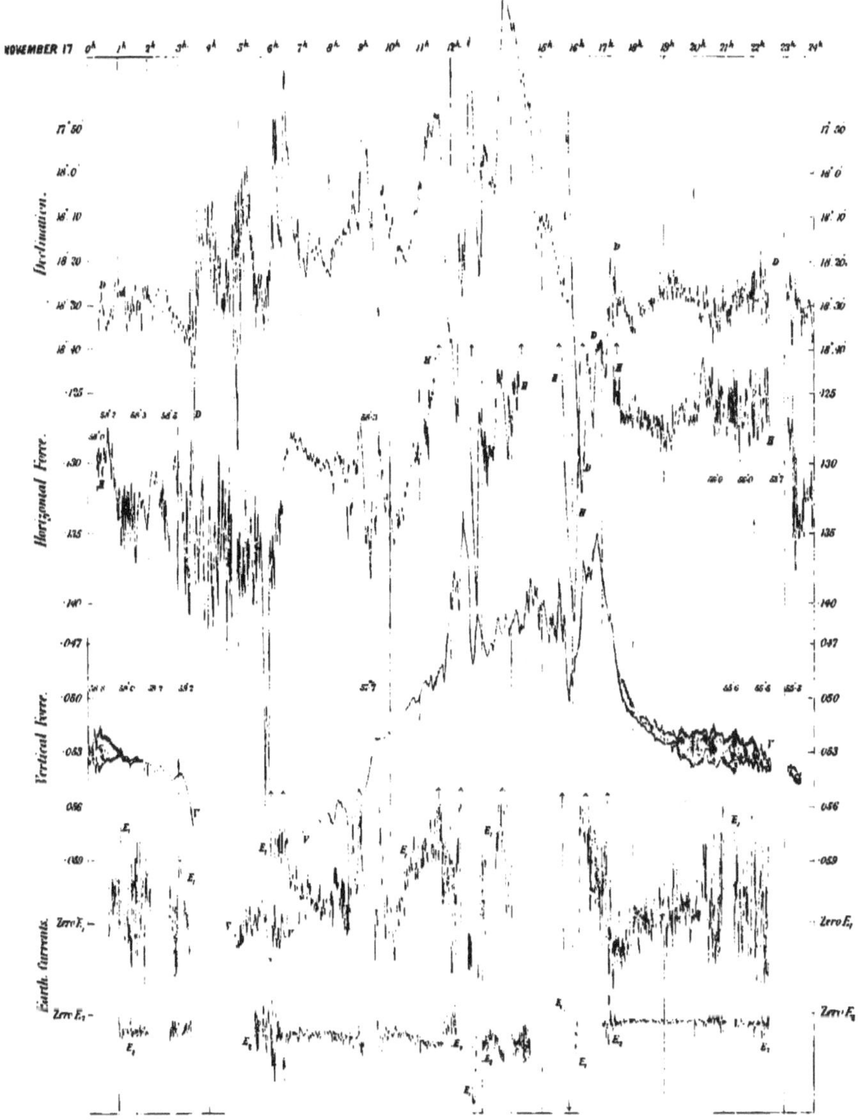

NOVEMBER 17

Magnetic Disturbances and Earth Currents recorded at the Royal Observatory Greenwich, 1882.

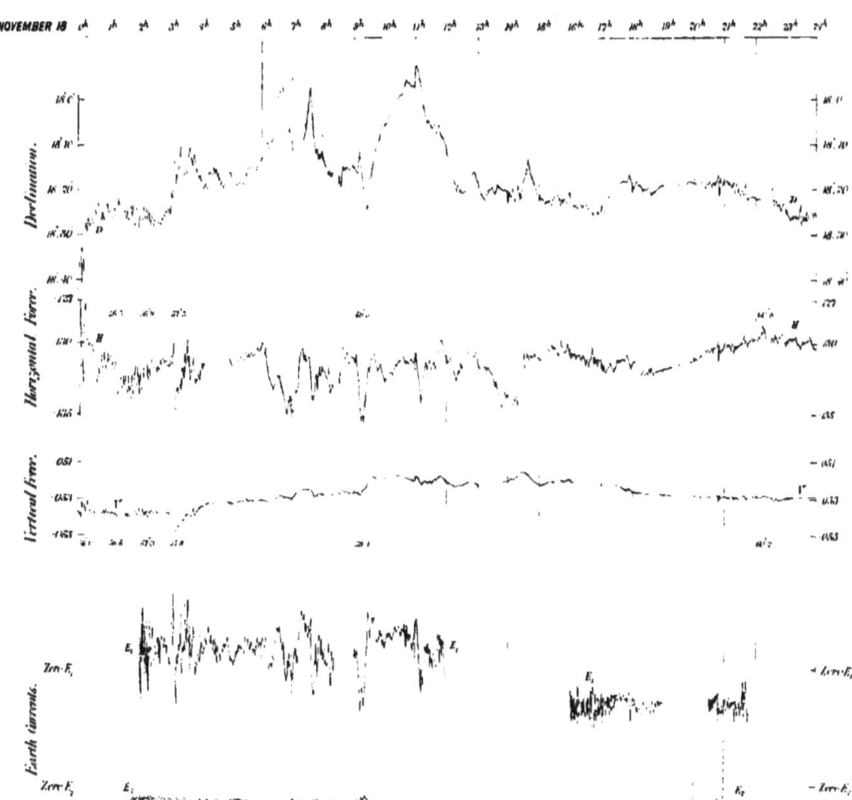

Plate XVII.

Magnetic Disturbances and Earth Currents recorded at the Royal Observatory Greenwich, 1882.

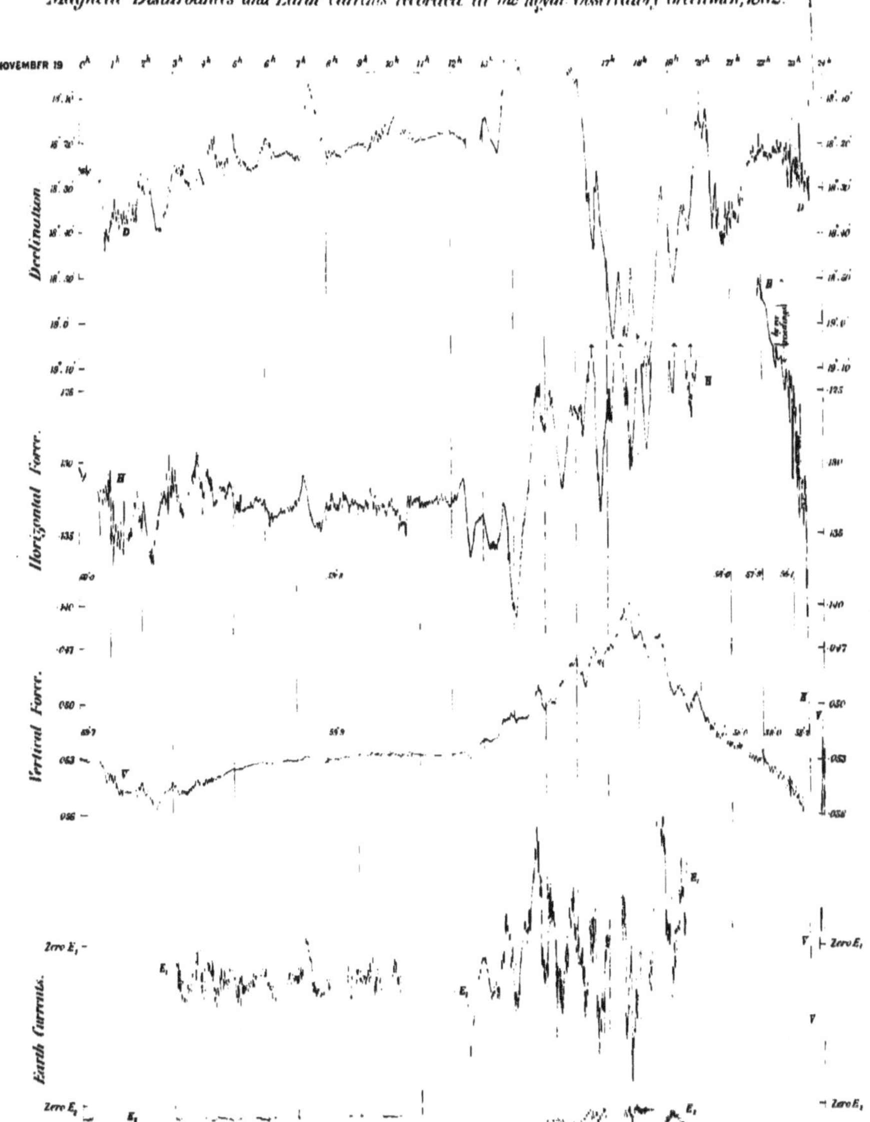

Magnetic Disturbances and Earth Currents recorded at the Royal Observatory Greenwich, 1882.

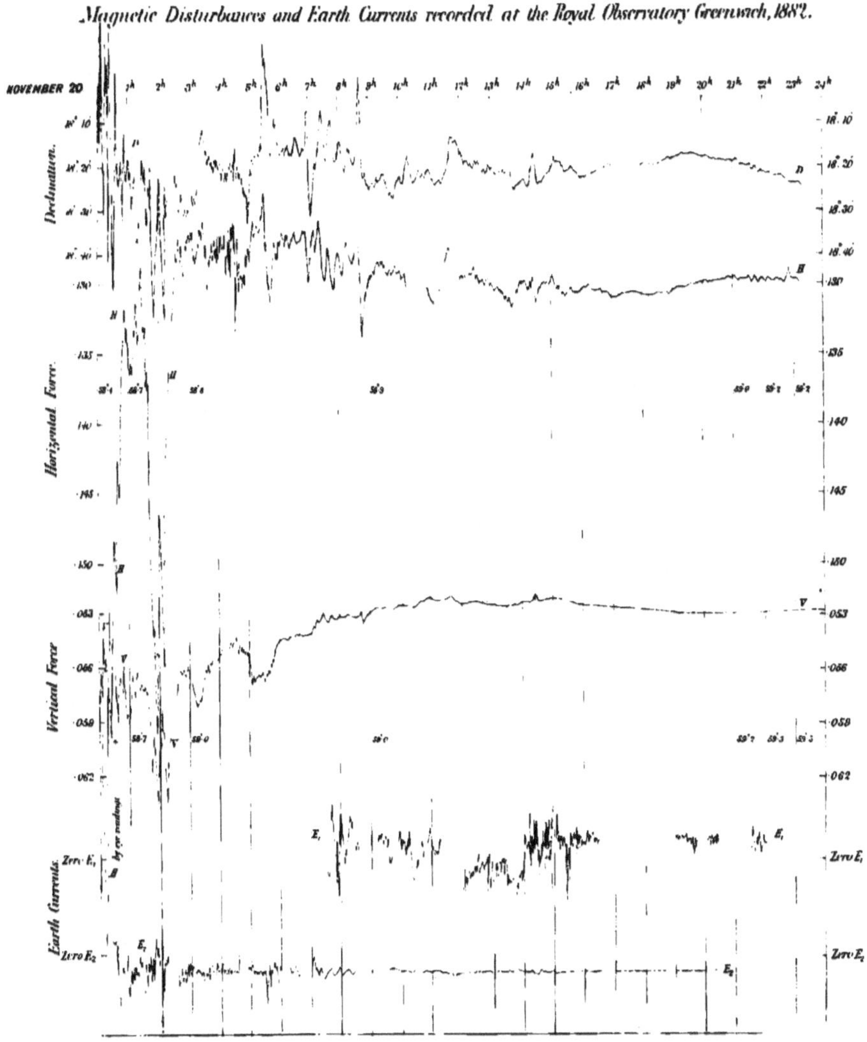

Magnetic Disturbances and Earth Currents recorded at the Royal Observatory Greenwich, 1882.

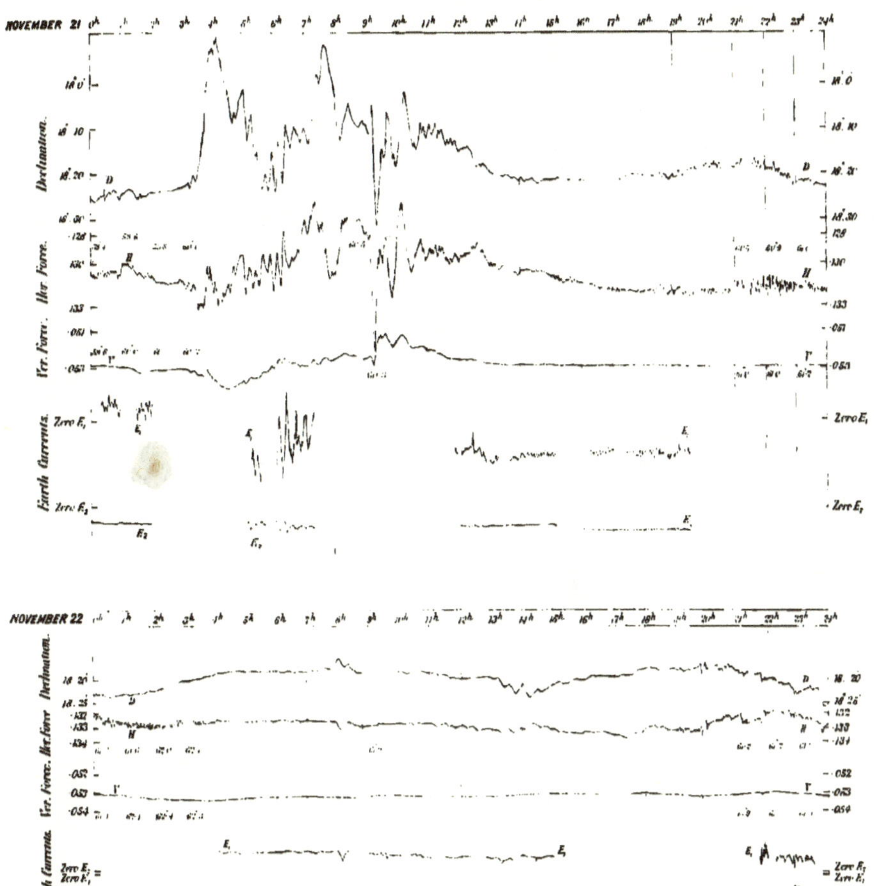

Magnetic Disturbances and Earth Currents recorded at the Royal Observatory Greenwich, 1882.

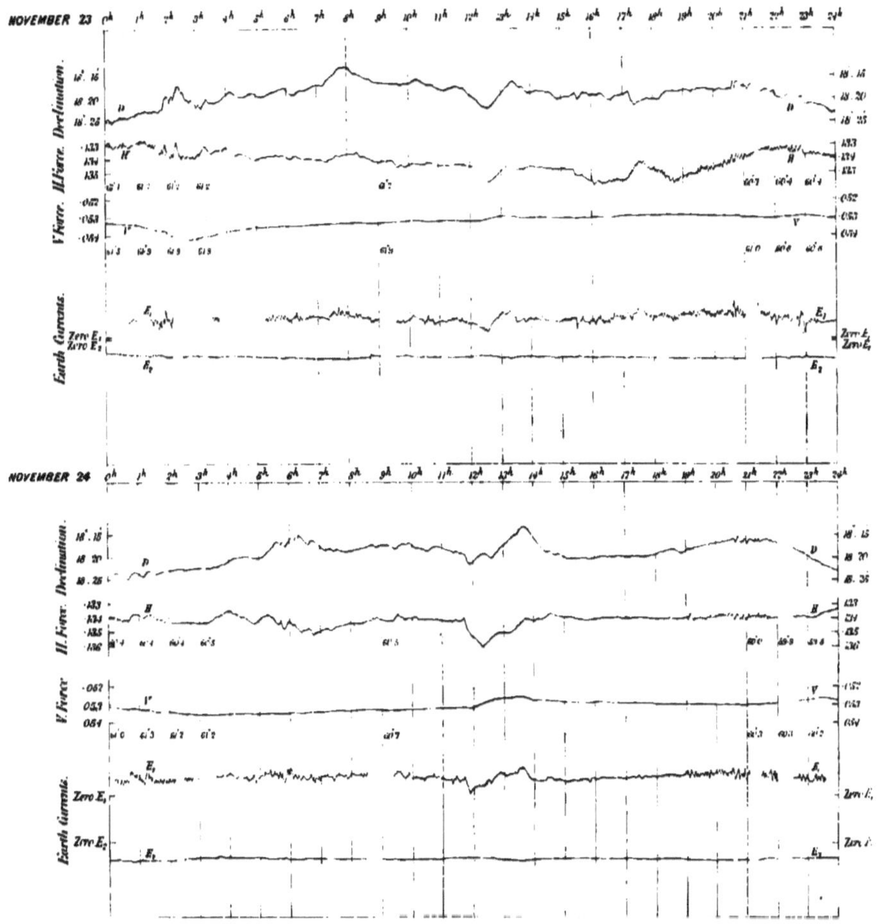

Magnetic Disturbances and Earth Currents recorded at the Royal Observatory Greenwich, 1882.

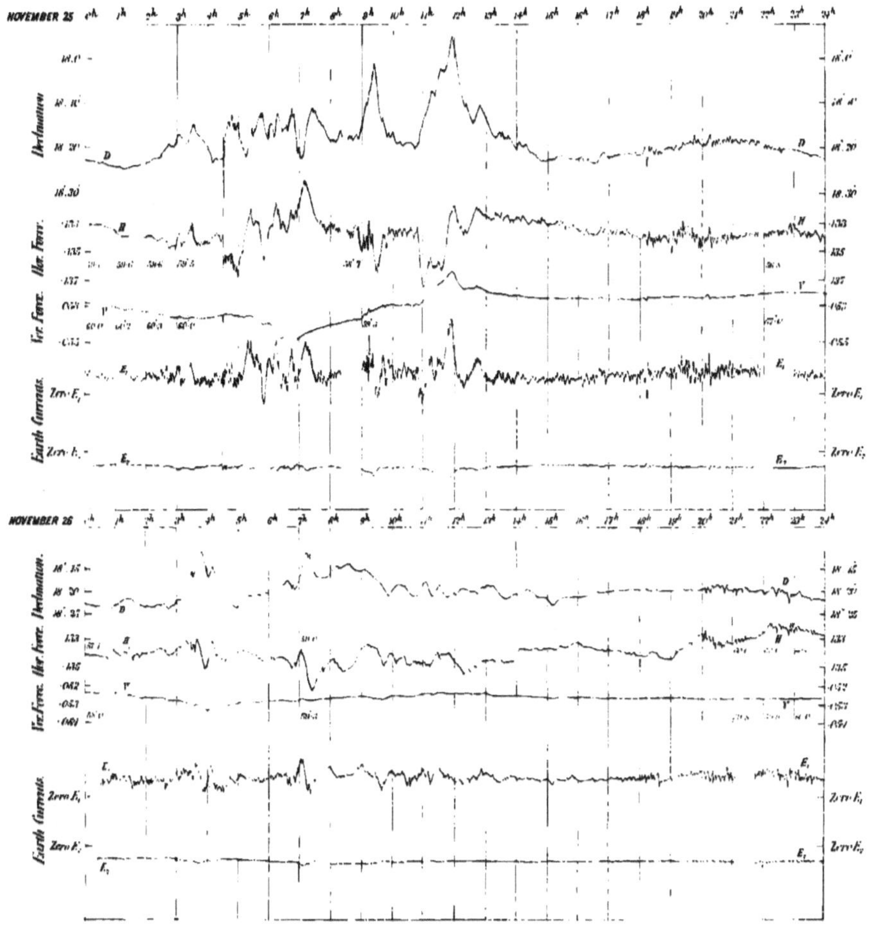

Danielsfield Lith 22 Bedford St Covent Garden

Magnetic Disturbances and Earth Currents recorded at the Royal Observatory Greenwich, 1882.

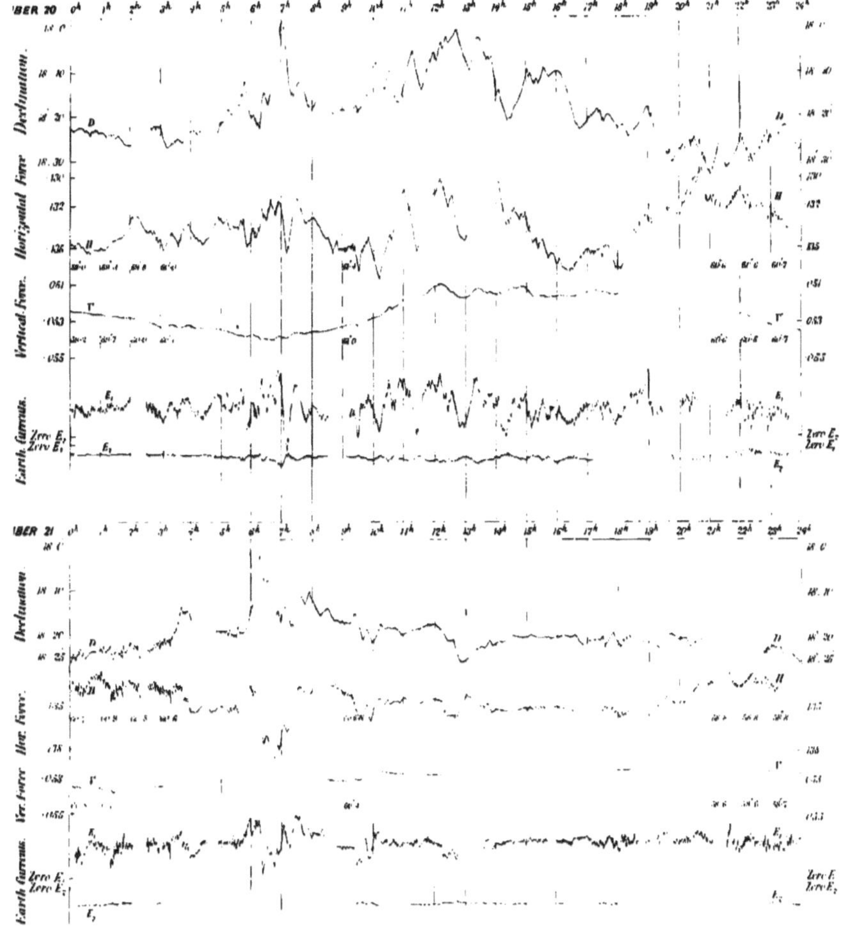

ROYAL OBSERVATORY, GREENWICH.

RESULTS

OF

METEOROLOGICAL OBSERVATIONS.

1882.

MONTH and DAY. 1882.	Phases of the Moon.	BAROMETER. Mean of 24 Hourly Values (corrected and reduced to 32° Fahrenheit).	TEMPERATURE. Of the Air. Highest.	Lowest.	Daily Range.	Mean of 24 Hourly Values.	Excess of Mean above Average of 20 Years.	Of Evaporation. Mean of 24 Hourly Values.	Of the Dew Point. Deduced Mean Daily Value.	Difference between the Air Temperature and Dew Point Temperature. Mean Daily Value.	Greatest of 24 Hourly Values.	Least of 24 Hourly Values.	Degree of Humidity (Saturation = 100).	TEMPERATURE. Highest in the Sun's Rays as shown by a Self-Registering Maximum Thermometer with blackened bulb in vacuo placed on the Grass.	Lowest on the Grass as shown by a Self-Registering Minimum Thermometer.	Daily Duration of Sunshine.	Sun above Horizon.	Rain collected in Gauge No. 6, whose receiving surface is 5 inches above the Ground.	Daily Amount of Ozone.	Electricity.
		in.	°	°	°	°	°	°	°	°	°	°		°	°	h.	hours.	in.		
Jan. 1	..	29·663	48·8	36·8	12·0	43·6	+ 5·5	42·2	40·5	3·1	5·9	1·1	89	85·0	30·0	1·5	7·9	0·210	4·8	wP: wP, wN
2	Greatest Declination N	29·558	51·0	37·6	13·4	46·3	+ 8·4	44·4	42·3	4·0	5·7	2·5	87	58·3	30·6	0·0	7·9	0·019	12·0	wP: —
3	..	29·167	49·9	35·1	14·8	45·7	+ 7·9	43·3	40·6	5·1	9·9	1·7	83	82·1	27·5	2·3	7·9	0·190	9·0	— : sP
4	Full	29·698	41·3	33·6	7·7	36·9	− 0·8	35·6	33·8	3·1	5·9	0·8	89	57·0	25·9	0·4	7·9	0·006	10·5	sP
5	..	29·601	52·2	40·1	12·1	47·2	+ 9·6	45·8	44·3	2·9	5·0	1·5	90	54·3	34·0	0·0	7·9	0·098	8·5	wP
6	..	29·572	52·9	41·6	11·3	48·0	+10·4	45·4	42·5	5·5	9·9	2·3	82	58·3	35·0	0·1	8·0	0·075	3·0	wP: mP
7	..	29·789	48·6	36·9	6·7	41·1	+ 3·5	38·1	34·3	6·8	11·9	3·7	77	76·7	30·6	5·4	8·0	0·000	3·5	mP: sP
8	Apogee	29·949	49·4	37·3	12·1	44·4	+ 6·7	42·2	39·6	4·8	7·1	2·7	83	58·9	31·1	0·0	8·0	0·040	10·5	mP: vP
9	In Equator	29·938	49·9	36·7	13·2	43·5	+ 5·8	41·8	39·8	3·7	8·8	1·0	87	69·9	30·0	1·9	8·1	0·335	3·0	wP, wN: mP
10	..	30·094	46·7	36·0	10·7	41·7	+ 3·9	40·2	38·3	3·4	8·2	1·2	89	53·7	29·2	0·2	8·1	0·002	0·0	mP: sP: wP
11	..	30·022	52·9	44·8	8·1	48·6	+10·7	47·2	45·7	2·9	4·4	0·6	90	76·1	38·1	0·7	8·1	0·005	0·0	mP: vP, wN: mP
12	Last Qr.	30·219	48·6	39·9	8·7	45·7	+ 7·6	45·1	44·5	1·2	2·7	0·7	96	54·1	29·8	0·0	8·2	0·000	0·0	wP
13	..	30·248	48·4	40·0	8·4	43·8	+ 5·6	42·2	40·3	3·5	6·9	1·5	87	82·8	36·1	1·2	8·2	0·000	3·0	vP: sP
14	..	30·379	42·4	38·0	4·4	40·1	+ 1·8	38·7	36·9	3·2	4·8	2·1	89	48·7	37·0	0·0	8·2	0·000	3·0	vP: mP
15	..	30·521	43·2	36·9	6·3	39·8	+ 1·4	38·8	37·5	2·3	3·5	0·2	92	47·7	36·1	0·0	8·3	0·003	0·0	vP
16	Greatest Declination S	30·669	41·2	34·8	6·4	39·3	+ 0·8	38·8	38·2	1·1	2·1	0·0	96	46·0	34·8	0·0	8·3	0·000	0·0	vP: ssP
17	..	30·741	34·8	30·5	4·3	33·0	− 5·6	32·9	32·7	0·3	1·9	0·0	98	38·3	30·5	0·0	8·3	0·000	0·0	sP: sP: vP
18	..	30·760	34·2	30·1	4·1	32·4	− 6·4	32·4	32·4	0·0	1·0	0·0	100	35·7	30·1	0·0	8·4	0·000	0·0	vP, wN
19	New	30·704	41·9	32·1	9·8	36·9	− 2·0	36·2	35·2	1·7	4·4	0·0	94	50·9	31·0	0·0	8·4	0·000	0·0	wP: vP
20	Perigee	30·563	40·9	34·6	6·3	38·9	− 0·2	37·7	36·1	2·8	5·3	0·7	91	45·7	31·0	0·0	8·5	0·000	0·0	wP: vP, wN
21	..	30·533	38·6	29·7	8·9	35·0	− 4·3	33·8	31·9	3·1	4·6	1·4	88	67·2	22·3	0·8	8·5	0·000	0·5	mP: vP, wN
22	In Equator	30·436	42·7	28·5	14·2	37·5	− 2·0	36·6	35·4	2·1	4·6	0·8	92	53·6	22·6	0·0	8·6	0·000	1·5	wP: mP
23	..	30·391	38·2	25·8	12·4	33·8	− 5·8	32·8	31·0	2·8	3·6	1·3	88	44·0	21·8	0·0	8·6	0·000	0·0	vP: sP
24	..	30·524	42·1	28·0	14·1	35·2	− 4·5	33·6	31·1	4·1	8·1	1·3	84	66·9	20·6	1·0	8·7	0·000	0·0	vP: ssP
25	..	30·531	34·7	25·4	9·3	31·0	− 8·8	30·7	29·9	1·1	7·0	0·0	94	34·7	18·3	0·0	8·7	0·000	0·0	vP
26	First Qr.	30·380	34·6	29·6	5·0	32·3	− 7·6	31·7	30·4	1·9	4·0	0·0	92	39·6	29·5	0·0	8·8	0·000	0·0	wP: mP
27	..	30·216	47·0	34·1	12·9	41·4	+ 1·4	40·8	40·1	1·3	4·4	0·0	96	54·7	32·4	0·0	8·8	0·000	1·8	wP
28	..	30·137	50·5	43·2	7·3	46·9	+ 6·8	45·2	43·3	3·6	4·8	2·4	88	56·3	37·4	0·3	8·9	0·000	5·2	wP
29	Greatest Declination N	29·985	49·3	40·7	8·6	45·6	+ 5·4	43·7	41·5	4·1	7·4	1·9	86	55·3	35·5	0·0	8·9	0·169	0·0	wP: wP, mN
30	..	30·129	43·0	37·9	5·1	41·4	+ 1·1	40·3	38·9	2·5	4·2	0·7	92	49·0	29·8	0·0	9·0	0·000	0·5	wP
31	..	30·453	40·8	38·2	2·6	39·3	− 1·1	37·8	35·9	3·4	4·4	2·5	88	47·0	37·0	0·0	9·0	0·000	1·5	wP: mP
Means	..	30·180	44·4	35·3	9·1	40·5	+ 1·8	39·2	37·6	2·9	5·6	1·2	89·6	56·4	30·5	0·5	8·4	Sum 1·352	2·6	..
Number of Column for Reference	1	2	3	4	5	6	7	8	9	10	11	12	13	14	15	16	17	18	19	20

The results apply to the civil day.

The mean reading of the Barometer (Column 2) and the mean temperatures of the Air and Evaporation (Columns 6 and 8) are deduced from the photographic records. The average temperature (Column 7) is that determined from the reduction of the photographic records from 1849 to 1868. The temperature of the Dew Point (Column 9) and the Degree of Humidity (Column 13) are deduced from the corresponding temperatures of the Air and Evaporation by means of Glaisher's Hygrometrical Tables. The mean difference between the Air and Dew Point Temperatures (Column 10) is the difference between the numbers in Columns 6 and 9, and the Greatest and Least Differences (Columns 11 and 12) are deduced from the 24 hourly photographic measures of the Dry-bulb and Wet-bulb Thermometers.

The values given in Columns 3, 4, 5, 14, and 15 are derived from eye-readings of self-registering thermometers.

The mean reading of the *Barometer* for the month was 30in·180, being 0in·451 *higher* than the average for the 20 years, 1854–1873.

TEMPERATURE OF THE AIR.

The highest in the month was 52°·9 on January 6 and 11; the lowest in the month was 25°·4 on January 25; and the range was 27°·5.

The mean of all the highest daily readings in the month was 44°·4, being 1°·4 *higher* than the average for the 41 years, 1841–1881.

The mean of all the lowest daily readings in the month was 35°·3, being 1°·9 *higher* than the average for the 41 years, 1841–1881.

The mean of the daily ranges was 9°·1, being 0°·5 *less* than the average for the 41 years, 1841–1881.

The mean for the month was 40°·5, being 1°·8 *higher* than the average for the 20 years, 1849–1868.

MONTH and DAY. 1881.	WIND AS DEDUCED FROM SELF-REGISTERING ANEMOMETERS. OSLER'S. General Direction. A.M.	P.M.	Pressure on the Square Foot. Greatest.	Least.	Mean of 24 Hourly Measures.	ROBINSON'S. Horizontal Movement of the Air.	CLOUDS AND WEATHER. A.M.	P.M.
			lbs.	lbs.	lbs.	miles.		
Jan. 1	S : SSW	SSW : WSW : NW	5·7	0·0	0·4	337	v, sc : 9, li.-sc, ci	9, sc : 9, r : th.-cl, lu.-ha
2	SW	SW	14·0	0·0	2·7	660	10 : 10, sc, w	10 : 10, sc, r, st.-w
3	SW : WSW	WSW	14·0	0·0	2·0	510	10, hy.-r, st.-w : 10	3, cu, ci.-cu, cu.-s : 1, li.-cl, lu.-co
4	WSW	SW : SSW	0·3	0·0	0·0	267	c, ho.-fr : 0, m, ho.-fr : 2, li.-cl, m	2, ci.-cu, ci, h, m : 1, h, ho.-fr : v, r, lu.-ha, m
5	SSW : SW	WSW : SW	9·6	0·0	1·9	547	10, c.-r : 10, sc, w : 10, sc	10, sc : v, ci.-cu, cu.-s, sc, li.-cl, lu.-ha
6	SW	WSW : SW	12·0	0·0	3·1	628	10 : 10 : 10, m.-r, sc, sq.	10, sc, r, w : 1, ci : 0
7	SW : WSW	WSW : SW	7·3	0·0	1·1	503	0 : s, li.-cl : 0, h	2, ci.-cu : 0 : 0
8	SW : SSW	SW : WSW	13·5	0·0	2·9	611	0 : 7, ci	10, tq.-r, w : 10, st.-w : 10, sc, st.-w
9	WSW : NNE-NW : W	W : WSW	9·3	0·0	1·0	394	10, sc, hy.-r : 10, hy.-r : 10, ci.-cu, ci.-s, h, slt.-f	4, ci, ci.-cu, ci.-s, cu.-s, h : 0
10	SW	SW	4·2	0·0	0·5	375	li.-cl : 6, ci, ci.-s, ho.-fr	9, cu.-s, ci.-cu : 10, oc.-m.-r
11	WSW : SW	SW	2·4	0·0	0·2	287	10 : 7, ci, cu.-s, slt.-sh	8, ci.-cu, ci.-s, sh.-r : vv : 10
12	SW : SE : S	S : SSE	0·0	0·0	0·0	140	10 : 10, f	10, m.-r : 10
13	SSE	SSE : SSW	0·4	0·0	0·0	186	10 : 10	7, ci, ci.-s, cu.-s, ci.-cu : 10
14	SSW : S	SSW : S	0·0	0·0	0·0	166	10 : 10	10 : 10
15	S : SE	SSE : SE	0·0	0·0	0·0	113	10 : 10	10 : 10, oc.-m.-r
16	ESE : SSE : SE	SE : SSE	0·0	0·0	0·0	85	10 : 10	10 : 10, f
17	SSE : SW	SW : WSW	0·0	0·0	0·0	110	10, f : 10, f	10, f : 10, tk.-f
18	W : Calm : SSW	SW : WSW : ENE	0·0	0·0	0·0	89	10, tk.-f : 10, tk.-f	10, tk.-f : 10, tk.-f
19	NE : Calm : SW	SSW : Calm	0·0	0·0	0·0	60	10, tk.-f : 10, slt.-f	10 : 10
20	Calm	SSW : WSW : NW	0·0	0·0	0·0	67	10 : 10, slt.-f	10 : 10
21	NNW : WSW	W : SW : Calm	0·0	0·0	0·0	121	10 : v, h, slt.-f	f, h : 10, f
22	SW : E	SE : E	0·0	0·0	0·0	63	10, f : 10, slt.-f	10 : 4, ho.-fr : 0, ho.-fr, f
23	W : SW	SW	0·0	0·0	0·0	139	0, ho.-fr, f : 9, cu.-s, ci.-cu, f, ho.-fr	10 : 10, slt.-f : 0, slt.-f, fr
24	SW	SW	0·0	0·0	0·0	180	0, ho.-fr : 9, ci.-cu, ci.-s, slt.-f, ho.-fr	3, cu.-s, ci.-cu : 0, slt.-f : 0, ho.-fr
25	SW : WSW	WSW : ESE	0·0	0·0	0·0	86	0, ho.-fr, slt.-f : tk.-f, ho.-fr	tk.-f : tk.-f : 10
26	SE : S	SSE : SE	0·0	0·0	0·0	104	10 : 10	10 : 10, sl?.-f
27	SE : S	S : SSW	1·0	0·0	0·0	200	10, slt.-f : 10, slt.-f	9, cu.-s, ci.-cu : 0 : 10, sc
28	SSW	SSW : SW	4·8	0·0	0·7	420	10, sc : 7, sc, ci, ci.-s, s	10, sc : 10, th.-cl, lu.-ha
29	SSW : SSE	SSE : SW	2·5	0·0	0·1	283	10 : 10	10, fq.-r : 10, oc.-slt.-r
30	WSW : NNE	NE : ENE	1·6	0·0	0·1	240	10 : 10	10, oc.-m.-r : 10, m.-r
31	E : ESE	ESE : E	2·1	0·0	0·2	236	10 : 10	10 : 10
Means	...	...	..	..	0·6	265		
Number of Column for Reference.	21	22.	23	24	25	26	27	28

The mean *Temperature of Evaporation* for the month was 39°·2, being 1°·8 *higher* than
The mean *Temperature of the Dew Point* for the month was 37°·6, being 2°·2 *higher* than
The mean *Degree of Humidity* for the month was 89·6, being 2·3 *greater* than
The mean *Elastic Force of Vapour* for the month was 0in·225, being 0in·018 *greater* than
The mean *Weight of Vapour in a Cubic Foot of Air* for the month was 2grs·6, being 0gr·2 *greater* than
The mean *Weight of a Cubic Foot of Air* for the month was 559 grains, being 7 grains *greater* than
} the average for the 20 years, 1849-1868.

The mean amount of *Cloud* for the month (a clear sky being represented by 0 and an overcast sky by 10) was 8·2.

The mean proportion of *Sunshine* for the month (constant sunshine being represented by 1) was 0·06. The maximum daily amount of *Sunshine* was 5·4 hours on January 7.

The highest reading of the *Solar Radiation Thermometer* was 85°·0 on January 1; and the lowest reading of the *Terrestrial Radiation Thermometer* was 18°·3 on January 25.

The mean daily distribution of *Ozone* was, for the 12 hours ending 9 a.m., 1·7; for the 6 hours ending 3 p.m., 0·3; and for the 6 hours ending 9 p.m., 0·6.

The *Proportions of Wind* referred to the cardinal points were N. 1, E. 4, S. 14, and W. 9. Three days were calm.

The *Greatest Pressure of the Wind* in the month was 14lbs·0 on the square foot on January 2 and 3. The mean daily *Horizontal Movement of the Air* for the month was 265 miles; the greatest daily value was 660 miles on January 2; and the least daily value 60 miles on January 19.

Rain fell on 10 days in the month, amounting to 1in·352, as measured by gauge No. 6 partly sunk below the ground; being 0in·710 *less* than the average fall for the 41 years, 1841-1881.

DAILY RESULTS OF THE METEOROLOGICAL OBSERVATIONS

Temperature. Of the Air. Highest.	Temperature. Of the Air. Lowest.	Temperature. Of the Air. Daily Range.	Temperature. Of the Air. Mean of 24 Hourly Values.	Temperature. Of the Air. Excess of Mean above Average of 20 Years.	Temperature. Of Evaporation. Mean of 24 Hourly Values.	Temperature. Of the Dew Point. Deduced Mean Daily Value.	Difference between the Air Temperature and Dew Point Temperature. Mean Daily Value.	Difference between the Air Temperature and Dew Point Temperature. Greatest of 24 Hourly Values.	Difference between the Air Temperature and Dew Point Temperature. Least of 24 Hourly Values.	Degree of Humidity (Saturation = 100).	Temperature. Highest in the Sun's Rays as shown by a Self-Registering Maximum Thermometer with blackened bulb in vacuo placed on the Grass.	Temperature. Lowest on the Grass as shown by a Self-Registering Minimum Thermometer.	Daily Duration of Sunshine.	Sun above Horizon.	Rain collected in Gauge No. 6, whose receiving surface is 5 inches above the Ground.	Daily Amount of Ozone.	Electricity.
			°	°				°					hours.	hours.	in.		
40·1	26·8	13·3	33·7	− 6·8	32·4	30·1	3·6	10·4	0·0	86	93·3	16·4	3·8	9·1	0·000	0·0	sP
36·5	24·8	11·7	32·3	− 8·3	31·8	30·7	1·6	5·5	0·0	94	49·7	16·3	0·0	9·2	0·000	0·0	vP
44·9	28·1	16·8	35·2	− 5·5	35·2	35·2	0·0	3·3	0·0	100	79·0	23·1	0·7	9·2	0·006	0·0	wP : vP
36·9	25·7	11·2	30·9	− 9·8	30·9	30·9	0·0	2·8	0·0	100	37·3	21·0	0·0	9·3	0·000	0·0	vP
37·8	26·5	11·3	33·4	− 7·2	32·7	31·4	2·0	6·2	0·0	92	51·3	21·7	0·0	9·3	0·000	0·0	wP : vP
42·3	33·1	9·2	37·3	− 3·1	37·0	36·6	0·7	2·6	0·0	97	50·1	29·6	0·0	9·4	0·010*	0·0	wP : vP
45·0	38·4	6·6	40·4	+ 0·2	40·1	39·7	0·7	3·1	0·0	98	59·3	35·5	0·0	9·4	0·000	2·0	wP : mP
41·2	33·0	8·2	38·2	− 1·7	37·2	35·8	2·4	5·1	0·0	91	51·0	30·5	0·0	9·5	0·000	8·7	wP : sP
36·9	29·8	7·1	34·9	− 4·7	33·8	32·1	2·8	4·9	1·0	89	42·8	28·3	0·0	9·6	0·000	6·7	wP : mP
46·0	32·5	13·5	37·4	− 1·9	35·8	33·6	3·8	9·2	0·8	87	115·0	23·0	2·2	9·6	0·000	1·5	wP : sP
52·8	34·6	18·2	42·8	+ 3·7	40·8	38·5	4·3	9·8	1·9	85	117·3	24·5	2·8	9·7	0·000	3·5	wP : mP
55·2	41·0	14·2	46·6	+ 7·7	44·7	42·6	4·0	11·2	0·4	87	103·8	33·0	3·0	9·8	0·000	3·2	wP : wP : vP
51·9	40·0	11·9	47·2	+ 8·4	45·9	44·5	2·7	4·4	0·9	91	36·4	32·4	0·0	9·8	0·003	5·8	wP
55·4	47·0	8·4	50·7	+ 12·0	47·9	45·0	5·7	13·0	0·6	81	96·3	40·5	3·9	9·9	0·130	6·5	wP : vP
51·1	35·5	15·6	43·7	+ 5·0	42·3	40·6	3·1	5·8	0·0	89	72·0	29·0	0·1	9·9	0·356	6·0	wP : vP, vN : vP
48·8	32·4	16·4	41·3	+ 2·5	39·7	37·7	3·6	5·3	2·6	88	80·8	27·0	1·4	10·0	0·003	2·0	mP : wP
52·1	44·7	7·4	47·5	+ 8·6	44·9	42·1	5·4	9·2	2·3	82	83·7	39·8	0·4	10·1	0·000	2·0	wP : mP
51·4	40·5	10·9	46·8	+ 7·8	44·3	41·5	5·3	9·2	1·1	83	87·6	35·0	1·7	10·1	0·013	0·8	wP : vP, vN
48·6	35·8	12·8	42·6	+ 3·4	38·8	34·2	8·4	14·9	3·2	73	97·8	29·0	6·6	10·2	0·000	2·2	mP
47·4	32·4	15·0	40·6	+ 1·3	38·8	36·5	4·1	10·3	0·3	86	81·2	25·9	0·2	10·3	0·000	4·8	mP : vP
51·5	41·8	9·7	47·2	+ 7·7	45·4	43·4	3·8	5·7	1·5	88	59·0	35·5	0·0	10·3	0·002	2·2	vP : wP : mP
54·9	38·7	16·2	46·5	+ 6·9	44·7	42·7	3·8	9·0	0·0	87	83·1	30·0	3·8	10·4	0·000	0·0	wP : wN, vP
45·0	40·1	4·9	42·5	+ 2·8	39·8	36·5	6·0	7·9	4·4	80	46·7	36·3	0·0	10·5	0·000	0·0	mP : mN, mP : mP
49·2	39·8	9·4	42·9	+ 3·1	40·7	38·1	4·8	10·1	1·8	84	87·0	27·9	2·2	10·5	0·000	0·5	wP, wN : vP
54·1	41·4	12·7	49·9	+ 10·0	47·9	45·8	4·1	6·8	1·4	87	71·2	37·1	0·0	10·6	0·050	6·8	wP, wN : wP
55·4	47·5	7·9	51·2	+ 11·2	49·3	47·4	3·8	7·2	1·6	87	86·3	43·5	0·9	10·7	0·137	13·7	o : wP
53·1	42·5	10·6	48·0	+ 7·9	46·1	44·0	4·0	7·6	1·0	87	86·2	41·2	0·2	10·7	0·147	6·0	wP : wN, wP
50·1	38·2	11·9	44·2	+ 4·0	43·3	42·2	2·0	6·9	0·0	93	77·3	38·2	0·1	10·8	0·234	2·2	wP : wP, wN
47·7	36·2	11·5	42·0	+ 2·3	40·4	38·5	3·4	7·5	1·0	88·3	75·2	30·4	1·3	9·9	Sum 1·153	3·2	..
3	4	5	6	7	8	9	10	11	12	13	14	15	16	17	18	19	20

MONTH and DAY, 1881.	WIND AS DEDUCED FROM SELF-REGISTERING ANEMOMETERS. Osler's. General Direction. A.M.	P.M.	Pressure on the Square Foot. Greatest.	Least.	Mean of 24 Hourly Measures.	Robinson's. Horizontal Movement of the Air.	CLOUDS AND WEATHER. A.M.	P.M.
			lbs.	lbs.	lbs.	miles.		
Feb. 1	E : ESE	E	0·3	0·0	0·0	154	v : 0, ho.-fr	0 : 0, ho.-fr
2	Calm : SW	SE : SW	0·0	0·0	0·0	104	0, ho.-fr, slt.-f : ci.-cu, cu.-s, slt.-f, ho.-fr	10, slt.-f : 9, cu.-s, ci.-cu, f
3	Calm : SW	NE : SE : Calm	0·0	0·0	0·0	104	10, f : 10, f	5, tk.-f : 0, tk.-f
4	Calm	Calm	0·0	0·0	0·0	49	tk.-f, ho.-fr : tk.-f, ho.-fr	tk.-f : tk.-f
5	Variable : Calm	SW : SE : Calm	0·0	0·0	0·0	114	tk.-f : 9	10 : 10, slt.-f : 10, slt.-f
6	Calm	NE	0·0	0·0	0·0	84	10, slt.-f : 10, f	10, m : 10, slt.-f : 10
7	NE : E	E : ENE	0·0	0·0	0·0	126	10 : 10, f	10 : 10, oc.-m.-r : 10
8	E : ESE	E : SE : S	0·0	0·0	0·0	140	10 : 10	10 : 10 : p.-cl
9	S : SSW	SSW : S	0·0	0·0	0·0	235	p.-cl : 10	10, oc.-m.-r : 10
10	SSW	S : SSE	0·0	0·0	0·0	180	10 : th.-cl	6, ci, ci.-cu, ci.-s : 0, ho.-fr
11	SSE : S	SSE : S	0·0	0·0	0·0	222	c, ho.-fr : 7, ci, ci.-s, slt.-m	6, ci, ci.-cu, ci.-s : 10, th.-cl
12	S : SW	SW : SSW	0·5	0·0	0·0	293	10, th.-cl : 10, oc.-m.-r	9, cu.-s : 0 : 0, d
13	SSW	SW	9·5	0·0	1·5	573	0, d : 10, th.-cl, sc	10, sc, oc.-slt.-r, w : vv, sc, oc.-slt.-r
14	SW : WSW	WSW : SW : SSW	3·0	0·0	0·3	396	vv : 10, r : 8, ci	5, cu.-s, ci.-cu, ci, sc : 10, sc, oc.-slt.-r
15	SW : N	N : NW : WNW	9·6	0·0	1·1	466	10, sc, oc.-r, w : 10, sc, hy.-r, w, gt.-glm	9, sc, glm, r : 10, sh.-r : 0
16	WSW : SW	SW : WSW	6·4	0·0	1·1	509	0 : 0, ho.-fr : v	10, slt.-r : 10
17	WSW : W	WSW	4·5	0·0	0·9	526	10 : 10	8, ci.-s, cu.-s : v, th.-cl
18	WSW : SW	SW : NW : W	13·0	0·0	1·0	534	vv, th.-cl : 6, cu.-s, ci.-cu, w	9, cu.-s, sc, w : 10, slt.-r : v
19	NW : NNW	NNW	3·7	0·0	0·6	397	0 : 0, h	vv, li.-cl : 0
20	WSW	WNW : WSW	1·0	0·0	0·1	302	0, ho.-fr : 10	9, th.-cl : 10 : 9
21	WSW : NNW : N	N : NNE	0·0	0·0	0·0	216	10 : 10, m, glm, slt.-r	10 : 10 : v
22	Calm : WSW	WSW : NW	0·3	0·0	0·0	216	0, d : p.-cl, m, slt.-f	6, cu.-s, ci.-cu, f : 10 : 10
23	NW : NNW	NE : SE	0·0	0·0	0·0	130	10 : 10, glm	10, glm : 10
24	SE : Calm : WSW	WNW : SW : S	1·0	0·0	0·0	154	10 : 10, slt.-f	7, cu.-s, ci.-cu, h : 9
25	S	SSW	12·5	0·0	2·3	365	10, slt.-r : 9, fq.-th.-r	9, ci.-s, li.-shs, w : 9, sc, sqs, fq.-r
26	SW : SSW	SW	11·0	0·3	3·0	659	10, sc, w : 10, r : 10, sc, li.-shs, w	9, cu.-s, ci.-cu, w : 7, sc, ci.-cu
27	WSW	WSW : N	4·1	0·0	0·6	388	v, s : 9, cu.-s, ci.-s, ci.-cu, sc	9, r : 10, fq.-r
28	NE : SE	SSE : SE	5·0	0·0	0·5	246	10 : 10, oc.-slt.-r, m	10, cu.-s : 10, hy.-r
Means	...	...	..	..	0·5	289		
Number of Column for Reference.	21	22	23	24	25	26	27	28

The mean *Temperature of Evaporation* for the month was 40°·4, being 2°·5 *higher* than
The mean *Temperature of the Dew Point* for the month was 38°·5, being 3°·1 *higher* than
The mean *Degree of Humidity* for the month was 88·3, being 3·5 *greater* than
The mean *Elastic Force of Vapour* for the month was 0in·233, being 0in·026 *greater* than
The mean *Weight of Vapour in a Cubic Foot of Air* for the month was 2grs·7, being 0gr·3 *greater* than
The mean *Weight of a Cubic Foot of Air* for the month was 555 grains, being 1 grain *greater* than
} the average for the 20 years, 1849–1868.

The mean amount of *Cloud* for the month (a clear sky being represented by 0 and an overcast sky by 10) was 8·0.

The mean proportion of *Sunshine* for the month (constant sunshine being represented by 1) was 0·13. The maximum daily amount of *Sunshine* was 6·6 hours on February 19.

The highest reading of the *Solar Radiation Thermometer* was 117°·3 on February 11; and the lowest reading of the *Terrestrial Radiation Thermometer* was 16°·3 on February 2.

The mean daily distribution of *Ozone* was, for the 12 hours ending 9 a.m., 1·1; for the 6 hours ending 3 p.m., 0·5; and for the 6 hours ending 9 p.m., 0·6.

The *Proportions of Wind* referred to the cardinal points were N. 3, E. 5, S. 9, and W. 7. Four days were calm.

The *Greatest Pressure of the Wind* in the month was 13lbs·0 on the square foot on February 18. The mean daily *Horizontal Movement of the Air* for the month was 289 miles; the greatest daily value was 659 miles on February 26; and the least daily value 49 miles on February 4.

Rain fell on 9 days in the month, amounting to 1in·153, as measured by gauge No. 6 partly sunk below the ground; being 0in·338 *less* than the average fall for the 41 years, 1841–1881.

MONTH and DAY, 1891.	Phases of the Moon.	BAROMETER. Mean of 24 Hourly Values (corrected and reduced to 32° Fahrenheit).	TEMPERATURE. Of the Air. Highest.	Of the Air. Lowest.	Of the Air. Daily Range.	Of the Air. Mean of 24 Hourly Values.	Of the Air. Excess of Mean above Average of 20 Years.	Of Evaporation. Mean of 24 Hourly Values.	Of the Dew Point. Deduced Mean Daily Value.	Difference between the Air Temperature and Dew Point Temperature. Mean Daily Value.	Greatest of 24 Hourly Values.	Least of 24 Hourly Values.	Degree of Humidity (Saturation = 100).	TEMPERATURE. Highest in the Sun's Rays shown by a Self-Registering Maximum Thermometer with blackened bulb in vacuo placed on the Grass.	Lowest on the Grass shown by a Self-Registering Minimum Thermometer.	Daily Duration of Sunshine.	Sun above Horizon.	Rain collected in Gauge No. 6, whose receiving surface is 5 inches above the Ground.	Daily Amount of Ozone.	Electricity.
		in.	°	°	°	°	°	°	°	°	°	°		°	°	hours.	hours.	in.		
Mar. 1	..	28·833	51·9	42·2	9·7	46·7	+ 6·4	44·3	41·6	5·1	13·0	0·2	83	92·3	38·4	2·6	10·8	0·193	19·7	wP : vP, vN
2	..	29·143	51·7	37·8	13·9	43·7	+ 3·3	40·5	36·7	7·0	16·0	2·5	76	115·3	31·8	6·5	10·9	0·041	11·2	mP : vP, mN : mP
3	Apogee	29·264	48·7	32·7	16·0	39·6	− 0·9	37·9	35·7	3·9	9·7	0·7	86	119·7	25·0	6·2	11·0	0·000	5·8	wP : mP
4	..	29·480	49·4	29·7	19·7	38·5	− 2·0	37·0	35·0	3·5	11·8	0·0	87	90·2	19·0	4·1	11·1	0·000	5·8	mP : wP : mP
5	Full: In Equator.	29·546	52·4	39·6	12·8	46·4	+ 5·9	44·7	42·8	3·6	8·0	0·7	88	96·9	33·3	1·5	11·1	0·025	3·0	wP
6	..	29·705	50·4	35·0	15·4	46·6	+ 6·1	42·7	38·3	8·3	13·9	2·3	74	80·6	27·0	1·3	11·2	0·000	2·2	vP, wN : vP
7	..	30·056	54·0	33·4	20·6	46·1	+ 5·5	44·7	43·1	3·0	7·7	0·8	90	67·6	26·1	0·1	11·2	0·007	7·0	mP : wP : wP
8	..	30·087	55·4	46·0	9·4	50·8	+ 10·2	49·0	47·1	3·7	7·4	1·4	87	69·2	39·2	0·0	11·3	0·000	0·0	wP
9	..	30·163	55·1	47·7	7·4	50·3	+ 9·6	48·7	47·0	3·3	7·2	0·6	89	89·0	44·2	1·1	11·4	0·000	4·0	wP
10	..	30·149	55·4	48·8	6·6	51·0	+ 10·3	50·0	49·0	2·0	3·8	1·0	93	66·0	46·6	0·0	11·4	0·000	10·0	wP
11	..	30·257	54·4	44·4	10·0	49·1	+ 8·3	48·4	47·6	1·5	4·6	0·0	95	71·3	44·0	0·0	11·5	0·107	0·0	wP, wN
12	Greatest Dec. S. Last Quarter.	30·331	52·2	38·6	13·6	45·8	+ 5·0	44·3	42·6	3·2	9·2	0·0	89	98·4	30·0	1·5	11·6	0·005	0·0	wP
13	..	30·381	55·7	33·8	21·9	44·3	+ 3·4	41·8	38·9	5·4	13·6	0·0	79	89·4	27·3	5·2	11·6	0·000	0·0	wP : wP, wN : vP, wN
14	..	30·264	60·2	33·2	27·0	46·6	+ 5·6	43·6	40·2	6·4	13·7	0·0	80	108·8	28·0	9·0	11·7	0·000	4·0	wP : mP
15	..	30·347	59·5	35·6	23·9	46·8	+ 5·7	44·2	41·3	5·5	14·1	0·0	82	108·0	27·8	4·8	11·8	0·000	0·0	wP : vP
16	..	30·438	63·1	36·4	26·7	49·4	+ 8·2	46·1	42·6	6·8	16·2	0·5	77	113·9	29·6	9·3	11·8	0·000	0·0	mP : vP, wN
17	..	30·359	63·8	36·9	26·9	49·4	+ 8·1	46·0	42·4	7·0	18·1	0·0	77	104·0	29·5	7·1	11·9	0·000	0·0	mP : mP, mN
18	Perigee: In Equator.	30·136	65·0	31·4	33·6	48·4	+ 7·0	44·9	41·1	7·3	18·9	0·0	76	110·2	25·5	6·8	12·0	0·000	0·8	wP, wN : sP
19	New	29·880	60·0	37·2	22·8	47·6	+ 6·2	44·7	41·5	6·1	17·7	0·0	80	114·2	28·8	8·5	12·0	0·000	4·2	mP : sP
20	..	29·642	63·1	34·5	28·6	48·7	+ 7·2	45·1	41·2	7·5	17·1	0·0	76	116·0	27·1	9·3	12·1	0·000	7·5	mP : vP
21	..	29·563	50·0	33·2	16·8	43·0	+ 1·4	39·8	36·0	7·0	14·7	0·3	77	113·1	31·0	6·1	12·2	0·076	1·5	vP, wN
22		29·824	45·4	30·8	14·6	36·[illegible]	− 5·0	34·5	31·3	5·4	10·3	2·7	82	93·9	25·3	5·9	12·2	0·032	5·0	mP : vP, wN : sP
23		30·003	50·3	28·8	21·5	40·1	− 1·7	37·1	33·2	6·9	14·1	2·3	76	118·0	21·3	1·4	12·3	0·000	1·0	sP : vP
24		29·590	55·1	43·6	11·5	49·1	+ 7·1	47·8	46·4	2·7	8·6	0·0	91	89·1	41·5	0·0	12·4	0·075	5·0	wP : vP
25	Greatest Declination N.	29·513	56·4	39·5	16·9	46·6	+ 4·3	42·8	38·6	8·0	16·8	0·7	74	112·2	32·0	6·7	12·4	0·410	7·2	mP : wP, wN : vP, vN
26	First Qr.	29·287	49·9	33·8	16·1	44·7	+ 2·1	42·0	38·8	5·9	13·9	0·0	80	98·2	32·2	6·5	12·5	0·173	6·7	vP, vN : mP
27	..	29·935	53·2	37·0	16·2	44·5	+ 1·5	41·5	38·0	6·5	10·7	1·6	78	97·1	29·0	2·4	12·6	0·000	0·0	mP : vP
28	..	30·001	54·7	39·2	15·5	47·5	+ 4·1	45·3	42·9	4·6	10·2	0·2	85	104·1	34·3	0·4	12·6	0·000	3·2	mP : vP
29	..	29·786	57·1	45·9	11·2	50·6	+ 6·8	48·7	46·7	3·9	8·0	2·3	87	90·1	41·0	0·1	12·7	0·000	5·8	wP : wP : vP
30	Apogee	29·479	57·6	40·0	17·6	47·8	+ 3·5	44·2	40·2	7·6	15·8	1·3	76	125·0	31·5	7·3	12·8	0·000	0·0	mP : vP, wN : vP
31	..	29·412	57·3	38·3	19·0	45·6	+ 0·8	42·5	38·9	6·7	16·0	0·9	78	121·6	28·5	6·2	12·8	0·000	1·5	vP, mN
Means	..	29·834	55·1	37·6	17·5	46·2	+ 4·6	43·7	40·9	5·3	12·3	0·7	82·2	99·5	31·5	4·1	11·8	Sum 1·144	3·9	....
Number of Column for Reference.	1	2	3	4	5	6	7	8	9	10	11	12	13	14	15	16	17	18	19	20

The results apply to the civil day.

The mean reading of the Barometer (Column 2) and the mean temperatures of the Air and Evaporation (Columns 6 and 8) are deduced from the photographic records. The average temperature (Column 7) is that determined from the reduction of the photographic records from 1849 to 1868. The temperature of the Dew Point (Column 9) and the Degree of Humidity (Column 13) are deduced from the corresponding temperatures of the Air and Evaporation by means of Glaisher's Hygrometrical Tables. The mean difference between the Air and Dew Point Temperatures (Column 10) is the difference between the numbers in Columns 6 and 9, and the Greatest and Least Differences (Columns 11 and 12) are deduced from the 24 hourly photographic measures of the Dry-bulb and Wet-bulb Thermometers.

The values given in Columns 3, 4, 5, 14, and 15 are derived from eye-readings of self-registering thermometers.

The mean reading of the *Barometer* for the month was 29in·834, being 0in·112 *higher* than the average for the 20 years, 1834–1873.

MONTH and DAY, 1882.	WIND AS DEDUCED FROM SELF-REGISTERING ANEMOMETERS.						CLOUDS AND WEATHER.	
	OSLER'S.					ROBINSON'S.		
	General Direction.		Pressure on the Square Foot.			Horizontal Movement of the Air.		
	A.M.	P.M.	Greatest.	Least.	Mean of 24 Hourly Measures.		A.M.	P.M.
			lbs.	lbs.	lbs.	miles.		
Mar. 1	S : SW	SW	15·0	0·0	3·6	643	10, r : 7, ci, ci.-cu, sc, fq.-shs, st.-w	7, ci.-s, ci.-cu, cu.-s, sc, shs.-r, st.-w, hl : v, sc, hy.-sh, st.-w
2	SW	SW : SSW	16·5	0·0	3·3	622	v, st.-w : 1, ci.-s, ci, st.-w	6, cu, cu.-s, ci.-cu, fq.-shs, hl, w : 1, li.-cl
3	SSE : SE : E	E : NE	1·5	0·0	0·1	240	0, ho.-fr : 4, ci, ci.-s, ci.-cu	4, cu, cu.-s : 1, li.-cl
4	N : NNW : SW	WSW : SW	1·4	0·0	0·2	232	0, ho.-fr : 10, f, glm	1, ci.-cu : 1, ci.-s, li.-cl, lu.-co
5	WSW : SW	SW	7·0	0·0	1·6	495	0 : p.-cl, ci.-s : 8, cu.-s, cu, ci	10, w : 10, fq.-shs, w
6	WSW : NW	NW : NNW	7·5	0·0	1·1	389	10, w : 8, li.-cl, cu.-s, ci.-cu	9, cu.-s, ci.-cu, ci.-s, h, so.-ha : 0, h
7	S : SSW	SW	4·2	0·0	0·8	397	li.-cl : 10, li.-shs	10 : p.-cl : 2, ci.-cu, li.-cl
8	SW	SW	7·0	0·0	1·2	465	li.-cl : 10	10 : v, li.-cl
9	SW	SW	4·0	0·0	0·7	402	10 : 10, oc.-m.-r, sc	10 : 10
10	SW	SW	4·8	0·0	1·1	477	10 : 10	10 : 10
11	WSW	NE	0·6	0·0	0·0	147	10 : 10, m, glm	10, r : 10, c.-r : 10, slt.-r
12	Calm : NNE : NE	SW : SSW	0·0	0·0	0·0	100	10, slt.-r : 9, ci.-cu, ci.-s	10, glm, slt.-f : 10, slt.-f : 0, h, slt.-f
13	SW : WSW	WSW : SW	0·0	0·0	0·0	163	0, slt.-f, d : 0, h, f	2, ci.-s, ci.-cu, ci : 0, d
14	Calm : SW	SW	0·0	0·0	0·0	142	0, ho.-fr : 0, slt.-f	2, li.-cl, ci : 0 : 0, d, m
15	NW : SW : N	N : NNE : SSW	0·0	0·0	0·0	122	th.-cl, d : th.-cl, slt.-f	4, li.-cl : 0, slt.-f, m
16	SW : WSW	WSW : SW	0·6	0·0	0·0	119	0, d : 0, slt.-m, d	0 : 0, slt.-h, d
17	SW : WSW	SW : Calm	0·0	0·0	0·0	126	0, d : 0, h	0, h, slt.-f : 0, h, m, d
18	Calm : WSW	SW : SSW	0·0	0·0	0·0	115	0, ho.-fr : 0, f	1, li.-cl, h : 0
19	SW : WSW	SW : SSW	1·4	0·0	0·0	216	0, d : 0, f, h	0 : 0
20	S : SSW	SW : WSW	2·5	0·0	0·2	260	0, d : 1, li.-cl	4, ci.-s, ci, so.-ha : v, ci.-cu, cu.-s
21	WSW	WSW : NW	15·0	0·0	2·3	590	0 : p.-cl, cu.-s, ci.-s : 9, cu.-s, ci.-cu, w	5, cu.-s, cu, w : 10, li.-shs, oc.-sn, sl : 10, r, oc.-sn
22	W : NW : NNW	N	22·0	0·0	2·9	554	0 : 5, ci.-cu, ci.-s, st.-w	9, cu.-s, ci.-cu, cu, sc, slt.-m, shs.-r : 0
23	NNW : WSW	SW : SSW	1·9	0·0	0·2	294	0 : 8, ci, ci.-s, m, fr	8, ci, ci.-cu : 10 : 10
24	SSW : SW	SW : W	6·0	0·0	1·4	494	10, slt.-r : 10, sc	10 : 10, slt.-r : v, li.-cl, hy.-sh
25	WNW : WSW : W	WSW : SW : SSE	5·0	0·0	0·8	434	li.-cl : 2, cu.-s, ci.-cu	7, cu.-s, cu : 10, hy.-r
26	SW : NNW	NNW	29·0	0·0	3·5	674	10, r : v, sc, r, hl, fr.-r, hy.-s, so.-ha	2, ci.-cu, st.-w, slt.-sh : 0, w
27	NW : WSW : WNW	W : SW	3·6	0·0	0·4	364	0 : 7, ci, ci.-cu, m	9, ci.-cu, cu.-s : v, li.-cl, s, ci.-s
28	SW : WSW	WSW	3·3	0·0	0·6	426	li.-cl : 9, ci.-cu, ci.-s	9, cu.-s, cu, ci.-s, sc : v, th.-cl, sc
29	SW	SW : WSW	4·8	0·0	1·1	485	10 : 10, li.-shs	10, li.-shs : 7, ci.-cu, s, slt.-sh
30	SW : WSW	SW	1·6	0·0	0·2	271	10, s : 2, li.-cl	6, cu, ci.-cu, cu.-s : 8, ci.-cu, li.-cl, h
31	NW : SW	SW : SSW : SSE	2·3	0·0	0·0	215	10 : 7, li.-cl, h, m	6, cu.-s, cu, ci.-cu : li.-cl
Means	...	...	..	..	0·9	348		
Number of column for reference.	21	22	23	24	25	26	27	28

The mean *Temperature of Evaporation* for the month was 43°·7, being 4°·7 *higher* than
The mean *Temperature of the Dew Point* for the month was 40°·9, being 4°·9 *higher* than
The mean *Degree of Humidity* for the month was 82·2, being 1·3 *greater* than
The mean *Elastic Force of Vapour* for the month was 0in·256, being 0in·044 *greater* than
The mean *Weight of Vapour in a Cubic Foot of Air* for the month was 3grs·0, being 0grs·5 *greater* than
The mean *Weight of a Cubic Foot of Air* for the month was 546 grains, being 4 grains *less* than
} the average for the 20 years, 1849–1868.

The mean amount of *Cloud* for the month (a clear sky being represented by 0 and an overcast sky by 10) was 5·6.

The mean proportion of *Sunshine* for the month (constant sunshine being represented by 1) was 0·35. The maximum daily amount of *Sunshine* was 9·3 hours on March 16 and 20.

The highest reading of the *Solar Radiation Thermometer* was 123°·0 on March 30; and the lowest reading of the *Terrestrial Radiation Thermometer* was 19°·0 on March 4.

The mean daily distribution of *Ozone* was, for the 12 hours ending 9 a.m., 1·9; for the 6 hours ending 3 p.m., 1·3; and for the 6 hours ending 9 p.m., 0·7.

The *Proportions of Wind* referred to the cardinal points were N. 4, E. 1, S. 11, and W. 13. Two days were calm.

The *Greatest Pressure of the Wind* in the month was 29lbs·0 on the square foot on March 26. The mean daily *Horizontal Movement of the Air* for the month was 348 miles; the greatest daily value was 674 miles on March 26; and the least daily value 100 miles on March 12.

Rain fell on 11 days in the month, amounting to 1in·144, as measured by gauge No. 6 partly sunk below the ground; being 0in·312 *less* than the average fall for the 41 years, 1841–1881.

MONTH and DAY, 1882.	Phases of the Moon.	BAROMETER. Mean of 24 Hourly Values (corrected and reduced to 32° Fahrenheit).	TEMPERATURE. Of the Air. Highest.	Of the Air. Lowest.	Of the Air. Daily Range.	Of the Air. Mean of 24 Hourly Values.	Of the Air. Excess of Mean above Average of 20 Years.	Of Evaporation. Mean of 24 Hourly Values.	Of the Dew Point. Deduced Mean Daily Value.	Difference between the Air Temperature and Dew Point Temperature. Mean Daily Value.	Difference. Greatest of 24 Hourly Values.	Difference. Least of 24 Hourly Values.	Degree of Humidity (Saturation = 100).	TEMPERATURE. Highest in the Sun's Rays as shown by a Self-Registering Maximum Thermometer with blackened bulb in vacuo placed on the Grass.	TEMPERATURE. Lowest on the Grass as shown by a Self-Registering Minimum Thermometer.	Daily Duration of Sunshine.	Sun above Horizon.	Rain collected in Gauge No. 6, whose receiving surface is 5 inches above the Ground.	Daily Amount of Ozone.	Electricity.
		in.	°	°	°	°	°	°	°	°	°	°		°	°	hours.	hours.	in.		
Apr. 1	In Equator	29·598	60·0	39·6	20·4	48·4	+ 3·1	44·4	40·0	8·4	17·7	1·8	73	129·9	32·9	9·0	12·9	0·000	9·2	mP
2	..	29·694	56·6	41·6	15·0	47·8	+ 2·1	45·7	43·4	4·4	9·8	1·8	86	113·9	36·4	4·5	13·0	0·000	9·2	mP : vP
3	Full	29·773	52·9	44·2	8·7	47·8	+ 1·7	46·3	44·6	3·2	6·4	1·7	90	100·8	38·0	3·5	13·0	0·000	15·2	wP : mP
4	..	29·880	54·9	39·7	15·2	47·2	+ 0·8	44·2	40·8	6·4	12·6	0·7	79	119·1	33·0	10·9	13·1	0·000	8·8	mP : vP
5	..	29·905	54·3	38·5	15·8	45·4	− 1·2	42·9	40·0	5·4	10·1	1·1	82	119·8	24·8	1·6	13·2	0·000	2·0	vP
6	..	30·042	62·0	37·9	24·1	48·2	+ 1·5	45·2	41·9	6·3	13·7	0·9	79	121·1	24·1	8·2	13·2	0·000	0·5	wP : mP
7	..	30·120	57·4	35·8	21·6	47·7	+ 0·9	44·4	40·8	6·9	13·5	1·7	78	120·7	27·0	11·1	13·3	0·000	2·5	mP : vP
8	Greatest Declination S	30·157	60·4	36·8	23·6	48·6	+ 1·8	45·1	41·3	7·3	14·4	1·4	76	125·8	28·6	11·4	13·4	0·000	1·2	mP : sP
9	..	30·075	58·9	34·9	24·0	45·7	− 1·2	43·1	40·1	5·6	11·6	0·7	82	129·0	25·0	5·7	13·4	0·000	8·8	mP : sP
10	..	29·940	55·6	33·2	22·4	44·2	− 2·7	41·7	38·7	5·5	9·8	1·5	81	133·9	24·8	3·9	13·5	0·000	0·5	vP : vP, wN
11	Last Qr.	29·732	59·1	36·7	22·4	47·0	0·0	43·0	38·5	8·5	19·4	1·2	73	112·8	27·0	7·2	13·6	0·000	9·3	vP : vP, wN
12	..	29·611	59·0	36·4	22·6	48·3	+ 1·2	43·8	38·9	9·4	20·0	2·1	70	105·6	28·9	1·0	13·6	0·000	10·8	mP : vP
13	..	29·177	54·0	46·4	7·6	49·6	+ 2·4	47·9	46·1	3·5	5·8	2·2	89	81·2	41·5	0·0	13·7	0·297	10·2	wP, wN
14	..	29·094	59·5	42·8	16·7	50·9	+ 3·5	48·0	45·0	5·9	9·9	1·1	81	125·1	34·5	8·5	13·7	0·066	11·3	wN, vP: vP, sN : sP
15	In Equator: Perigee.	29·270	54·4	39·3	15·1	47·2	− 0·3	45·3	43·2	4·0	6·4	0·7	87	80·1	32·8	1·9	13·8	0·003	2·0	vP, sN : vP
16	..	29·571	54·4	31·8	22·6	43·6	− 4·0	40·6	37·1	6·5	11·8	3·1	77	126·0	24·5	7·2	13·9	0·000	3·5	sP
17	New	29·281	58·4	42·0	16·4	48·5	+ 0·7	47·0	45·4	3·1	6·4	0·9	89	111·8	38·0	0·2	13·9	0·094	14·5	wP, wN : vP, vN
18	..	29·595	55·5	41·3	14·2	48·1	+ 0·2	44·9	41·4	6·7	14·1	1·8	78	99·0	31·0	3·0	14·0	0·007	0·2	vP, vN
19	..	29·866	57·1	42·5	14·6	50·0	+ 2·0	48·0	45·9	4·1	5·8	2·4	86	78·1	33·5	0·0	14·1	0·000	2·0	vP : wP
20	..	29·896	65·2	44·3	20·9	54·5	+ 6·4	50·7	47·0	7·5	12·9	1·9	76	127·1	34·0	8·1	14·1	0·016	8·8	wP : wP, wN ; vP
21	Greatest Declination N	30·013	65·7	39·7	26·0	52·9	+ 4·7	49·0	45·1	7·8	14·3	2·0	76	125·4	29·8	7·8	14·2	0·000	7·8	mP
22	..	29·501	61·0	49·5	11·5	53·2	+ 5·0	50·9	48·6	4·6	7·2	2·2	84	110·4	41·5	1·6	14·2	0·161	4·3	mP : wP, vN : mP
23	..	29·190	59·3	46·8	12·5	51·6	+ 3·3	49·6	47·6	4·0	7·4	1·5	87	110·2	40·8	2·4	14·3	0·266	13·7	wP, wN : vP, sN
24	..	29·323	59·8	42·2	17·6	49·3	+ 1·0	47·1	44·7	4·6	10·0	1·9	85	124·2	36·6	5·3	14·4	0·159	8·5	wP, wN : vP, vN : vP, wN
25	First Qr.	29·170	54·6	38·8	15·8	45·1	− 3·3	43·8	42·3	2·8	9·0	0·5	90	104·8	34·3	3·3	14·4	0·704	5·8	mP : vN
26	..	29·234	52·1	37·8	14·3	44·1	− 4·3	42·2	39·9	4·2	7·8	1·1	85	87·7	34·0	0·8	14·5	0·087	5·0	vN, vP : wN, vP
27	Apogee	29·557	53·3	35·8	17·5	45·1	− 3·3	42·3	39·0	6·1	10·5	1·6	79	90·5	26·0	3·3	14·5	0·000	2·0	mP, mN : wN, vP
28	In Equator	29·165	59·1	40·0	19·1	47·6	− 0·9	45·2	42·6	5·0	10·2	1·3	84	135·1	32·0	5·3	14·6	0·177	12·0	vP, vN
29	..	29·156	53·8	39·2	14·6	45·4	− 3·1	43·1	40·5	4·9	7·6	2·1	83	99·6	32·2	3·2	14·7	0·350	21·5	mP : vN ; wP, wN
30	..	29·554	59·9	37·0	22·9	46·6	− 2·0	43·8	40·6	6·0	11·8	2·4	81	131·0	31·0	11·5	14·7	0·016	15·0	mP
Means	..	29·605	57·6	39·8	17·9	48·0	+ 0·5	45·3	42·4	5·6	10·9	1·6	81·5	112·7	32·0	5·0	13·8	Sum 2·403	7·5	..
Number of Column for Reference.	1	2	3	4	5	6	7	8	9	10	11	12	13	14	15	16	17	18	19	20

The results apply to the civil day.

The mean reading of the Barometer (Column 2) and the mean temperatures of the Air and Evaporation (Columns 6 and 8) are deduced from the photographic records. The average temperature (Column 7) is that determined from the reduction of the photographic records from 1849 to 1868. The temperature of the Dew Point (Column 9) and the Degree of Humidity (Column 13) are deduced from the corresponding temperatures of the Air and Evaporation by means of Glaisher's Hygrometrical Tables. The mean difference between the Air and Dew Point Temperatures (Column 10) is the difference between the numbers in Columns 6 and 9, and the Greatest and Least Differences (Columns 11 and 12) are deduced from the 24 hourly photographic measures of the Dry-bulb and Wet-bulb Thermometers.

The values given in Columns 3, 4, 5, 14, and 15 are derived from eye-readings of self-registering thermometers.

The mean reading of the *Barometer* for the month was 29in·605, being 0in·198 *lower* than the average for the 20 years, 1854–1873.

TEMPERATURE OF THE AIR.

The highest in the month was 65°·7 on April 21; the lowest in the month was 31°·8 on April 16; and the range was 33°·9.

The mean of all the highest daily readings in the month was 57°·6, being *the same as* the average for the 41 years, 1841–1881.

The mean of all the lowest daily readings in the month was 39°·8, being 0°·6 *higher* than the average for the 41 years, 1841–1881.

The mean of the daily ranges was 17°·9, being 0°·5 *less* than the average for the 41 years, 1841–1881.

The mean for the month was 48°·0, being 0°·5 *higher* than the average for the 20 years, 1849–1868.

MONTH and DAY. 1882.	WIND AS DEDUCED FROM SELF-REGISTERING ANEMOMETERS. Osler's. General Direction. A.M.	P.M.	Pressure on the Square Foot. Greatest.	Least.	Mean of 24 Hourly Measures.	Robinson's. Horizontal Movement of the Air.	CLOUDS AND WEATHER. A.M.	P.M.
			lbs.	lbs.	lbs.	miles.		
April 1	SE	SE : E	3·8	0·0	1·1	341	p.-cl, s, d : 5, ci.-cu, ci	7,cu.-s,cu,ci.-cu,ci.-s : 2, ci.-cu, li.-cl
2	ENE : E	E : ENE	3·6	0·0	0·8	362	0 : 4, ci, ci.-cu	6, ci, cu, ci.-s : 10 : 10
3	ENE : E	E : ENE	3·7	0·0	0·7	334	10 : 10	7,cu.-s,ci.-cu,ci : 0 : 10, sc
4	ENE : E	E : ENE	4·9	0·0	1·0	363	10 3, li.-cl, ci.-cu	1, cu, ci.-cu : 1 : 3,cu.-s,ci.-cu,li.-cl
5	NNE : N	E : NE : N	1·4	0·0	0·0	201	v : 10, oc.-th.-r	9, cu.-s, cu, ci.-cu : 0, h, m, l
6	N : NE	E : ENE : NE	3·4	0·0	0·2	246	p.-cl, m : p.-cl, li.-sc, ci, ci.-cu	0 : 0
7	NE : ENE	ENE	4·8	0·0	0·9	390	0, d : 0	0 : 0
8	NE : ENE	ENE : NE	3·9	0·0	0·5	328	0 : 0	0 : 0, d
9	NE : NNE	NE : E : ENE	1·8	0·0	0·0	262	0, d : 3, cu	2, ci.-cu : 0
10	NE : N : SE	E : S : SSW	0·0	0·0	0·0	135	0 : 5, ci.-cu, ci, slt.-m	9, ci.-cu, cu.-s : v
11	SSW : WSW : N	N : SW	0·0	0·0	0·0	152	10 : 10, m : 0, m, h	4,li.-cl,cu.-s,cu,ci.-cu,h : p.-cl, h : v, th.-cl
12	SSW : SE : S	S	2·8	0·0	0·2	284	0 : 8, li.-cl, ci.-cu, cu.-s	9,ci.-cu,cu.-s,th.-cl,slt.-r : 10, ci.-s, s, slt.-sh
13	S : SSE	SSE : SSW	..	..	..	398	10 : 10, shs.-r	10, fq.-r : v, sc, oc.-shs, w
14	SW	SW : SSW	..	..	..	612	10, r, st.-w : 6, cu, cu.-s, w, shs.-r	7, cu, ci.-cu, cu.-s, shs.-r : 0
15	SSW : W : NE	NNE	..	..	..	305	10 : 10, f, glm, t	10 : 10
16	N : NE	S : SSE	..	..	..	189	10 : 4, cu	3, cu.-s : p.-cl : 10, slt.-r
17	S : SSW	SSW : W	..	..	..	346	10 : 10, m.-r	9 : 10, fq.-shs : 10, oc.-r
18	WSW : W : NW	NW : SW	3·9	0·0	0·7	397	10, oc.-r : 9, cu.-s	7, cu.-s, cu : p.-cl : 2,th.-cl,h,m
19	SSW	SW	3·2	0·0	0·6	371	10 : 10, sc, oc.-slt.-r	10, oc.-th.-r : v, th.-cl, h
20	W : WNW	W : WSW	5·9	0·0	1·2	475	10, slt.-r : 9, cu.-s	4, cu, ci.-cu : 0
21	SW : SSW	S : SE	0·0	0·0	0·0	201	0 : 7, li.-cl, ci, ci.-s, so.-ha	8,ci,ci.-s,ci.-cu,so.-ha : 10
22	SSE : SE	SSE : SW : S	2·3	0·0	0·1	235	10 : 10, r	9,ci.-cu,ci.-s,oc.-r : p.-cl : 0
23	SSE : SSW	SW : WSW	12·0	0·0	1·5	539	li.-cl, w : 9,cu.-s,cu,ci.-cu,fq.-shs,w	9,cu.-s,cu,ci.-cu,shs.-r : p.-cl,cu.-s,hy.-shs : v,cu.-s,li.-cl
24	SW : WSW	W : WSW	5·2	0·0	0·9	481	10 : 8, cu.-s, cu, fq.-shs	8,cu,cu.-s,ci.-cu,shs.-r,hl : 1, ci.-s, li.-cl
25	WSW : SW	Variable	6·3	0·0	0·5	338	0 : 8, li.-cl, ci, ci.-cu, slt.-r	10, hy.-r : 10, r, w
26	WNW : WSW : NW	NNW : NNE	3·7	0·0	0·2	325	10, r : 10, slt.-r : 9, cu.-s	10 : 10
27	W : NW	WSW : SW : SSW	1·4	0·0	0·0	226	10 : 7, li.-cl, h, glm	9, cu.-s : p.-cl : 0
28	SSE : SW	WSW	16·5	0·0	1·4	513	v, hy.-r, hy.-sqs : 10, sc, li.-shs	6,cu.-s,cu,slt.-r : p.-cl,slt.-r,w : v, li.-cl
29	SW : SSE	SSE : SW : WSW	49·5	0·0	4·0	748	p.-cl, ci : 10, sc, r	10, sc, fq.-r, g : 10, sc, hy.-g : 10, g
30	WSW	SW : S : SSE	8·0	0·0	1·0	521	li.-cl, w : 6, cu	6, cu.-s, cu, slt.-r : v, cu.-s
Means	...	...	..	..	0·7 (25 dys)	354		
Number of Column for Reference.	21	22	23	24	25	26	27	28

The mean *Temperature of Evaporation* for the month was 45°·3, being 1°·4 *higher* than the average for the 20 years, 1849–1868.
The mean *Temperature of the Dew Point* for the month was 42°·4, being 2°·1 *higher* than the average for the 20 years, 1849–1868.
The mean *Degree of Humidity* for the month was 81·5, being 4·6 *greater* than the average for the 20 years, 1849–1868.
The mean *Elastic Force of Vapour* for the month was 0in·271, being 0in·021 *greater* than the average for the 20 years, 1849–1868.
The mean *Weight of Vapour in a Cubic Foot of Air* for the month was 3grs·1, being 0gr·2 *greater* than the average for the 20 years, 1849–1868.
The mean *Weight of a Cubic Foot of Air* for the month was 540 grains, being 4 grains *less* than the average for the 20 years, 1849–1868.

The mean amount of *Cloud* for the month (a clear sky being represented by 0 and an overcast sky by 10) was 6·4.

The mean proportion of *Sunshine* for the month (constant sunshine being represented by 1) was 0·36. The maximum daily amount of *Sunshine* was 11·5 hours on April 30.

The highest reading of the *Solar Radiation Thermometer* was 135°·1 on April 28; and the lowest reading of the *Terrestrial Radiation Thermometer* was 24°·1 on April 6.

The mean daily distribution of *Ozone* was, for the 12 hours ending 9 a.m., 3·6; for the 6 hours ending 3 p.m., 2·1; and for the 6 hours ending 9 p.m., 1·8.

The *Proportions of Wind* referred to the cardinal points were N. 5, E. 8, S. 9, and W. 8.

The *Greatest Pressure of the Wind* in the month was 49lbs·5 on the square foot on April 29. The mean daily *Horizontal Movement of the Air* for the month was 354 miles; the greatest daily value was 748 miles on April 29; and the least daily value 135 miles on April 10.

Rain fell on 13 days in the month, amounting to 2in·403, as measured by gauge No. 6 partly sunk below the ground; being 0in·754 *greater* than the average fall for the 41 years, 1841–1881.

MONTH and DAY, 1882.	Phases of the Moon.	BAROMETER. Mean of 24 Hourly Values (corrected and reduced to 32° Fahrenheit).	TEMPERATURE. Of the Air. Highest.	TEMPERATURE. Of the Air. Lowest.	TEMPERATURE. Of the Air. Daily Range.	TEMPERATURE. Of the Air. Mean of 24 Hourly Values.	TEMPERATURE. Of the Air. Excess of Mean above Average of 20 Years.	TEMPERATURE. Of Evaporation. Mean of 24 Hourly Values.	TEMPERATURE. Of the Dew Point. Deduced Mean Daily Value.	Difference between the Air Temperature and Dew Point Temperature. Mean Daily Value.	Difference between the Air Temperature and Dew Point Temperature. Greatest of 24 Hourly Values.	Difference between the Air Temperature and Dew Point Temperature. Least of 24 Hourly Values.	Degree of Humidity (Saturation = 100).	TEMPERATURE. Highest in the Sun's Rays, as shown by a Self-Registering Maximum Thermometer with blackened bulb in vacuo placed on the Grass.	TEMPERATURE. Lowest on the Grass as shown by a Self-Registering Minimum Thermometer.	Daily Duration of Sunshine.	Sun above Horizon.	Rain collected in Gauge No. 6, whose receiving surface is 5 inches above the Ground.	Daily Amount of Ozone.	Electricity.
		in.	°	°	°	°	°	°	°	°	°	°		°	°	hours.	hours.	in.		
May 1	..	29·588	59·0	40·3	18·7	49·1	+ 0·4	47·4	45·5	3·6	9·0	0·0	88	130·0	32·5	8·6	14·8	0·120	18·2	wP, wN : vP, wN
2	..	29·754	62·2	43·1	19·1	51·3	+ 2·4	49·6	47·9	3·4	7·6	0·0	88	133·9	36·0	5·8	14·8	0·087	12·8	vN, wP : mP
3	Full	29·614	70·4	45·0	25·4	56·1	+ 7·0	53·6	51·2	4·9	15·5	0·0	84	133·4	32·9	4·2	14·9	0·178	4·5	wP : vP, vN : mP
4	..	29·510	58·7	48·0	10·7	51·2	+ 1·8	50·7	50·2	1·0	7·8	0·0	97	83·2	42·0	0·0	14·9	0·209	1·5	vP, vN : wP
5	..	29·681	65·4	46·1	19·3	54·2	+ 4·5	51·2	48·3	5·9	14·6	0·0	81	135·9	41·2	3·2	15·0	0·047	9·5	wP : wP, mN
6	Greatest Declination S.	29·722	65·8	48·3	17·5	54·9	+ 4·9	50·5	46·3	8·6	18·9	0·5	73	125·5	47·2	4·4	15·1	0·277	0·0	wN, wP : vP
7	..	29·779	68·2	42·2	26·0	55·6	+ 5·3	49·3	43·3	12·3	21·6	1·8	63	137·6	32·0	7·8	15·1	0·000	0·0	mP : vP, wN
8	..	29·896	60·7	42·0	18·7	49·8	− 0·8	46·5	43·0	6·8	15·8	0·0	77	131·5	28·6	6·9	15·2	0·000	5·5	mP : vP, wN : vP
9	..	30·211	60·7	39·2	21·5	49·2	− 1·6	45·7	41·9	7·3	16·3	0·5	76	109·8	27·5	6·0	15·2	0·000	2·0	mP, mN : wN, vP
10	Last Qr.	30·186	67·1	46·4	20·7	54·6	+ 3·5	51·8	49·1	5·5	18·0	0·0	82	130·2	38·0	4·4	15·3	0·000	1·5	wP, wN
11	..	30·091	71·6	44·5	27·1	58·0	+ 6·6	54·4	51·2	6·8	18·4	0·0	78	153·8	33·4	3·5	15·3	0·000	2·0	vP : mP
12	In Equator	30·058	66·4	44·0	22·4	55·9	+ 4·1	51·4	47·1	8·8	22·1	0·0	73	136·2	33·0	10·6	15·4	0·000	0·0	vP : mP
13	Perigee	30·153	68·4	37·4	31·0	53·8	+ 1·7	48·4	43·1	10·7	22·5	0·0	67	141·7	25·1	12·4	15·4	0·000	0·8	vP
14	..	30·123	61·9	38·7	23·2	49·8	− 2·7	45·2	40·3	9·5	18·2	0·0	70	149·8	30·8	10·8	15·5	0·000	2·2	mP
15	..	30·076	56·7	39·0	17·7	47·8	− 5·1	43·5	38·8	9·0	14·6	3·1	72	136·5	29·3	6·7	15·5	0·008	0·0	mP : vP, mN : mP
16	..	30·210	61·1	36·1	25·0	48·9	− 4·4	44·2	39·1	9·8	20·7	0·0	69	142·0	26·4	11·5	15·6	0·000	0·3	mP
17	New	30·277	63·4	34·5	28·9	50·0	− 3·7	45·7	41·2	8·8	18·2	0·0	72	133·8	23·7	11·5	15·6	0·000	2·7	ssP : vP : sP
18	Greatest Declination N	30·194	67·1	35·8	31·3	52·2	− 1·9	47·5	42·7	9·5	20·7	0·0	70	137·8	24·9	12·8	15·7	0·000	0·0	vP
19		29·973	64·2	40·0	24·2	53·7	− 0·7	48·7	43·8	9·9	18·6	0·2	69	132·0	34·3	12·5	15·7	0·000	0·0	vP : wP, mN : vP
20		29·710	64·1	43·8	20·3	54·0	− 0·7	49·9	45·9	8·1	19·0	1·1	73	131·9	37·5	13·2	15·8	0·000	4·0	mP : mP, vN : mP
21		29·706	67·3	46·8	20·5	56·9	+ 1·9	53·2	49·8	7·1	14·6	1·1	77	129·8	42·1	6·9	15·8	0·002	11·0	mP
22	..	29·652	76·1	44·8	31·3	59·9	+ 4·6	54·6	49·9	10·0	22·5	0·2	70	144·7	37·8	6·8	15·9	0·020	4·8	vP, vN
23	..	29·417	70·9	52·1	18·8	58·5	+ 3·0	55·2	52·2	6·3	15·8	0·0	80	136·2	45·1	3·8	15·9	0·110	12·7	vP, sN : vP
24	..	29·319	67·0	49·7	17·3	56·9	+ 1·2	52·4	48·3	8·6	16·9	3·2	73	133·1	43·7	9·2	16·0	0·024	11·5	wP : wP, vN : mP
25	First Quarter Apogee.	29·302	58·9	49·0	9·9	53·3	− 2·6	51·5	49·7	3·6	6·7	0·4	88	92·0	43·2	1·0	16·0	0·285	15·7	wP : wN, wP : wP
26	In Equator	29·643	68·0	51·4	16·6	57·5	+ 1·4	53·6	50·0	7·5	13·5	1·6	76	134·3	47·1	9·7	16·0	0·000	12·2	wP : vP
27	..	29·872	70·1	50·8	19·3	59·5	+ 3·2	54·8	50·6	8·9	16·7	1·0	73	138·3	45·7	13·1	16·1	0·000	10·8	vP, wN
28	..	30·001	73·8	48·5	25·3	59·9	+ 3·4	55·6	51·8	8·1	18·9	0·4	75	136·2	42·7	3·5	16·1	0·000	10·7	vP : mP
29	..	30·117	76·5	48·8	27·7	60·6	+ 3·8	55·4	50·9	9·7	21·1	0·0	70	140·5	42·1	8·2	16·1	0·000	5·3	vP, vN
30	..	30·098	71·1	49·8	21·3	60·3	+ 3·3	54·3	49·0	11·3	21·4	2·4	66	136·1	40·2	8·7	16·2	0·000	4·3	vP, wN
31	..	30·106	68·4	44·0	24·4	55·9	− 1·4	51·2	46·8	9·1	18·3	1·5	72	139·2	37·1	10·1	16·2	0·000	0·2	vP
Means	..	29·873	66·2	44·2	22·0	54·5	+ 1·4	50·5	46·7	7·8	17·0	0·6	75·5	132·5	36·2	7·7	15·6	Sum 1·367	5·4	..
Number of Column for Reference.	1	2	3	4	5	6	7	8	9	10	11	12	13	14	15	16	17	18	19	20

The results apply to the civil day.

The mean reading of the Barometer (Column 2) and the mean temperatures of the Air and Evaporation (Columns 6 and 8) are deduced from the photographic records. The average temperature (Column 7) is that determined from the reduction of the photographic records from 1849 to 1868. The temperature of the Dew Point (Column 9) and the Degree of Humidity (Column 13) are deduced from the corresponding temperatures of the Air and Evaporation by means of Glaisher's Hygrometrical Tables. The mean difference between the Air and Dew Point Temperatures (Column 10) is the difference between the numbers in Columns 6 and 9, and the Greatest and Least Differences (Columns 11 and 12) are deduced from the 24 hourly photographic measures of the Dry-bulb and Wet-bulb Thermometers. The results from May 4 to 10 for Air and Evaporation Temperatures are deduced entirely from eye-observations, the driving clock of the photographic apparatus being away for repair.

The values given in Columns 3, 4, 5, 14, and 15 are derived from eye-readings of self-registering thermometers.

The mean reading of the *Barometer* for the month was 29^in·873, being 0^in·096 *higher* than the average for the 20 years, 1854–1873.

TEMPERATURE OF THE AIR.

The highest in the month was 76°·5 on May 29; the lowest in the month was 34°·5 on May 17; and the range was 42°·0.
The mean of all the highest daily readings in the month was 66°·2, being 2°·0 *higher* than the average for the 41 years, 1841–1881.
The mean of all the lowest daily readings in the month was 44°·2, being 0°·5 *higher* than the average for the 41 years, 1841–1881.
The mean of the daily ranges was 22°·0, being 1°·5 *greater* than the average for the 41 years, 1841–1881.
The mean for the month was 54°·5, being 1°·4 *higher* than the average for the 20 years, 1849–1868.

MONTH and DAY, 1882.	Wind as deduced from Self-registering Anemometers. Osler's. General Direction. A.M.	P.M.	Pressure on the Square Foot. Greatest.	Least.	Mean of 24 Hourly Measures.	Robinson's. Horizontal Movement of the Air.	Clouds and Weather. A.M.	P.M.
			lbs.	lbs.	lbs.	miles.		
May 1	SSE : SW	SSW : S	6·0	0·0	0·6	358	p.-cl : 10, fq.-shs : 9, cu.-s cu	5, cu, cu.-s, hy.-sh : v, ci.-cu, li.-cl
2	S : SSW	SSW : ESE	2·2	0·0	0·2	293	10, sh.-r : 9, cu.-s, sc, shs.-r	6, cu.-s, cu : 8, li.-cl
3	ENE	SE : SW	1·4	0·0	0·0	214	10, th.-cl : 10, hy.-sh	7, s, ci.-cu, ci.-s, ci : 9
4	WSW : N	SSW	0·0	0·0	0·0	131	10 : 10, m, r	10, glm, oc.-slt.-r: p.-cl : 0, h
5	SW	S : SSW	0·0	0·0	0·0	171	v : 10 : 9, cu.-s	8,ci.-cu,cu,cu.-s,slt.-h: v, sh.-r : 10, r
6	SSE : WSW : W	SW	0·8	0·0	0·0	182	10, c.-r : 10	5, ci.-cu, cu.-s, h : 9, d
7	SW	Variable	0·0	0·0	0·0	125	li.-cl, lu.-ha : 6, ci.-s, li.-cl, so.-ha	7, cu, cu.-s : v, l
8	Variable : NNW	N	3·5	0·0	0·4	302	0 : 0, h : 4,ci.-cu,li.-cl,m	6,cu.-s,cu,ci.-cu: 10 : v
9	N	W : SW	0·3	0·0	0·0	194	10 : 0, h	8,th.-cl,cu,cu.-s,h: 10, slt.-r : 10
10	WSW : WNW	NW : ESE	0·3	0·0	0·0	238	10 : 10	5, cu, h : p.-cl : 1, li.-cl, h, d
11	S : SW	SW	0·8	0·0	0·0	202	p.-cl, d : 10	8, cu, cu.-s, ci.-cu : 0
12	WSW : N : NNE	NE : ESE	0·6	0·0	0·0	202	v : 1, th.-cl	1, ci : 0 : 0, d
13	Calm : NE	NE : E	2·2	0·0	0·1	178	0, d : 0, h, m	0 : 0
14	NE	NE : NNE	2·9	0·0	0·3	328	0 : 6, cu, ci.-cu, cu.-s	5,cu.-s,ci.-cu: p.-cl : 10
15	NNE : NE	ENE : NE	2·8	0·0	0·4	367	10 : 6, cu, cu.-s	7,cu.-s,cu,ci.-cu,li-shs: v : 0
16	NNE : NE	NE : ESE	2·0	0·0	0·3	280	0 : 1, li.-cl, cu	6, cu, cu.-s, ci.-cu : 4, cu, cu.-s
17	NE	NNE : ESE	0·0	0·0	0·0	157	0 : 7, cu.-s, cu	4, cu, ci.-cu : 3, ci.-s : 0
18	Calm : NE	NE : ESE : E	0·0	0·0	0·0	162	0 : 0, slt.-h : 3, cu	0 : 0, d
19	NE : E	E : ENE	12·5	0·0	0·8	350	0, d : 2, li.-cl, ci, ci.-cu, w	4, cu, cu.-s, w : 0, h
20	ENE : E	E : ENE	10·5	0·0	1·6	444	0, h : 0, w	1, cu, ci, w : 0
21	ENE : E : ESE	E	1·1	0·0	0·1	225	0 : 9, oc.-slt.-r	8, cu.-s, ci.-cu, ci : 2, li.-cl
22	ENE : E	S : SSW : SE	1·1	0·0	0·0	196	v : 7,cu.-s,ci.-s,ci.-cu,ci	7,cu.-s,cu,ci.-cu,ci : v, lu.-co, r
23	E : SE	SSW	3·3	0·0	0·2	304	10, r : li.-cl	9, cu.-s, oc.-shs: 8, ci.-cu, n : 3, li.-cl
24	SSW	SSW : S	9·6	0·0	1·6	537	p.-cl : 8,li.-cl,cu.-s,cu,ci.-cu,w	7, cu, cu.-s, sh.-r : v,ci.-s,ci.-cu: 8,cu.-s,ci.-cu
25	SSE : SE : E	SW	5·2	0·0	0·7	358	10 : 10, sc, r	10, sc, oc.-r : vv, oc.-shs : v,ci-cu,cu.-s,ci.-s
26	SSW	SSW : SSE	5·3	0·0	0·5	393	p.-cl : li.-cl : 10,th.-cl,sc,so.-ha	7, cu, cu.-s, ci.-cu : v, cu.-s, li.-cl, slt.-r
27	S : SSW	SSW : S	5·9	0·0	1·1	449	li.-cl : 5 cu, cu.-s	5, cu, ci.-cu : 0
28	SSE : SSW	SW	0·0	0·0	0·0	199	0 : 6, ci, ci.-cu	8,ci.-cu,ci.-s : p.-cl,s,slt.-r : 0
29	WSW	W : SW : NE	0·0	0·0	0·0	148	0 : 3, li.-cl, h	5,cu,ci.-cu,cu.-s,h: p.-cl : 10,cu.-s,ci.-s,li.-cl
30	NNE : NE	NE	2·5	0·0	0·3	308	10, ci.-s, li.-cl : 5, li.-cl, ci, ci.-s	8, cu, ci, ci.-cu, cu.-s : 5, ci.-cu, ci.-s, li.-cl
31	N : NE	ENE	1·6	0·0	0·1	298	li.-cl : 2, li.-cl, ci.-cu	6,cu,cu.-s,ci.-cu: p.-cl : 0
Means	...	...	..	..	0·3	268		
Number of Column for Reference.	21	22	23	24	25	26	27	28

The mean *Temperature of Evaporation* for the month was 50°·5, being 1°·6 *higher* than the average for the 20 years, 1849–1868.
The mean *Temperature of the Dew Point* for the month was 46°·7, being 1°·6 *higher* than the average for the 20 years, 1849–1868.
The mean *Degree of Humidity* for the month was 75·5, being 0·1 *greater* than the average for the 20 years, 1849–1868.
The mean *Elastic Force of Vapour* for the month was 0in·319, being 0in·018 *greater* than the average for the 20 years, 1849–1868.
The mean *Weight of Vapour in a Cubic Foot of Air* for the month was 3grs·6, being 0gr·2 *greater* than the average for the 20 years, 1849–1868.
The mean *Weight of a Cubic Foot of Air* for the month was 538 grains, being *the same as* the average for the 20 years, 1849–1868.

The mean amount of *Cloud* for the month (a clear sky being represented by 0 and an overcast sky by 10) was 5·5.

The mean proportion of *Sunshine* for the month (constant sunshine being represented by 1) was 0·49. The maximum daily amount of *Sunshine* was 13·2 hours on May 20.

The highest reading of the *Solar Radiation Thermometer* was 153°·8 on May 11; and the lowest reading of the *Terrestrial Radiation Thermometer* was 23°·7 on May 17.

The mean daily distribution of *Ozone* was, for the 12 hours ending 9 a.m., 2·5; for the 6 hours ending 3 p.m., 1·3; and for the 6 hours ending 9 p.m., 1·6.

The *Proportions of Wind* referred to the cardinal points were N. 6, E. 9, S. 10, and W. 5. One day was calm.

The *Greatest Pressure of the Wind* in the month was 12lbs·5 on the square foot on May 19. The mean daily *Horizontal Movement of the Air* for the month was 268 miles; the greatest daily value was 537 miles on May 24; and the least daily value 125 miles on May 7.

Rain fell on 11 days in the month, amounting to 1in·367, as measured by gauge No. 6 partly sunk below the ground; being 0in·651 *less* than the average fall for the 41 years, 1841–1881.

MONTH and DAY. 1881.	Phases of the Moon.	BAROMETER. Mean of 24 Hourly Values (corrected and reduced to 32° Fahrenheit).	TEMPERATURE. Of the Air. Highest.	Lowest.	Daily Range.	Mean of 24 Hourly Values.	Excess of Mean above Average of 20 Years.	Of Evaporation. Mean of 24 Hourly Values.	Of the Dew Point. Deduced Mean Daily Value.	Difference between the Air Temperature and Dew Point Temperature. Mean Daily Value.	Greatest of 24 Hourly Values.	Least of 24 Hourly Values.	Degree of Humidity (Saturation = 100).	TEMPERATURE. Highest in the Sun's Rays, as shown by a Self-Registering Maximum Thermometer with blackened bulb in vacuo placed on the Grass.	Lowest on the Grass, as shown by a Self-Registering Minimum Thermometer.	Daily Duration of Sunshine.	Sun above Horizon.	Rain collected in Gauge No. 6, whose receiving surface is 5 inches above the Ground.	Daily Amount of Ozone.	Electricity.
		in.	°	°	°	°	°	°	°	°	°	°		°	°	hours.	hours.	in.		
June 1	Full	30·114	63·3	43·0	20·3	53·7	− 3·8	49·6	45·6	8·1	16·3	0·9	74	130·0	37·9	6·3	16·2	0·000	3·3	wP
2	Greatest Declination S.	29·912	62·4	48·7	13·7	55·9	− 1·8	53·3	50·9	5·0	11·6	0·8	84	108·9	43·3	0·8	16·3	0·053	7·5	wP, wN
3	..	29·627	72·7	53·9	18·8	61·3	+ 3·4	58·7	56·5	4·8	10·8	0·2	85	120·3	50·1	1·5	16·3	0·043	1·8	wP, wN : wP
4	..	29·554	70·5	50·1	20·4	58·0	− 0·1	55·1	52·5	5·5	14·4	0·6	82	135·0	45·2	6·2	16·3	0·137	11·5	wP : wP : wP, wN
5	..	29·634	66·2	48·3	17·9	56·9	− 1·3	54·3	51·9	5·0	12·1	1·2	83	132·8	43·0	2·7	16·4	0·000	19·0	..
6	..	29·556	65·2	53·8	11·4	58·1	− 0·2	56·2	54·5	3·6	9·3	0·0	88	105·0	50·0	1·1	16·4	0·195	11·5	— : wP
7	Perigee	29·587	69·5	51·7	17·8	58·8	+ 0·4	54·2	50·1	8·7	17·3	0·6	73	136·2	47·4	10·8	16·4	0·036	7·2	wP, wN : vP, sN
8	Last Quarter In Equator.	29·626	66·1	47·9	18·2	55·4	− 3·1	53·3	51·3	4·1	10·3	0·0	8[illegible]	126·7	42·1	0·7	16·4	0·321	2·0	wP : vP, vN : wP, wN
9	..	29·287	63·6	49·0	14·6	53·8	− 4·7	52·0	50·2	3·6	9·1	0·0	87	126·4	45·8	3·9	16·4	0·360	16·0	wP, vN : ssP, ssN
10	..	29·450	59·2	51·3	7·9	54·6	− 4·0	51·8	49·1	5·5	11·2	0·4	81	87·4	48·0	1·3	16·5	0·033	3·0	wP, wN
11	..	29·801	61·6	47·1	14·5	53·2	− 5·5	49·0	44·8	8·4	16·5	2·1	73	121·4	42·6	7·5	16·5	0·065	3·0	wP : wP, sN : vP
12	..	29·655	60·0	45·3	14·7	52·0	− 6·8	47·6	43·1	8·9	16·7	1·0	72	121·3	42·0	6·9	16·5	0·150	3·0	vP, vN : wN, mP
13	..	29·746	56·6	42·2	14·4	49·4	− 9·5	46·2	42·8	6·6	14·8	0·0	78	85·8	37·2	2·5	16·5	0·113	2·0	mP, wN : vN, wP
14	..	29·626	65·1	48·6	16·5	55·8	− 3·3	53·3	50·9	4·9	10·1	0·0	85	122·6	48·6	1·0	16·5	0·093	0·8	wP
15	Greatest Decl. N. New.	29·738	63·1	46·4	16·7	54·1	− 5·2	49·5	45·0	9·1	16·3	2·7	71	107·4	38·5	4·4	16·5	0·004	2·2	wP, wN : vP, vN
16	..	30·004	63·4	40·9	22·5	53·5	− 6·0	49·2	44·9	8·6	18·2	2·0	73	130·8	33·0	6·3	16·5	0·000	0·0	wP, wN : wP, mN
17	..	29·911	67·8	44·9	22·9	56·6	− 3·1	51·1	46·0	10·6	21·2	0·4	68	130·1	39·7	9·0	16·6	0·000	2·0	wP : wP, wN : mP
18	..	29·537	65·1	49·2	15·9	54·5	− 5·4	51·5	48·6	5·9	12·9	1·2	80	119·4	45·5	2·9	16·6	0·190	13·5	vP : vN
19	..	29·597	69·1	47·9	21·2	55·5	− 4·7	51·7	48·1	7·4	16·9	0·8	77	132·9	43·9	3·0	16·6	0·017	10·5	vP, wN : wP, vN
20	..	29·726	72·0	48·9	23·1	58·7	− 1·8	54·4	50·5	8·2	16·4	1·3	75	133·8	43·2	6·4	16·6	0·000	7·5	wP
21	..	29·730	67·1	49·9	17·2	58·0	− 2·8	55·3	52·9	5·1	12·2	0·0	83	110·0	46·3	0·6	16·6	0·000	9·0	wP
22	Apogee: In Equator.	29·607	63·4	50·3	13·1	58·0	− 3·1	55·9	54·0	4·0	10·6	1·5	86	86·3	45·5	2·0	16·6	0·078	11·5	wP : wP,wN : wP
23	First Qr.	29·710	68·3	46·0	22·3	56·6	− 4·8	52·2	48·1	8·5	16·2	1·2	73	132·3	41·2	6·1	16·6	0·000	12·8	wP : mP
24	..	29·794	70·3	49·6	20·7	59·0	− 2·7	55·1	51·6	7·4	15·7	0·2	77	132·1	44·1	2·4	16·6	0·268	11·0	wP : wP : vP, mN
25	..	29·825	72·2	54·1	18·1	59·3	− 2·6	55·8	52·7	6·6	16·2	0·2	79	132·7	53·2	6·5	16·6	0·104	9·0	vP, vN : wP : mP
26	..	29·833	68·1	48·2	19·9	57·5	− 4·5	54·9	52·6	4·9	12·1	0·4	84	131·6	40·2	3·0	16·5	0·031	5·2	wP : vvP, vvN
27	..	29·904	74·1	50·1	24·0	61·8	− 0·2	56·2	51·4	10·4	21·1	1·0	69	127·1	44·2	12·0	16·5	0·000	3·0	mP : wN : wN, wP
28	..	29·989	71·8	53·9	17·9	62·0	+ 0·1	57·2	53·1	8·9	14·8	3·6	73	127·1	46·9	3·4	16·5	0·000	5·0	mP : wP,wN : vN,wP
29	Greatest Declination S.	29·960	69·6	56·0	13·6	61·5	− 0·3	59·3	57·4	4·1	8·3	0·2	87	105·9	50·0	0·0	16·5	0·065	0·0	wP : wN : wN, wP
30	..	29·933	62·0	50·0	12·0	57·1	− 4·6	56·2	55·4	1·7	4·8	0·0	94	81·7	41·5	0·2	16·5	0·000	0·0	wP
Means	..	29·732	66·3	48·9	17·4	56·7	− 3·1	53·3	50·2	6·5	13·8	0·8	79·4	119·4	44·0	4·0	16·5	Sum 2·356	6·5	..
Number of Column for Reference.	1	2	3	4	5	6	7	8	9	10	11	12	13	14	15	16	17	18	19	20

The results apply to the civil day.

The mean reading of the Barometer (Column 2) and the mean temperatures of the Air and Evaporation (Columns 6 and 8) are deduced from the photographic records. The average temperature (Column 7) is that determined from the reduction of the photographic records from 1849 to 1868. The temperature of the Dew Point (Column 9) and the Degree of Humidity (Column 13) are deduced from the corresponding temperatures of the Air and Evaporation by means of Glaisher's Hygrometrical Tables. The mean difference between the Air and Dew Point Temperatures (Column 10) is the difference between the numbers in Columns 6 and 9, and the Greatest and Least Differences (Columns 11 and 12) are deduced from the 24 hourly photographic measures of the Dry-bulb and Wet-bulb Thermometers.

The values given in Columns 3, 4, 5, 14, and 15 are derived from eye-readings of self-registering thermometers.

The mean reading of the *Barometer* for the month was 29^in·732, being 0^in·096 *lower* than the average for the 20 years, 1854–1873.

TEMPERATURE OF THE AIR.

The highest in the month was 74°·1 on June 27; the lowest in the month was 40°·9 on June 16; and the range was 33°·2.

The mean of all the highest daily readings in the month was 66°·3, being 4°·7 *lower* than the average for the 41 years, 1841–1881.

The mean of all the lowest daily readings in the month was 48°·9, being 1°·0 *lower* than the average for the 41 years, 1841–1881.

The mean of the daily ranges was 17°·4, being 3°·7 *less* than the average for the 41 years, 1841–1881.

The mean for the month was 56°·7, being 3°·1 *lower* than the average for the 20 years, 1849–1868.

MONTH and DAY. 1882.	WIND AS DEDUCED FROM SELF-REGISTERING ANEMOMETERS. OSLER'S. General Direction. A.M.	P.M.	Pressure on the Square Foot. Greatest.	Least.	Mean of 24 Hourly Measures.	ROBINSON'S. Horizontal Movement of the Air.	CLOUDS AND WEATHER. A.M.	P.M.
			lbs.	lbs.	lbs.	miles.		
June 1	ENE	ENE	7·6	0·0	1·0	405	p.-cl : 10	5,cu.-s,cu,ci.-cu,ci,w : v,ci.-cu,s,ci.-s,lu.-co
2	ENE	ENE : E	8·0	0·0	1·2	394	10 : 9,ci.-cu,ci.-s,cu.-s,w	10, slt.-r, w : 10, hy.-sh : 10
3	NE	E : SW	3·7	0·0	0·0	158	10 : 10, sh.-r : 6, ci, ci.-cu	10, slt.-r : v, cu.-s, oc.-shs
4	SSW	SSW : SW	3·3	0·0	0·6	355	v : 9, cu, ci.-cu, cu.-s, shs.-r	7, cu, cu.-s : v, s, cu.-s, fq.-shs
5	SSW : SW	SW : SSW	9·0	0·0	1·7	548	p.-cl : li.-cl : 10, li.-shs, w	10, w : 10, sc, w, oc.-slt.-r
6	SSW	SW	3·3	0·0	0·7	392	10 : 10, sc, hy.-r	10, oc.-slt.-r : 10, cu.-s, s
7	SW : WSW	W : WSW	2·9	0·0	0·3	363	v : 6, li.-cl, cu, cu.-s	6, cu, cu.-s, hy.-sh : v, s, ci.-s
8	SW : WSW	SW : SSW	4·2	0·0	0·1	298	p.-cl : 10, hy.-shs	10 : 10, sc, fq.-r
9	WSW	WSW : W	3·1	0·0	0·5	437	v, s, li.-cl : v, cu, fq.-hy.-shs	7,cu.-s,ci.-cu,n,hy.-shs,t.-sn : v, n, shs.-r
10	WSW : W : NW	NNW	4·0	0·0	0·5	428	10 : 10, oc.-slt.-r	10, li.-shs : 0 : 9,cu.-s,th.-cl,sh.-r
11	NNW : NW	WNW : W : WSW	2·8	0·0	0·2	384	10, sh.-r : 5,li.-cl,ci,ci.-cu,cu.-s,slt.-h	8, cu.-s, m, shs.-r : v, s, cu.-s, ci.-cu
12	WSW : W : WNW	NW : WNW	3·0	0·0	0·3	381	10, shs.-r : v, hy.-shs, t	5, cu, cu.-s, ci.-cu,m : 0, h
13	W : WNW	W : SW	5·0	0·0	0·7	488	v, li.-cl : 10, m	10, slt.-r : 10, r
14	WNW : WSW	WSW	7·8	0·0	1·0	539	10, r : 9, cu,-s, ci.-cu, sc	9, cu.-s, w : 3, ci.-cu, h
15	WSW : WNW	NW : N : NE	4·9	0·0	1·2	433	v : 10, slt.-r	9 cu.-s, th.-cl, shs.-r, l, t : 2, h
16	NE : NNE	NNE : SE : S	0·0	0·0	0·0	160	v : 10 : 7,cu.-s,ci.-cu,cu,h	6, cu.-s, ci.-cu, cu : 10
17	SSW : SW	SSW : S	2·6	0·0	0·2	282	0, h : 5, ci, li.-cl	3,cu,ci.-cu,ci.-s,so.-ha : 10
18	SSW : SW	SSW : W : WSW	4·1	0·0	0·1	309	10, r : 10, r, m	10, r : v
19	WSW : WNW	WNW : NW : WSW	4·3	0·0	0·6	445	10, slt.-r : 10, m	9,cu.-s,ci.-cu,li.-shs : 10
20	WSW : SW	SW : SSW	0·0	0·0	0·0	240	10 : 6,li.-cl,cu,ci,ci.-s,so.-ha	10, cu.-s, cu, ci.-cu : 6, cu.-s, ci.-cu, s
21	SSW	SW : SSW	2·6	0·0	0·1	326	v : 10, ci.-s, s, sc, slt.-r	9, cu, n : 10, oc.-m.-r
22	SSE	S : SW	2·7	0·0	0·1	283	10, r : 10, shs.-r	10, shs.-r : v, ci.-cu
23	SW	SSW : S : SSE	2·0	0·0	0·1	269	0 : 8, cu, ci.-cu, cu.-s	8, cu, ci.-cu, so.-ha : v, s, ci.-s, slt.-r
24	SSE	S : SSE	1·0	0·0	0·0	196	10, sh.-r : 8, ci.-cu, cu, ci	10, th.-cl, cu, so.-ha : 10, r
25	SE : SW	SSW : S	0·6	0·0	0·0	197	10, hy.-r : 10, slt.-r	v, cu.-s, cu, ci.-cu : 1, s, li.-cl
26	SE	SE : E : SW	0·2	0·0	0·0	143	v : v, ci, ci.-s, r	10,cu.-s,cu,shs.-r,t,m : v, ci.-s, h, d
27	WSW : W	W : WNW : WSW	2·1	0·0	0·2	329	v, d : 2, cu, ci.-cu, h, m	5, cu, ci.-cu, cu.-s, h : 1, ci.-s, li.-cl
28	WSW	WNW : WSW	0·9	0·0	0·0	276	v : 10 : 9,cu.-s,cu,ci.-cu,h	9, cu.-s, cu, ci.-cu : 10, ci.-cu, cu.-s
29	WSW : NE	SW : Calm	0·0	0·0	0·0	125	10 : 10, m	10, slt.-r, m : 10, glm, r : 10, m
30	NNE : NE	NE : NNE	0·0	0·0	0·0	134	10, m : 10, m	10, m : 0, h, m, d
Means	...	...	..	..	0·4	325		
Number of Column for Reference.	21	22	23	24	25	26	27	28

The mean *Temperature of Evaporation* for the month was 53°·3, being 1°·9 *lower* than
The mean *Temperature of the Dew Point* for the month was 50°·2, being 1°·0 *lower* than
The mean *Degree of Humidity* for the month was 79·4, being 6·1 *greater* than
The mean *Elastic Force of Vapour* for the month was 0in·364, being 0in·013 *less* than
The mean *Weight of Vapour in a Cubic Foot of Air* for the month was 4grs·1, being 0gr·1 *less* than
The mean *Weight of a Cubic Foot of Air* for the month was 532 grains, being 1 grain *greater* than
} the average for the 20 years, 1849–1868.

The mean amount of *Cloud* for the month (a clear sky being represented by 0 and an overcast sky by 10) was 8·1.

The mean proportion of *Sunshine* for the month (constant sunshine being represented by 1) was 0·24. The maximum daily amount of *Sunshine* was 12·0 hours on June 27.

The highest reading of the *Solar Radiation Thermometer* was 136°·2 on June 7; and the lowest reading of the *Terrestrial Radiation Thermometer* was 33°·0 on June 16.

The mean daily distribution of *Ozone* was, for the 12 hours ending 9 a.m., 3·1; for the 6 hours ending 3 p.m., 1·5; and for the 6 hours ending 9 p.m., 1·9.

The *Proportions of Wind* referred to the cardinal points were N. 3, E. 4, S. 10, and W. 12. One day was calm.

The *Greatest Pressure of the Wind* in the month was 9lbs·0 on the square foot on June 5. The mean daily *Horizontal Movement of the Air* for the month was 325 miles; the greatest daily value was 548 miles on June 5; and the least daily value 125 miles on June 29.

Rain fell on 19 days in the month, amounting to 2in·336, as measured by gauge No. 6 partly sunk below the ground; being 0in·310 *greater* than the average fall for the 41 years, 1841–1881.

MONTH and DAY. 1882.	Phases of the Moon.	BAROMETER. Mean of 24 Hourly Values (corrected and reduced to 32° Fahrenheit).	TEMPERATURE. Of the Air. Highest.	Lowest.	Daily Range.	Mean of 24 Hourly Values.	Excess of Mean above Average of 20 Years.	Of Evaporation. Mean of 24 Hourly Values.	Of the Dew Point. Deduced Mean Daily Value.	Difference between the Air Temperature and Dew Point Temperature. Mean Daily Value.	Greatest of 24 Hourly Values.	Least of 24 Hourly Values.	Degree of Humidity (Saturation = 100).	TEMPERATURE. Highest in the Sun's Rays as shown by a Self-Registering Maximum Thermometer with blackened bulb in vacuo placed on the Grass.	Lowest on the Grass as shown by a Self-Registering Minimum Thermometer.	Daily Duration of Sunshine.	Sun above Horizon.	Rain collected in Gauge No. 6, whose receiving surface is 5 inches above the Ground.	Daily Amount of Ozone.	Electricity.
		in.	°	°	°	°	°	°	°	°	°	°		°	°	hours.	hours.	in.		
July 1	Full	29·924	73·4	45·7	27·7	59·3	− 2·3	54·7	50·6	8·7	19·3	0·2	73	136·4	36·9	9·3	16·5	0·000	2·0	wP : vP
2	. .	29·931	74·1	50·9	23·2	62·1	+ 0·6	57·4	53·4	8·7	21·1	0·2	73	132·0	45·3	9·2	16·5	0·000	1·0	mP : wP
3	. .	29·897	78·7	55·1	23·6	63·0	+ 3·6	60·2	56·3	8·7	16·5	2·9	74	138·7	51·0	7·9	16·4	0·005	6·5	wP
4	Perigee	29·634	69·1	56·8	12·3	59·8	− 1·6	56·1	52·8	7·0	11·5	1·1	79	120·2	54·9	1·6	16·4	0·000	14·7	mP : vP
5	. .	29·353	68·7	54·8	13·9	59·1	− 2·4	55·7	52·6	6·5	15·8	1·5	80	133·4	52·0	4·7	16·4	0·143	6·3	wP : vvP, vvN
6	In Equator	29·280	64·5	52·8	11·7	57·1	− 4·6	54·3	51·7	5·4	10·1	2·7	82	116·3	47·3	1·8	16·4	0·121	8·3	wP : wP, sN : mP
7	Last Qr.	29·212	68·2	51·9	16·3	58·6	− 3·3	54·5	50·8	7·8	13·5	3·6	75	135·2	46·2	11·7	16·3	0·144	13·7	wP : vP, wN : mP
8	. .	29·331	67·5	50·2	17·3	56·8	− 5·4	54·4	52·2	4·6	9·9	0·4	85	130·8	49·2	4·3	16·3	0·469	10·5	mP:vvP,vvN:sN,mP
9	. .	29·453	70·1	51·6	18·5	58·8	− 3·7	54·8	51·2	7·6	18·2	0·4	76	140·0	47·0	8·5	16·3	0·026	7·0	wP : vvP, vvN
10	. .	29·571	68·6	48·4	20·2	57·4	− 5·3	53·7	50·3	7·1	14·9	1·0	77	135·8	43·9	7·8	16·3	0·062	11·0	mP : vvP, vvN
11	. .	29·388	66·1	51·8	14·3	57·5	− 5·4	56·1	54·8	2·7	7·2	0·9	91	93·5	47·6	0·4	16·2	0·421	10·0	wP : o
12	Greatest Declination N.	29·581	70·5	53·8	16·7	60·9	− 2·2	56·6	52·9	8·0	16·4	0·6	75	132·1	53·6	4·2	16·2	0·066	0·0	o : wP,mN : wN,mP
13	. .	29·687	66·3	54·3	12·0	59·1	− 4·2	55·8	52·8	6·3	11·6	2·3	80	122·0	49·2	1·1	16·2	0·028	7·0	mP
14	. .	29·474	73·6	57·3	16·3	63·3	− 0·1	59·4	56·1	7·2	15·5	1·7	78	134·5	53·8	5·4	16·1	0·002	10·0	wP
15	New	29·339	72·7	54·0	18·7	62·7	− 0·7	59·8	57·4	5·3	10·6	1·5	83	132·1	50·0	2·6	16·1	0·238	12·5	wP : wN, wP : wP
16	. .	29·461	72·0	53·3	18·7	60·8	− 2·7	56·7	53·2	7·6	15·3	0·8	76	140·8	48·9	8·8	16·1	0·000	10·0	wP : mP
17	. .	29·639	71·4	54·8	16·6	60·3	− 3·2	56·3	52·8	7·5	18·2	0·6	76	140·9	49·2	7·8	16·0	0·183	7·0	mP : vP, wN
18	. .	29·717	71·2	55·0	16·2	62·1	− 1·3	57·8	54·1	8·0	14·8	0·6	75	135·1	54·2	9·6	16·0	0·058	6·0	wP : vP
19	Apogee. In Equator.	29·880	71·9	54·0	17·9	60·6	− 2·7	56·2	52·4	8·2	15·7	0·9	74	139·8	47·0	8·1	16·0	0·040	10·8	o : wP : vP
20	. .	29·979	73·4	50·1	23·3	60·6	− 2·6	55·6	51·3	9·3	18·9	1·4	71	142·9	43·3	12·0	15·9	0·000	4·8	o : wP : mP
21	. .	29·844	73·1	48·9	24·2	60·5	− 2·5	55·8	51·7	8·8	18·0	1·0	73	141·0	42·6	8·9	15·9	0·000	4·8	mP : vP
22	. .	29·651	68·3	55·6	12·7	61·4	− 1·5	58·9	56·8	4·6	8·1	0·9	85	104·0	54·5	1·4	15·8	0·065	9·3	o : mP
23	First Qr.	29·504	72·2	52·4	19·8	59·8	− 3·0	55·5	51·7	8·1	18·5	1·0	75	140·1	51·4	7·8	15·8	0·034	13·5	mP, vN : mP
24	. .	29·610	70·1	51·9	18·2	58·4	− 4·3	54·9	51·8	6·6	15·5	2·2	78	137·1	46·4	10·3	15·7	0·170	8·2	vP : ssP, ssN : mP
25	. .	29·701	67·4	51·8	15·6	57·0	− 5·7	54·7	52·6	4·4	13·9	0·0	85	120·1	46·8	0·3	15·7	0·120	3·0	wP, wN
26	. .	30·083	70·6	50·9	19·7	59·2	− 3·5	54·6	50·5	8·7	19·6	1·6	73	140·5	44·0	8·6	15·7	0·000	2·0	vP
27	Greatest Declination S.	30·252	78·2	48·0	30·2	61·5	− 1·1	56·1	51·5	10·0	18·9	1·0	70	143·8	40·2	7·6	15·6	0·000	7·0	wP : vP
28	. .	30·162	65·3	55·2	10·1	60·3	− 2·3	57·9	55·8	4·5	10·1	0·4	86	102·6	48·0	0·0	15·6	0·053	0·0	vP
29	. .	30·034	76·5	53·0	23·5	63·4	+ 0·8	59·2	55·7	7·7	19·0	0·2	76	141·6	46·0	8·0	15·5	0·000	3·0	wP : vP
30	Full	29·924	77·6	54·6	23·0	63·9	+ 1·3	59·5	55·8	8·1	21·4	0·2	76	129·0	47·0	4·9	15·5	0·003	0·0	vP
31	Perigee	30·092	74·1	49·8	24·3	62·0	− 0·6	55·1	49·2	12·8	21·2	4·0	62	127·3	40·0	10·1	15·4	0·000	4·0	vP : wP,wN : wN,wP
Means	. .	29·697	71·1	52·3	18·6	60·3	− 2·3	56·4	53·0	7·3	15·5	1·2	77·2	131·0	47·7	6·3	16·0	Sum 2·451	6·9	. . . .
Number of Column for Reference.	1	2	3	4	5	6	7	8	9	10	11	12	13	14	15	16	17	18	19	20

The results apply to the civil day.

The mean reading of the Barometer (Column 2) and the mean temperatures of the Air and Evaporation (Columns 6 and 8) are deduced from the photographic records. The average temperature (Column 7) is that determined from the reduction of the photographic records from 1849 to 1868. The temperature of the Dew Point (Column 9) and the Degree of Humidity (Column 13) are deduced from the corresponding temperatures of the Air and Evaporation by means of Glaisher's Hygrometrical Tables. The mean difference between the Air and Dew Point Temperatures (Column 10) is the difference between the numbers in Columns 6 and 9, and the Greatest and Least Differences (Columns 11 and 12) are deduced from the 24 hourly photographic measures of the Dry-bulb and Wet-bulb Thermometers.

The values given in Columns 3, 4, 5, 14, and 15 are derived from eye-readings of self-registering thermometers.

The mean reading of the *Barometer* for the month was 29in·697, being 0in·112 *lower* than the average for the 20 years, 1854–1873.

TEMPERATURE OF THE AIR.

The highest in the month was 78°·7 on July 3; the lowest in the month was 45°·7 on July 1; and the range was 33°·0.
The mean of all the highest daily readings in the month was 71°·1, being 3°·2 *lower* than the average for the 41 years, 1841–1881.
The mean of all the lowest daily readings in the month was 52°·3, being 0°·7 *lower* than the average for the 41 years, 1841–1881.
The mean of the daily range was 18°·6, being 2°·5 *less* than the average for the 41 years, 1841–1881.
The mean for the month was 60°·3, being 2°·3 *lower* than the average for the 20 years, 1849–1868.

MONTH and DAY. 1882.	WIND AS DEDUCED FROM SELF-REGISTERING ANEMOMETERS. Osler's. General Direction. A.M.	P.M.	Pressure on the Square Foot. Greatest.	Least.	Mean of 24 Hourly Measures.	Robinson's. Horizontal Movement of the Air.	CLOUDS AND WEATHER. A.M.	P.M.
			lbs.	lbs.	lbs.	miles.		
July 1	NNE	NE : ENE : SE	0·0	0·0	0·0	134	0, d, h : 1, li.-cl, h	2, ci, ci.-cu : p.-cl, so.-ha : 5 cu.-s, ci.-s, h, lu.-ha
2	SE : NE	NE : SE : S	0·0	0·0	0·0	125	v, th.-cl : 1, ci.-cu, h	1, li.-cl, h : 1, th.-cl, h
3	S : SW : WSW	SW : SSW	0·8	0·0	0·0	247	v, h : 6, ci, h	7, ci, cu, h : v : 10, slt.-r
4	SSW : SW	SW	..	..	..	310	10 : 10	10 : 10
5	SW : WSW	WSW	..	..	..	386	10 : 10, hy.-sh : 9, ci.-cu, cu, r	9, cu.-s, cu, ci.-cu, shs.-r : 9, cu.-s, n, shs.-r
6	WSW	WSW	..	..	..	468	4, ci.-cu : v, shs.-r	v, shs.-r, so.-ha : 1, s, ci.-s
7	SW	SW : SSW	..	..	..	467	p.-cl : 8, cu, ci.-cu, hy.-r, hl	5, cu, ci.-cu : v, cu, cu.-s, s, ci.-s, slt.-r
8	SSW : S	SSW : S	..	..	..	271	p.-cl : 8, shs.-r	10, hy.-r : v, hy.-sh : 0
9	SSW : WSW	WSW : SW	3·3	0·0	0·2	311	p.-cl : 6, cu, ci.-cu, shs.-r, t	7, cu, ci.-cu, ce.-shs : p.-cl : 1, li.-cl, s
10	SW : SSW : WSW	SW : NW	3·8	0·0	0·1	296	p.-cl : 9, cu, ci, sh.-r	7, cu, cu.-s, ci.-cu, ce.-shs : v, shs.-r : 5, cu.-s, ci.-cu, s, ci.-s, li.-cl
11	SSW : SE : E	SE : SSW	0·0	0·0	0·0	206	v, s : 10, r : 10, c.-r	10, fq.-r : p.-cl
12	WSW : NNW	NW : WSW	4·2	0·0	0·4	357	10, sh.-r : 10	6, cu, ci.-cu, h, sh.-r : li.-cl, so.-ha : v, h, ci.-s, s
13	SW	SSW	3·2	0·0	0·3	312	10 : 10, r	9, ci.-cu, cu.-s, shs.-r : 9, cu.-s, ci.-cu
14	SSW : SW	SW : SSW : SSE	2·9	0·0	0·6	337	10 . 10, r	6, cu.-s, ci.-cu, cu, ci : 10, r
15	SSW : S	SSW	2·9	0·0	0·3	344	10, slt.-r : 10, sc, hy.-r	8, cu, ci.-cu, ci, cu.-s : v, ci.-cu, ci, s
16	SSW	SSW	2·6	0·0	0·4	332	10 5, cu.-s, ci.-cu, cu	p.-cl, cu.-s, ci.-cu : 2, th.-cl
17	SW : WSW	SW : S	4·0	0·0	0·4	336	v 6, cu, ci-cu	6, cu, ci.-cu : 10, r
18	SSW : SW	SW : SSW	8·0	0·0	0·9	393	10, r 8, ci, cu, th.-cl	7, cu, ci.-cu, ci : p.-cl : 9, r
19	SW	SSW : SW	3·4	0·0	0·7	391	v, r p.-cl	7, cu, ci.-cu, cu.-s : 8, cu.-s, ci.-cu, cu
20	SW	SW : SSW	1·6	0·0	0·2	289	v 7, cu, ci.-cu, ci.-s, so.-ha	5, cu, ci.-cu, ci, ci.-s : v, th.-cl, s
21	SSW	SSW	2·8	0·0	0·6	299	s 7, cu.-s, cu, ci	6, cu, ci.-cu, ci, ci.-s : 8, ci.-cu
22	SSW : SW	SSW : SW	2·4	0·0	0·3	327	10, hy.-sh : 10, slt.-r	9, cu.-s, m.-r : 10
23	SSW : SSE	SW : SSW	4·8	0·0	1·0	395	10, r : 10, th.-r	6, cu, ci.-cu : 1, li.-cl
24	SSW : SW	SW : SSW	2·6	0·0	0·2	343	0 : v, cu, n, r, l, t	7, cu, cu.-s, ci.-cu, hy.-r : 5, ci.-cu
25	SSW : S	NE : NNW	1·2	0·0	0·1	126	th.-cl : 10, r : 10, r	9, cu, cu.-s, sh.-r : 9, fq.-r, m : v, li.-cl
26	NNW	N : NE : E	1·5	0·0	0·1	231	p.-cl : 8, cu, cu.-s, ci.-cu	6, cu, cu.-s : 1, h
27	SE : SW	WSW : SW	2·4	0·0	0·1	196	10 v : 0, slt.-h	8, cu, ci.-cu, cu.-s : 10 : 10, slt.-r
28	SW	WSW : SE	0·0	0·0	0·0	109	10 : 10, r : 10	10, glm : v : 1, h, m
29	Calm : NE	NE : SE : SW	0·0	0·0	0·0	90	m : f : 0, h, m	6, cu, ci.-cu, cu.-s : 1, cu.-s, h, m
30	WSW : NW	WNW : NW : NNW	2·3	0·0	0·1	253	0, h, m 0, h, m	4, cu.-s, ci.-cu, m : 9, r
31	NNW : WNW	WNW : WSW	0·9	0·0	0·1	275	1, ci.-cu, h, m	5, ci.-s, s, ci.-cu, h : 10, slt.-r
Means	...	...	..	..	0·3	290		

MONTH and DAY, 1882.	Phases of the Moon.	BAROMETER. Mean of 24 Hourly Values (corrected and reduced to 32° Fahrenheit).	TEMPERATURE. Of the Air. Highest.	Lowest.	Daily Range.	Mean of 24 Hourly Values.	Excess of Mean above Average of 20 Years.	Of Evaporation. Mean of 24 Hourly Values.	Of the Dew Point. Deduced Mean Daily Value.	Difference between the Air Temperature and Dew Point Temperature. Mean Daily Value.	Greatest of 24 Hourly Values.	Least of 24 Hourly Values.	Degree of Humidity (Saturation = 100).	TEMPERATURE. Highest in the Sun's Rays as shown by a Self-Registering Maximum Thermometer with blackened bulb in vacuo placed on the Grass.	Lowest on the Grass as shown by a Self-Registering Minimum Thermometer.	Daily Duration of Sunshine.	Sun above Horizon.	Rain collected in Gauge No. 6, whose receiving surface is 5 inches above the Ground.	Daily Amount of Ozone.	Electricity.
		in.	°	°	°	°	°	°	°	°	°	°		°	°	hours.	hours.	in.		
Aug. 1	..	30·007	75·2	58·6	16·6	65·2	+ 2·6	61·7	58·8	6·4	9·7	2·2	81	112·7	55·8	0·6	15·3	0·000	0·0	mP: wP,wN: wN,vP
2	In Equator	29·900	80·0	56·9	23·1	66·0	+ 3·3	62·0	58·8	7·2	17·3	0·8	78	144·2	48·0	6·5	15·3	0·050	0·0	mP, mN : wN, mP
3	..	29·990	68·9	50·9	18·0	58·8	− 3·9	53·8	49·4	9·4	16·6	2·2	71	121·1	41·7	6·6	15·2	0·000	0·0	vP: wP,wN: wN,mP
4	..	30·087	71·9	50·8	21·1	59·6	− 3·1	54·0	49·0	10·6	17·3	4·0	68	135·0	42·1	11·2	15·2	0·000	1·0	mP: wP,vN: wN,wP
5	..	30·055	71·0	52·5	18·5	61·4	− 1·3	57·7	54·5	6·9	13·0	2·3	78	123·0	42·4	0·8	15·1	0·000	2·5	vP, wN : wP, wN
6	Last Qr.	29·979	81·0	50·8	30·2	64·6	+ 1·9	58·9	54·1	10·5	23·0	0·8	69	133·2	40·8	9·1	15·1	0·000	2·5	vP
7	..	29·985	74·3	55·3	19·0	63·0	+ 0·3	58·3	54·3	8·7	15·5	1·9	74	139·8	45·6	2·4	15·0	0·000	1·0	wP : vP, wN
8	Greatest Declination N	30·013	72·6	50·5	22·1	59·8	− 2·9	55·4	51·5	8·3	18·9	0·2	74	131·0	39·0	5·5	15·0	0·000	0·0	wP : wP, wN : vP
9	..	30·036	71·1	46·7	24·4	58·4	− 4·3	54·8	51·6	6·8	14·9	1·9	78	134·8	35·0	5·5	14·9	0·000	0·0	vP : mP
10	..	30·079	64·8	53·5	11·3	58·0	− 4·7	55·3	52·9	5·1	8·7	1·3	83	91·3	43·9	0·0	14·9	0·000	3·0	wP : wP, wN : mP
11	..	30·004	70·5	53·4	17·1	60·6	− 2·1	57·2	54·3	6·3	14·9	1·2	80	123·0	43·0	0·8	14·8	0·000	0·0	mP
12	..	29·798	80·6	51·2	29·4	64·8	+ 2·2	61·1	58·0	6·8	18·7	0·0	79	145·8	40·8	10·3	14·7	0·012	5·7	vP : wP : mP
13	New	29·640	71·0	58·0	13·0	64·5	+ 2·0	61·8	59·5	5·0	9·9	0·2	84	106·9	49·0	0·1	14·7	0·000	11·0	vP, mN : mP
14	..	29·683	75·1	56·3	18·8	64·6	+ 2·2	60·9	57·8	6·8	14·0	1·1	78	141·9	46·9	5·1	14·6	0·000	13·5	wP : wP : mP
15	..	29·570	71·1	50·0	21·1	61·2	− 1·1	57·6	54·5	6·7	14·4	1·5	79	132·1	41·0	5·0	14·6	0·051	10·8	wP : wP, wN : vP
16	In Equator Apogee	29·472	68·1	49·1	19·0	56·9	− 5·2	53·7	50·7	6·2	14·2	0·2	80	123·4	40·0	4·2	14·5	0·197	2·0	vP, vN
17	..	29·661	66·2	53·7	12·5	58·6	− 3·3	56·5	54·6	4·0	8·8	0·4	86	76·2	47·2	0·5	14·4	0·069	0·0	vP : wN : wP
18	..	29·810	74·1	51·8	22·3	61·6	− 0·2	59·6	57·9	3·7	9·0	0·6	88	121·3	43·3	0·8	14·4	0·000	0·0	mP
19	..	29·777	71·8	55·8	16·0	62·2	+ 0·6	59·8	57·8	4·4	10·1	0·2	86	113·0	47·0	0·5	14·3	0·012	7·0	wP : wP, wN
20	..	29·791	73·1	47·8	25·3	59·3	− 2·1	55·0	51·2	8·1	20·0	0·4	75	144·6	37·0	6·3	14·3	0·045	1·0	mP
21	..	29·575	67·9	53·0	14·9	59·0	− 2·3	54·5	50·5	8·5	16·9	0·4	74	125·9	44·0	3·6	14·2	0·000	6·0	o : wP, vN : mP
22	First Qr.	29·580	67·0	50·0	17·0	57·7	− 3·6	53·1	48·9	8·8	16·0	0·2	72	126·0	39·9	4·4	14·1	0·136	4·0	wP : wP, wN : vP
23	Greatest Declination S.	29·220	66·8	50·7	16·1	58·0	− 3·2	53·2	48·9	9·1	18·2	0·4	72	124·3	43·5	6·6	14·1	0·082	15·0	wP : vvP, vvN
24	..	29·444	65·2	47·8	17·4	54·9	− 6·2	51·9	49·0	5·9	15·2	1·7	80	142·2	40·6	5·0	14·0	0·039	10·5	wP : vP, vvN : vP
25	..	29·247	67·0	51·8	15·2	56·5	− 4·5	54·1	51·9	4·6	10·4	0·2	85	124·9	45·3	3·8	13·9	0·124	15·5	wP
26	..	29·446	69·2	52·4	16·8	57·9	− 3·0	54·8	52·0	5·9	16·9	0·2	80	133·7	46·0	3·3	13·9	0·016	0·5	o : vP, vN
27	..	29·610	64·9	51·8	13·1	57·2	− 3·6	54·6	52·2	5·0	10·8	1·4	84	92·1	44·7	0·2	13·8	0·000	4·5	mP
28	Full	29·536	66·2	45·9	20·3	57·2	− 3·5	54·9	52·8	4·4	12·4	0·0	83	115·2	36·1	0·5	13·8	0·009	4·8	wP
29	Perigee In Equator	29·342	66·2	51·8	14·4	56·8	− 3·8	52·9	49·3	7·5	14·4	2·3	76	131·9	42·9	6·2	13·7	0·115	7·2	wP : vvP,vvN : vP
30	..	29·816	69·5	51·1	18·4	58·4	− 2·0	53·6	49·3	9·1	16·9	1·8	72	137·0	40·1	9·8	13·7	0·000	0·0	sP: wP,wN: wN,vP
31	..	29·844	63·8	44·0	19·8	54·8	− 5·5	52·7	50·7	4·1	13·5	0·0	86	111·8	33·0	1·1	13·6	0·202	1·0	vP
Means	..	29·742	70·5	51·7	18·8	59·9	− 1·9	56·3	53·1	6·8	14·5	1·0	78·5	124·5	42·8	4·1	14·5	Sum 1·139	4·2	..
Number of Column for Reference.	1	2	3	4	5	6	7	8	9	10	11	12	13	14	15	16	17	18	19	20

The results apply to the civil day.

The mean reading of the Barometer (Column 2) and the mean temperatures of the Air and Evaporation (Columns 6 and 8) are deduced from the photographic records. The average temperature (Column 7) is that determined from the reduction of the photographic records from 1849 to 1868. The temperature of the Dew Point (Column 9) and the Degree of Humidity (Column 13) are deduced from the corresponding temperatures of the Air and Evaporation by means of Glaisher's Hygrometrical Tables. The mean difference between the Air and Dew Point Temperatures (Column 10) is the difference between the numbers in Columns 6 and 9, and the Greatest and Least Differences (Columns 11 and 12) are deduced from the 24 hourly photographic measures of the Dry-bulb and Wet-bulb Thermometers. The results from August 18 to 30 for Barometer are deduced entirely from eye-observations, the driving clock of the photographic apparatus being away for repair.

The values given in Columns 3, 4, 5, 14, and 15 are derived from eye-readings of self-registering thermometers.

The mean reading of the *Barometer* for the month was 29in·742, being 0in·057 *lower* than the average for the 20 years, 1854–1873.

MONTH and DAY. 1881.	OSLER'S. General Direction.		Pressure on the Square Foot.			ROBINSON'S. Horizontal Movement of the Air.	CLOUDS AND WEATHER.	
	A.M.	P.M.	Greatest.	Least.	Mean of 24 Hourly Measures.		A.M.	P.M.
			lbs.	lbs.	lbs.	miles.		
Aug. 1	WSW	W : WSW	2·6	0·0	0·3	386	10 : 10	10, m, th.-r : 10
2	WSW	WSW : NW	4·5	0·0	0·7	436	v : 0, h : v, ci.-cu, cu	9, cu, ci.-cu : 10, r : 0
3	WSW : NNW	NNW	2·5	0·0	0·1	305	0 : 10	8, cu, ci.-cu, th.-cl : 1 li.-cl
4	NW : NNW	NNW	1·8	0·0	0·1	301	p.-cl : 5, cu, ci.-cu, h	7, cu, ci.-cu, cu.-s : 1, li.-cl
5	NW:WSW:NNW	NNW : NW	1·0	0·0	0·0	207	v : 10 : 10	10 : 1, m, h
6	W : NW	NW : NNW	1·3	0·0	0·1	280	v : 3, th.-cl, m	0 : 1, li.-cl
7	NNW	N : NE : E	1·2	0·0	0·0	221	v : 10 : 10	9, cu.-s : v, li.-cl : v, h, th.-cl
8	Calm : NNE	NNE : NE	1·9	0·0	0·1	190	v : 10	6, cu, ci.-cu, ci: p.-cl : 0
9	NE	NE : SE	0·0	0·0	0·0	136	0, hy.-d : 10 : 10	v, li.-cl : 0 : v, h
10	NE	ENE : E	0·5	0·0	0·0	175	v : 10	10 : 10
11	ENE : SE	ESE : E	0·2	0·0	0·0	147	10 : 10, slt.-r	9, cu, ci.-cu, li.-cl : 0, hy.-d
12	E : NE	E : ESE	..	..	..	134	0, m, hy.-d : 0, f	1, ci.-cu, cu: 1, li.-cl, l : v, l, r
13	SE	SW	..	..	..	257	10 : 10	10, slt.-r : 9 : 1, li.-cl
14	SSW	SSW	..	..	..	278	p.-cl : 10	8, cu, cu.-s, ci.-cu : p.-cl
15	SSW	SW : WSW	..	..	..	347	10 : 10, slt.-r : p.-cl, r	9, cu.-s, ci.-cu, shs.-r : 0, hy.-d
16	SSE : NW	NNW : WSW	2·3	0·0	0·1	252	p.-cl : 10, r : 10, m, shs.-r	7, cu.-s, cu, ci.-cu, h, m: 10
17	WSW : W	NW : SW	0·2	0·0	0·0	204	10 : 10, hy.-sh, glm	10 : v, th.-cl
18	S : SW	SW : SSW	0·0	0·0	0·0	153	p.-cl, ci, ci.-s : 9, li.-cl, ci.-s, ci.-cu	8, cu.-s : p.-cl : p.-cl
19	SSW : SW	WSW : W : WNW	1·8	0·0	0·1	266	10 : 10	10, n, cu.-s, sh.-r : 10 : v, li.-cl
20	WSW : SW	SW	4·0	0·0	0·3	312	v, li.-cl : 10	7, cu, ci : 8 : 10, hy.-sh
21	SW : WSW : W	W : WSW	7·3	0·0	0·9	497	10 : 10	9, cu.-s, ci.-cu, w : p.-cl, w : 0
22	WSW : W	W : WSW : SSW	6·3	0·0	0·8	492	0, w : 4, li.-cl	10 : 10, r, w
23	SW : WSW	WSW	28·0	0·2	2·6	699	10, r, w : 8, cu.-s, g	6, cu, ci.-cu, cu.-s, w, shs.-r: 4, cu.-s, ci.-s
24	WSW	SW	9·0	0·0	0·8	472	0 : 3, cu, ci.-cu, ci, li.-cl	9, cu.-s, cu, th.-cl, r, w : 7, ci.-cu
25	SW : S : SSE	S : SW : SSW	3·5	0·0	0·3	308	10, s : 10, r	8, cu, cu.-s, r : 8, ci.-s
26	WSW : W : NW	WNW : WSW	3·0	0·0	0·3	337	10 : 8, ci.-cu, h, m	9, cu.-s, ci.-cu, slt.-r : v, cu.-s, r
27	WSW : W	WNW : W : SW	1·0	0·0	0·0	264	10 : 10	10 : 9, cu.-s, ci.-s
28	SW	SSW : SW	2·7	0·0	0·3	291	p.-cl : 8, ci.-cu, ci	10, sh.-r : 10, li.-shs : 4, sc, ci, n, cu.
29	SW : WSW	NW : WSW	9·1	0·0	1·1	496	p.-cl : v, r	4, ci.-cu, li.-cl, cu, shs.-r, w: 4, ci, ci.-s, li.-cl
30	W : NW	NW	4·2	0·0	0·6	397	0, h : 6, ci.-cu, cu.-s, li.-cl	7, cu, ci.-cu, cu.-s: p.-cl : 1, ci.-cu, h, m
31	SW	SW : SSE	0·2	0·0	0·0	142	p.-cl, m : 10, th.-cl, ci.-s, ci.-cu, m	10, r : 10, c.-r
Means	...	...	..	..	0·4	303		
Number of Column for Reference	21	22	23	24	25	26	27	28

MONTH and DAY, 1882.	Phases of the Moon.	BAROMETER. Mean of 24 Hourly Values (corrected and reduced to 32° Fahrenheit).	TEMPERATURE. Of the Air. Highest.	Lowest.	Daily Range.	Mean of 24 Hourly Values.	Excess of Mean above Average of 20 Years.	Of Evaporation. Mean of 24 Hourly Values.	Of the Dew Point. Deduced Mean Daily Value.	Difference between the Air Temperature and Dew Point Temperature. Mean Daily Value.	Greatest of 24 Hourly Values.	Least of 24 Hourly Values.	Degree of Humidity (Saturation = 100).	TEMPERATURE. Highest in the Sun's Rays as shown by a Self-Registering Maximum Thermometer with blackened bulb in vacuo placed on the Grass.	Lowest on the Grass as shown by a Self-Registering Minimum Thermometer.	Daily Duration of Sunshine.	Sun above Horizon.	Rain collected in Gauge No. 6, whose receiving surface is 5 inches above the Ground.	Daily Amount of Ozone.	Electricity.
		in.	°	°	°	°	°	°	°	°	°	°		°	°	hours.	hours.	in.		
Sept. 1	..	29·555	65·7	54·4	11·3	61·3	+ 1·2	60·2	59·2	2·1	5·0	0·6	93	90·3	52·1	0·1	13·5	0·043	14·5	o : wP
2	..	29·382	70·1	57·5	12·6	63·0	+ 3·0	59·3	56·2	6·8	13·5	1·7	79	132·7	51·0	7·3	13·4	0·063	18·8	wP : mP
3	..	29·602	71·1	56·0	15·1	61·1	+ 1·3	56·6	52·7	8·4	17·1	2·7	74	140·2	46·0	6·6	13·4	0·000	12·2	wP : mP
4	Last Qr.	29·936	69·7	53·0	16·7	59·1	− 0·6	55·7	52·7	6·4	14·8	1·2	80	126·2	42·0	3·3	13·3	0·000	5·0	o : wP : vP
5	Greatest Declination N	30·011	65·2	51·4	13·8	57·4	− 2·1	55·5	53·8	3·6	10·3	0·2	88	127·1	40·2	2·2	13·2	0·300	0·0	o, mP : vP
6	..	30·051	65·4	52·2	13·2	57·4	− 1·9	53·0	49·0	8·4	17·5	0·4	73	136·7	46·0	6·9	13·2	0·036	0·0	vP
7	..	30·183	67·5	45·9	21·6	56·1	− 2·9	52·0	48·1	8·0	15·7	2·1	75	139·3	36·1	9·7	13·1	0·000	0·0	mP : vP
8	..	30·191	68·6	44·9	23·7	56·3	− 2·5	51·8	47·6	8·7	19·4	1·5	72	136·1	37·3	9·9	13·0	0·000	0·0	vP
9	..	30·133	66·4	43·8	22·6	55·0	− 3·5	51·7	48·5	6·5	14·2	1·0	79	132·8	32·8	6·0	13·0	0·000	0·0	wP : vP
10	..	29·765	69·4	46·8	22·6	57·7	− 0·6	55·6	53·7	4·0	10·1	0·6	86	108·8	36·8	0·3	12·9	0·000	0·0	o : wP
11	..	29·329	65·2	45·6	19·6	55·4	− 2·7	53·4	51·5	3·9	8·7	0·4	87	95·0	37·7	0·0	12·9	0·023	0·0	wP : wP, wN
12	In Equator New Apogee	29·435	57·5	44·6	12·9	50·3	− 7·7	47·8	45·2	5·1	10·1	2·3	83	107·9	37·0	1·2	12·8	0·256	0·0	wP, vN : vP
13	..	29·491	61·0	39·6	21·4	49·0	− 8·8	46·1	43·0	6·0	14·4	0·4	80	106·3	30·3	2·9	12·7	0·000	0·0	wP : wN, wP : wN, wP
14	..	29·447	54·4	39·7	14·7	46·0	−11·6	44·7	43·2	2·8	8·2	0·2	91	74·2	29·0	0·0	12·7	0·178	0·0	wP : vN, sP : sN, vP
15	..	29·584	65·7	36·7	29·0	49·6	− 7·8	46·4	43·0	6·6	19·6	0·0	78	134·7	30·8	6·6	12·6	0·000	0·0	mP : mP : vP, wN
16	..	29·753	63·3	40·9	22·4	52·9	− 4·4	50·2	47·5	5·4	11·2	0·4	82	101·3	32·6	0·9	12·6	0·000	0·5	vP : wN, wP : mP
17	..	29·812	68·1	45·8	22·3	55·2	− 1·9	52·0	48·9	6·3	13·7	2·4	80	121·3	36·8	4·7	12·5	0·000	2·5	mP : vP, wN
18	..	29·831	63·9	47·0	16·9	53·7	− 3·2	51·0	48·4	5·3	11·2	1·6	82	123·2	35·0	2·8	12·4	0·000	0·0	mP : vP
19	Greatest Declination S.	29·705	57·0	43·7	13·3	50·8	− 6·0	50·1	49·4	1·4	2·3	0·0	95	60·0	33·0	0·0	12·3	0·306	0·0	mP, mN : wN, wP
20	First Qr.	29·555	60·8	47·5	13·3	55·2	− 1·4	54·1	53·0	2·2	5·9	0·4	93	97·5	36·5	0·3	12·3	0·282	0·0	vP, vN : wP : mP
21	..	29·629	60·4	45·9	14·5	53·4	− 3·0	51·7	50·0	3·4	8·9	0·2	88	79·9	34·3	1·3	12·2	0·006	0·0	vP
22	..	29·714	64·7	46·3	18·4	54·3	− 1·9	51·2	48·2	6·1	12·4	1·9	79	124·4	36·0	5·6	12·2	0·000	0·0	mP : vP
23	..	29·837	59·4	39·0	20·4	50·4	− 5·7	48·5	46·5	3·9	10·5	0·0	87	64·1	31·1	3·1	12·1	0·000	0·0	mP : wP, wN : wP
24	..	29·837	65·1	47·8	17·3	55·2	− 0·7	52·7	50·3	4·9	9·9	1·3	84	84·6	39·1	0·6	12·0	0·000	1·3	wP : mP
25	..	29·650	67·9	49·6	18·3	56·5	+ 0·7	53·7	51·1	5·4	15·1	0·6	82	126·5	39·0	4·1	11·9	0·000	9·7	wP : mP
26	In Equator Perigee	29·296	64·1	48·3	15·8	54·7	− 1·0	52·7	50·8	3·9	6·2	1·6	87	116·9	36·2	2·7	11·9	0·016	1·3	mP : vP, wN
27	Full	29·143	60·7	47·4	13·3	52·8	− 2·7	50·8	48·8	4·0	7·8	1·3	87	109·0	36·8	2·3	11·8	0·052	3·7	wP : vP, vN
28	..	29·488	62·1	43·5	18·6	51·3	− 4·1	47·8	44·2	7·1	16·5	1·9	77	123·2	37·3	7·7	11·7	0·010	0·0	vP
29	..	29·347	57·2	48·1	9·1	52·2	− 3·0	50·6	49·0	3·2	6·4	0·4	89	75·0	44·0	0·2	11·7	0·831	5·0	vN : vP : vP, wN
30	..	29·712	61·3	44·9	16·4	54·0	− 0·9	52·3	50·6	3·4	8·7	0·6	88	83·9	40·8	0·1	11·6	0·003	5·5	mP : wP
Means	..	29·687	64·0	46·6	17·4	54·6	− 2·9	52·0	49·5	5·1	11·5	1·0	83·3	110·2	37·8	5·3	12·6	Sum 2·405	2·7	..
Number of Column for Reference.	1	2	3	4	5	6	7	8	9	10	11	12	13	14	15	16	17	18	19	20

The results apply to the civil day.

The mean reading of the Barometer (Column 2) and the mean temperatures of the Air and Evaporation (Columns 6 and 8) are deduced from the photographic records. The average temperature (Column 7) is that determined from the reduction of the photographic records from 1849 to 1868. The temperature of the Dew Point (Column 9) and the Degree of Humidity (Column 13) are deduced from the corresponding temperatures of the Air and Evaporation by means of Glaisher's Hygrometrical Tables. The mean difference between the Air and Dew Point Temperatures (Column 10) is the difference between the numbers in Columns 6 and 9, and the Greatest and Least Differences (Columns 11 and 12) are deduced from the 24 hourly photographic measures of the Dry-bulb and Wet-bulb Thermometers.

The values given in Columns 3, 4, 5, 14, and 15 are derived from eye-readings of self-registering thermometers.

The mean reading of the *Barometer* for the month was 29in·687, being 0in·100 *lower* than the average for the 20 years, 1854–1873.

TEMPERATURE OF THE AIR.

The highest in the month was 71°·1 on September 3; the lowest in the month was 36°·7 on September 15; and the range was 34°·4.

The mean of all the highest daily readings in the month was 64°·0, being 3°·3 *lower* than the average for the 41 years, 1841–1881.

The mean of all the lowest daily readings in the month was 46°·6, being 2°·6 *lower* than the average for the 41 years, 1841–1881.

The mean of the daily ranges was 17°·4, being 0°·9 *less* than the average for the 41 years, 1841–1881.

The mean for the month was 54°·6, being 2°·9 *lower* than the average for the 20 years, 1849–1868.

MONTH and DAY. 1882.	WIND AS DEDUCED FROM SELF-REGISTERING ANEMOMETERS. OSLER'S. General Direction. A.M.	P.M.	Pressure on the Square Foot. Greatest.	Least.	Mean of 24 Hourly Measures.	ROBINSON'S. Horizontal Movement of the Air.	CLOUDS AND WEATHER. A.M.	P.M.
			lbs.	lbs.	lbs.	miles.		
Sept. 1	S : SSW	SSW	6·7	0·0	0·6	344	10 : 10, sh.-r	10, lt.-r : 10, sc, th.-r, w
2	SSW	SW	13·5	0·1	2·9	624	10, w : 6,ci.-cu,cu,w : [illegible]	8,cu,ci.-cu,cu.-s,w,r : 10, sqs : v
3	SSW : SW	SW	3·5	0·0	0·9	391	v, th.-cl : p.-cl	7, cu, cu.-s : v, li.-cl
4	W : N	N : NE : SSE	0·0	0·0	0·0	155	10 : 10	7, cu.-s, ci.-cu, cu : v, th.-cl, h
5	SW : WSW	SW	2·5	0·0	0·0	229	p.-cl : 10, li.-cl : p.-cl, r	10 : 10, r : 10, m.-r
6	N	NNE	1·8	0·0	0·2	303	10, r : 10 : 9,th.-cl,so.-ha	5, ci, cu, cu.-s : p.-cl, cu.-s
7	NNE : NE	ENE	3·0	0·0	0·1	259	1, li.-cl : 0 : p.-cl	5, cu.-s, cu, ci.-cu : 0, d
8	NNE	NE : E	0·3	0·0	0·0	172	v : 7,cu, ci.-cu, ci,m,so.-ha	2,ci.-cu,ci,cu,so.-ha : 0, m, d
9	NE : ENE	ENE : NE	1·5	0·0	0·1	217	0 : p.-cl, cu.-s, ci.-cu	5, cu.-s, ci.-cu, cu : 3, ci.-cu
10	NNE : N	Variable	0·0	0·0	0·0	92	v : 10, m	9, cu.-s, ci.-cu, h, m : 2, li.-cl, m, d
11	SW : WSW	SW : S : N	0·3	0·0	0·0	130	0, m, d : p.-cl, ci : 10	10, slt.-r : 10, slt.-r
12	N	N : NNE	0·2	0·0	0·0	170	10, hy.-r : 10, r : 10, oc.-r	7, cu, ci.-cu, slt.-h : v, ci.-cu, m
13	SW : WSW	NW : W : SW	1·3	0·0	0·1	182	p.-cl, m : 3, th.-cl, h, f	8,cu,cu.-s,h : p.-cl : 0, h, m, l
14	SW : SSE	Variable	0·5	0·0	0·0	149	1, th.-cl, h, m : li.-cl, h, slt.-f	[illegible] : p.-cl, f : 2, slt.-f
15	ENE	E : Calm	1·3	0·0	0·1	103	0, f : 0, f, ho.-fr	2,cu,ci.-cu,h : ci.-s, cu.-s : 1,th.-cl,h,slt.-f
16	WSW : W : NNE	NNE : Calm : WSW	1·0	0·0	0·0	129	p.-cl, slt.-f : 9,ci.-s,d,slt.-f : 2, ci, h, f	10 : 10, m
17	WSW	W : WNW	0·2	0·0	0·0	139	10 : 3, ci.-cu, h, slt.-f	p.-cl, ci.-cu, cu.-s, f : 10
18	NNW : N	NNE	1·0	0·0	0·1	179	10 : 10, m	9,cu.-s,cu,ci : p.-cl : v,h,slt.-m,d
19	N : NNW	NW : NNW : NNE	2·8	0·0	0·4	270	0 : v, li.-cl, s, sc : 10, r	10, sc, r : 10, slt.-r
20	NNE : NE	ENE : ESE : NE	2·5	0·0	0·3	241	10, r : 10, r : 9,cu,cu.-s,sc	10, sc, r : 0
21	NNE	NNE : N	3·3	0·0	0·6	323	v : 10, sc, ci.-s, oc.-th.-r	10, oc.-r, sc : v : v, li.-cl, slt.-h
22	N : NNE	N : NNE	2·0	0·0	0·4	245	0 : 0 : p.-cl,ci,ci.-cu	6, cu.-s, ci.-cu, cu : v, th.-cl
23	Calm : SW	SSE : SSW	0·1	0·0	0·0	123	0 : 0, tk.-f : 3, cu, h, m	9, h, m : p.-cl, slt.-h : p.-cl
24	S : SW	SSW : SE	1·5	0·0	0·0	169	10 : 10	p.-cl, ci.-cu, cu.-s : p.-cl, ci.-cu
25	SE : SSE	S : SE : ESE	3·4	0·0	0·3	207	v : 10 : 10, slt.-r	7,cu.-s,ci.-cu,ci : 0, mock suns : v, ci.-s, cu.-s
26	E : ENE : ESE	SSE : SE	2·2	0·0	0·2	181	p.-cl, cu.-s : 6,ci.-cu,ci.-s,s,li.-cl	10, r : 10 : th.-cl,ci.-cu,cu.-s,h.-r,lu.-ha
27	SE : SW	WSW	3·1	0·0	0·5	243	v : p.-cl, cu, cu.-s, ci	10, r : 10, shs.-r : 5,ci.-cu,li.-cl
28	WSW	WSW : S : SE	2·4	0·0	0·4	277	v, li.-cl : 0 : 1, li.-cl	5,cu,cu.-s,ci.-cu,so.-ha : 10, th.-cl, lu.-ha, r
29	ESE : WSW : NW	NW : SW	4·8	0·0	0·8	318	10, hy.-r : 10, c.-hy.-r : 10, sc	10 : 10 : v,li.-cl,lu.-ha
30	SW	S : SSW	3·0	0·0	0·6	273	0 : 9, m : 9,cl,ci.-s,m,slt.-r	10 : 10 : p.-cl, sc
Means	...	...	..	..	0·3	228		
Number of Column for Reference.	21	22	23	24	25	26	27	28

The mean *Temperature of Evaporation* for the month was 52°·0, being 1°·3 *lower* than
The mean *Temperature of the Dew Point* for the month was 49°·5, being 1°·9 *lower* than
The mean *Degree of Humidity* for the month was 83·3, being 3·2 *greater* than
The mean *Elastic Force of Vapour* for the month was 0in·355, being 0in·024 *less* than
The mean *Weight of Vapour in a Cubic Foot of Air* for the month was 4gr·0, being 0gr·2 *less* than
The mean *Weight of a Cubic Foot of Air* for the month was 534 grains, being 2 grains *greater* than
} the average for the 20 years, 1849–1868.

The mean amount of *Cloud* for the month (a clear sky being represented by 0 and an overcast sky by 10) was 6·9.

The mean proportion of *Sunshine* for the month (constant sunshine being represented by 1) was 0·26. The maximum daily amount of *Sunshine* was 9·9 hours on September 8.

The highest reading of the *Solar Radiation Thermometer* was 140°·2 on September 3; and the lowest reading of the *Terrestrial Radiation Thermometer* was 29°·0 on September 14.

The mean daily distribution of *Ozone* was, for the 12 hours ending 9 a.m., 1·4; for the 6 hours ending 3 p.m., 0·7; and for the 6 hours ending 9 p.m., 0·6.

The *Proportions of Wind* referred to the cardinal points were N. 9, E. 5, S. 8, and W. 7. One day was calm.

The *Greatest Pressure of the Wind* in the month was 13lbs·5 on the square foot on September 2. The mean daily *Horizontal Movement of the Air* for the month was 228 miles; the greatest daily value was 624 miles on September 2; and the least daily value 92 miles on September 10.

Rain fell on 14 days in the month, amounting to 2in·435, as measured by gauge No. 6 partly sunk below the ground; being 0in·113 *greater* than the average fall for the 41 years, 1841–1881.

MONTH and DAY. 188[illegible].	Phases of the Moon.	BAROMETER. Mean of 24 Hourly Values (corrected and reduced to 32° Fahrenheit).	TEMPERATURE. Of the Air. Highest.	Lowest.	Daily Range.	Mean of 24 Hourly Values.	Excess of Mean above Average of 20 Years.	Of Evaporation. Mean of 24 Hourly Values.	Of the Dew Point. Deduced Mean Daily Value.	Difference between the Air Temperature and Dew Point Temperature. Mean Daily Value.	Greatest of 24 Hourly Values.	Least of 24 Hourly Values.	Degree of Humidity (Saturation = 100).	TEMPERATURE. Highest in the Sun's Rays as shown by a Self-Registering Maximum Thermometer with blackened bulb in vacuo placed on the Grass.	Lowest on the Grass as shown by a Self-Registering Minimum Thermometer.	Daily Duration of Sunshine.	Sun above Horizon.	Rain collected in Gauge No. 6, whose receiving surface is 5 inches above the Ground.	Daily Amount of Ozone.	Electricity.
		in.	°	°	°	°	°	°	°	°	°	°		°	°	hours.	hours.	in.		
Oct. 1	..	29·679	71·1	59·1	12·0	63·3	+ 8·6	61·0	59·1	4·2	8·5	1·6	87	119·2	54·2	3·3	11·6	0·069	8·0	wP : wP : vP, wN
2	Greatest Declination N	29·834	67·0	49·3	17·7	56·9	+ 2·5	54·5	52·3	4·6	9·5	1·8	83	121·0	43·1	8·4	11·5	0·000	11·0	wP : mP
3	..	30·045	63·1	45·7	17·4	54·6	+ 0·6	52·3	50·1	4·5	9·9	0·4	84	113·0	40·0	5·7	11·4	0·129	1·5	vP, sN : vP, wN : vP
4	Last Qr.	30·279	58·9	43·3	15·6	51·6	− 2·1	50·0	48·4	3·2	6·3	1·3	89	75·1	37·6	0·0	11·4	0·000	0·0	vP
5	..	30·221	60·7	45·9	14·8	52·6	− 0·8	51·1	49·6	3·0	6·5	0·8	90	96·0	40·7	0·8	11·3	0·058	0·0	mP : vP, wN
6	..	29·977	58·8	51·6	7·2	54·4	+ 1·4	52·8	51·2	3·2	5·7	0·8	89	86·2	50·4	0·3	11·2	0·010	0·0	wP
7	..	29·895	65·1	47·8	17·3	54·7	+ 2·0	52·4	50·2	4·5	10·3	1·0	85	117·1	39·8	4·1	11·2	0·042	0·5	wP : mP
8	..	29·920	64·8	44·8	20·0	53·7	+ 1·2	51·7	49·8	3·9	8·9	0·0	87	116·8	37·1	4·0	11·1	0·000	4·5	wP : mP
9	Apogee In Equator	29·963	69·1	48·5	20·6	55·9	+ 3·6	54·0	52·2	3·7	10·1	0·4	88	126·4	42·1	4·3	11·0	0·000	2·0	mP
10	..	29·860	62·1	48·7	13·4	55·5	+ 3·4	54·5	53·6	1·9	4·9	0·0	94	81·8	45·1	0·0	11·0	0·024	0·0	vP : wP
11	..	29·494	61·3	53·1	8·2	57·3	+ 5·4	56·4	55·6	1·7	4·6	0·2	94	75·6	49·1	0·0	10·9	0·314	0·0	wP : wP, wN
12	New	29·360	56·8	48·5	8·3	51·5	− 0·2	50·0	48·5	3·0	7·4	0·6	90	78·0	44·3	0·0	10·9	0·116	1·0	wP, wN : vP, wN
13		29·593	60·0	44·1	15·9	52·9	+ 1·3	51·2	49·5	3·4	10·3	0·2	89	92·1	39·3	0·5	10·8	0·035	0·0	wN, mP : wP, wN
14		29·788	56·2	47·2	9·0	52·8	+ 1·4	50·7	48·6	4·2	6·4	0·4	86	67·9	40·5	0·0	10·7	0·010	0·0	wN, wP : mP
15		29·768	56·9	46·2	10·7	49·9	− 1·4	47·7	45·4	4·5	8·0	1·5	86	89·1	45·8	0·5	10·7	0·130	0·0	wP : wP, wN
16	..	29·419	49·4	45·2	4·2	47·4	− 3·8	46·7	45·9	1·5	2·3	0·4	95	53·8	45·0	0·0	10·6	0·916	3·0	wN : wN, wP
17	Greatest Declination S	29·627	49·7	44·5	5·2	48·4	− 2·7	47·7	46·9	1·5	3·8	0·4	95	54·2	40·0	0·0	10·5	0·039	0·0	o : wP : wP
18	..	29·925	51·0	42·2	8·8	46·2	− 4·8	45·7	45·2	1·0	2·7	0·0	97	61·9	35·0	0·0	10·5	0·000	1·5	wP : wP, wN : mP
19	First Qr.	29·701	54·4	47·1	7·3	51·2	+ 0·4	49·9	48·6	2·6	6·2	0·2	91	65·2	41·0	0·0	10·4	0·490	6·5	wP : vP, vN
20	..	29·622	61·2	44·8	16·4	52·2	+ 1·6	50·4	48·6	3·6	12·2	0·2	88	106·3	39·6	4·2	10·3	0·025	8·5	mP
21	..	29·401	57·0	46·8	10·2	53·5	+ 3·1	52·6	51·7	1·8	3·6	0·4	94	69·5	41·9	0·0	10·3	0·284	11·5	wP, wN : wP
22	..	29·148	55·0	43·3	11·7	50·5	+ 0·4	48·3	46·0	4·5	12·4	0·8	85	83·0	36·5	1·8	10·2	0·364	4·2	wP, wN : vP, wN : sP
23	In Equator	29·347	56·0	41·3	14·7	46·6	− 3·1	43·9	40·8	5·8	9·8	2·9	82	101·0	34·1	6·8	10·2	0·000	11·2	— : mP, sN : vP
24	..	29·134	54·9	39·3	15·6	45·7	− 3·7	44·0	42·0	3·7	5·8	0·0	87	88·7	35·0	0·4	10·1	0·649	13·5	— : wN : mP
25	Perigee	29·382	54·2	37·7	16·5	44·2	− 4·9	42·6	40·7	3·5	9·0	0·7	88	100·2	29·0	1·7	10·0	0·078	0·0	mP : vvP, vN
26	Full	29·355	53·7	30·6	23·1	42·5	− 6·3	40·9	39·0	3·5	11·4	0·0	88	100·6	27·0	4·9	10·0	0·156	2·2	vP : vvP, vvN
27	..	29·233	51·2	40·1	11·1	46·6	− 1·9	45·7	44·7	1·9	4·6	0·0	94	67·4	33·4	0·0	9·9	0·232	10·8	wP : wP, wN : wN
28	..	29·294	48·9	46·0	2·9	47·7	− 0·5	46·1	44·3	3·4	5·3	1·7	80	53·0	43·0	0·0	9·8	0·833	4·2	vN : vN : mP
29	Greatest Declination N	29·609	50·1	37·3	12·8	45·9	− 2·0	43·3	40·3	3·6	9·7	1·4	82	84·7	31·0	2·9	9·8	0·000	0·8	vP : sP
30	..	29·671	52·3	34·9	17·4	46·4	− 1·2	45·2	43·9	2·5	5·3	0·6	92	68·7	29·1	0·1	9·7	0·418	0·0	mP : wP, wN : —
31	..	29·812	56·5	41·8	14·7	49·1	+ 1·8	46·9	44·5	4·6	10·5	0·7	85	101·0	33·4	5·2	9·7	0·000	0·5	— : mP
Means	..	29·665	57·7	44·7	12·9	51·0	0·0	49·4	47·7	3·4	7·5	0·7	88·9	87·6	39·5	1·9	10·6	Sum 3·421	3·4	....
Number of Column for Reference.	1	2	3	4	5	6	7	8	9	10	11	12	13	14	15	16	17	18	19	20

The results apply to the civil day.

The mean reading of the Barometer (Column 2) and the mean temperatures of the Air and Evaporation (Columns 6 and 8) are deduced from the photographic records. The average temperature (Column 7) is that determined from the reduction of the photographic records from 1849 to 1868. The temperature of the Dew Point (Column 9) and the Degree of Humidity (Column 13) are deduced from the corresponding temperatures of the Air and Evaporation by means of Glaisher's Hygrometrical Tables. The mean difference between the Air and Dew Point Temperatures (Column 10) is the difference between the numbers in Columns 6 and 9, and the Greatest and Least Differences (Columns 11 and 12) are deduced from the 24 hourly photographic measures of the Dry-bulb and Wet-bulb Thermometers.

The values given in Columns 3, 4, 5, 14, and 15 are derived from eye-readings of self-registering thermometers.

MONTH and DAY, 1882.	WIND AS DEDUCED FROM SELF-REGISTERING ANEMOMETERS. Osler's. General Direction. A.M.	P.M.	Pressure on the Square Foot. Greatest.	Least.	Mean of 24 Hourly Measures.	Robinson's. Horizontal Movement of the Air.	CLOUDS AND WEATHER. A.M.	P.M.
			lbs.	lbs.	lbs.	miles		
Oct. 1	SW : SSW	S : SSW : WSW	3·7	0·0	1·1	361	10 : p.-cl	7 : 10, r, l
2	SW	SSW	2·9	0·0	0·5	311	v : o	3, cu, ci.-cu, cu.-s : o, a
3	SW : WSW : W	W : WNW : WSW	2·3	0·0	0·4	276	v, hy.-sh : 1, li.-cl, h	8, ci.-cu, cu.-s, cu, m : o, slt.-f
4	WSW : NNW	N : NNE	1·5	0·0	0·2	228	v, slt.-f : p.-cl, f	10 : p.-cl : o
5	NNE	NE	4·3	0·0	1·0	360	p.-cl : 9, cu.-s, ci.-cu	9, cu.-s, ci.-cu, oc.-r : 10, sh.-r
6	ENE	ENE	6·0	0·0	1·1	360	10 : 10	10, sc, slt.-r : 10, m.-r
7	ENE : SE	SE : E	0·2	0·0	0·0	144	10, r : 9, ci.-cu, ci.-s	5,cu.-s,cu,ci,ci.-cu : p.-cl : 1, l
8	NE : SE	SSE	0·1	0·0	0·0	86	v : 10, m.-r : 7,cu.-s,ci.-cu	4, cu, ci.-cu : 10, l
9	Calm : S : SSW	SSW : S	0·8	0·0	0·0	118	10 : v, ci, m	7,ci,cu,cu.-s,sc.-ha : p.-cl : p.-cl, f
10	NE : E	E : S : SSW	0·3	0·0	0·0	118	10, slt.-f : 10, f, slt.-r	10, m : 10, m, sh.-r : v
11	SSE : SSW : S	SSW	1·1	0·0	0·2	215	10 : 10, slt.-r : 10, fq.-r	10, r : 10, oc.-r : 10, hy.-r
12	WSW : W : N	N : NW : SW	0·3	0·0	0·0	143	10, shs.-r : 10, fq.-shs, m	10 : 10, f
13	SSW : WSW : SW	SW : NNE : NE	0·1	0·0	0·0	114	10, slt.-f, r : 8, ci.-cu, slt.-f	10 : 10, m.-r
14	NE	ENE : NE	2·1	0·0	0·2	228	10, oc.-th.-r : 10	10 : 10
15	NE : Calm : SSE	SE	2·0	0·0	0·1	148	10 : 9, ci.-cu	10 : 10, r
16	ESE	E : ENE	3·5	0·0	0·9	339	10, c.-r : 10, sc, c.-r	10, c.-r : 10, c.-r
17	NE : NNE	NNE : N	1·7	0·0	0·4	287	10, r : 10, sc, m.-r	10, sc, m.-r : 10, sc, fq.-m.-r : v, th.-cl
18	NNW : N	SSW : SSE : SE	0·3	0·0	0·0	103	th.-cl : 10, f, glm, m.-r	10, li.-cl, h, f : v, li.-cl, f : 6, slt.-f
19	SE : SSE	SE : SSE	1·4	0·0	0·3	173	10 : 10, r	10, sc, r : 10, sc, c.-r : 10, c.-r
20	WSW	SSW : S	1·6	0·0	0·2	221	10, sh.-r : o, f	5,ci,ci.-cu,cu : 10, shs.-r : v
21	SSE : SE : S	SSW : S	3·7	0·0	0·5	284	v : 10, sc, r	10, sc, r : 10, oc.-r
22	S : WSW	WSW	6·4	0·0	1·4	458	10, fq.-r : 8, sc, fq.-r	v, sc, m, shs.-r : o
23	SW : WSW	WSW : SW	3·7	0·0	0·7	368	o : 1, li.-cl	6, cu, cu.-s, slt.-r, w : 3, s, th.-cl, lu.-ha
24	SSW : SSE : S	WSW	29·0	0·0	4·1	632	8, th.-cl : 10, hy.-r : 10, c.-r, sc, g	10, sc, r, hy.-g : v, oc.-shs.-r, w : o
25	SW : SSW	SW : S	1·1	0·0	0·1	186	v : p.-cl, ci, ci.-s, slt.-f	7,cu,ci,ci.-cu,cu.-s,l,t,shs.-r : 1, li.-cl
26	Calm : S	SSE : SE	2·2	0·0	0·1	134	1, li.-cl, hy.-d, f : tk.-f, ho.-fr	6, ci, ci.-cu : 9, cu.-s, r : v, li.-shs
27	SE : ENE	ENE : NE	8·4	0·0	0·8	324	v : 10, r	10, fq.-r : 10, c.-r : 10, r, w
28	NNE	NNE	9·4	0·4	3·2	617	10, r, w : 10, c.-r, w	10, sc, c.-r, w : 10, sc, slt.-r
29	N : NNW	NNW : NW : SW	5·5	0·0	1·3	344	10 : 1, ci.-cu, h, slt.-m	4, ci.-cu, cu : v, h, slt.-f
30	SSW	SSW : W	3·8	0·0	1·1	377	o : o : 10, oc.-r	10, sc, fq.-r : 10, c.-r : p.-cl, r
31	WSW	SW : SSW : S	1·8	0·0	0·2	272	1, li.-cl : o : 1	5,cu,ci.-cu,cu.-s : 10, slt.-sh : v, li.-cl, m
Means	...	...	..	..	0·6	269		
Number of Column for Reference.	21	22	23	24	25	26	27	28

MONTH and DAY, 1882.	Phases of the Moon.	BAROMETER. Mean of 24 Hourly Values (corrected and reduced to 32° Fahrenheit).	TEMPERATURE. Of the Air. Highest.	Lowest.	Daily Range.	Mean of 24 Hourly Values.	Excess of Mean above Average of 20 Years.	Of Evaporation. Mean of 24 Hourly Values.	Of the Dew Point. Deduced Mean Daily Value.	Difference between the Air Temperature and Dew Point Temperature. Mean Daily Value.	Greatest of 24 Hourly Values.	Least of 24 Hourly Values.	Degree of Humidity (Saturation = 100).	TEMPERATURE. Highest in the Sun's Rays as shown by a Self-Registering Maximum Thermometer with blackened bulb in vacuo placed on the Grass.	Lowest on the Grass as shown by a Self-Registering Minimum Thermometer.	Daily Duration of Sunshine.	Sun above Horizon.	Rain collected in Gauge No. 6, whose receiving surface is 5 inches above the Ground.	Daily Amount of Ozone.	Electricity.
		in.	°	°	°	°	°	°	°	°	°	°		°	°	hours.	hours.	in.		
Nov. 1	..	29·488	58·4	47·9	10·5	52·4	+ 5·4	50·2	48·0	4·4	8·2	1·7	85	89·7	42·1	1·0	9·6	0·004	7·0	wP
2	Last Qr.	29·619	58·6	46·9	11·7	51·7	+ 5·0	49·7	47·7	4·0	6·8	1·6	87	97·2	41·8	1·7	9·5	0·066	15·8	wP
3	..	29·634	57·1	49·6	7·5	52·6	+ 6·2	50·5	48·4	4·2	8·6	1·8	86	97·1	43·9	4·5	9·5	0·089	14·8	wP : vP
4	..	29·555	57·1	47·4	9·7	53·3	+ 7·3	50·8	48·3	5·0	8·6	1·2	83	95·1	42·8	3·8	9·4	0·005	9·0	wN, wP : mP
5	..	29·752	60·1	46·9	13·2	53·9	+ 8·3	51·8	49·8	4·1	5·9	2·4	86	87·0	42·5	0·5	9·4	0·028	11·5	mP : wP
6	In Equator: Apogee.	29·835	56·0	44·2	11·8	49·0	+ 3·8	47·4	45·6	3·4	9·4	0·4	89	100·8	36·7	2·8	9·3	0·182	12·7	mP : mP, sN : vP
7	..	29·552	54·9	43·9	11·0	47·9	+ 3·2	46·3	44·5	3·4	4·8	1·4	89	59·9	43·2	0·0	9·2	0·383	2·5	wP, wN : vP, mN
8	..	29·283	49·6	39·9	9·7	45·4	+ 1·1	42·6	39·4	6·0	10·7	1·3	80	94·5	35·0	5·2	9·2	0·000	7·5	mP : sP
9	..	29·180	51·1	40·3	10·8	45·3	+ 1·5	41·3	36·7	8·6	13·4	3·9	72	79·4	34·6	2·4	9·1	0·000	0·7	mP : sP
10	New	29·434	50·9	36·4	14·5	43·5	+ 0·1	41·0	38·1	5·4	10·1	1·2	81	89·3	29·9	5·2	9·1	0·012	3·0	sP : sP, sN : sP, mN
11	..	29·559	46·3	35·6	10·7	41·7	− 1·3	38·6	34·8	6·9	12·0	4·8	78	66·3	28·0	4·1	9·0	0·000	0·0	mP : vP, wN : wN, vP
12	..	29·881	42·6	28·6	14·0	36·4	− 6·2	35·3	33·7	2·7	5·9	0·0	90	63·0	22·9	1·3	9·0	0·000	0·8	sP : sP : mP
13	Greatest Declination S.	29·789	45·1	35·9	9·2	41·6	− 0·7	39·1	36·0	5·6	9·5	2·8	81	56·2	31·1	0·0	8·9	0·085	10·2	wP, mN : vP
14	..	29·723	40·4	36·9	3·5	39·2	− 2·8	36·5	33·0	6·2	7·6	4·6	79	43·8	33·9	0·0	8·9	0·000	3·0	vP : sP
15	..	29·521	42·2	34·7	7·5	38·0	− 3·8	35·6	32·3	5·7	7·8	2·0	80	78·3	28·8	0·4	8·8	0·040	0·2	mP : vP : sP, ssN
16	..	29·086	39·3	32·7	6·6	37·6	− 4·0	36·6	35·3	2·3	4·6	1·1	91	42·7	32·2	0·0	8·8	0·394	0·8	ssP, ssN : vN : wP
17	..	29·697	41·4	29·8	11·6	37·3	− 4·2	35·5	33·0	4·3	7·4	1·9	83	64·4	21·0	1·0	8·7	0·000	0·0	vP : mP
18	First Qr.	29·771	41·4	24·4	17·0	33·8	− 7·7	32·5	30·2	3·6	9·4	0·0	86	71·3	18·2	2·4	8·7	0·169	0·2	wP : sP : vP, vN
19	In Equator	29·324	48·2	36·9	11·3	42·5	+ 1·1	40·4	37·9	4·6	10·7	0·0	84	75·7	29·9	3·3	8·6	0·084	3·2	wP : sP, ssN : mP
20	..	29·189	45·9	35·2	10·7	39·2	− 2·1	37·6	35·5	3·7	6·8	1·2	87	59·3	29·9	0·9	8·6	0·041	1·3	mP : wP, mN : mP
21	..	29·572	42·7	33·3	9·4	38·9	− 2·3	37·2	34·9	4·0	8·8	0·5	87	51·2	26·1	0·0	8·5	0·000	0·0	mP : vP, wN : wN, vP
22	Perigee	29·406	53·8	38·9	14·9	48·6	+ 7·5	46·9	45·1	3·5	7·4	1·3	88	66·4	36·9	0·1	8·5	0·098	0·0	mN, wP : wP
23	..	29·319	55·1	51·9	3·2	52·9	+ 11·9	51·4	49·9	3·0	5·2	1·4	90	65·6	47·1	0·1	8·4	0·116	1·8	wP : vP : wP, wN
24	..	29·150	53·5	43·8	9·7	48·5	+ 7·5	45·7	42·7	5·8	12·0	1·8	80	75·2	38·6	1·1	8·4	0·100	5·2	vP, sN : mP
25	Full	29·161	48·1	39·7	8·4	43·6	+ 2·7	41·2	38·4	5·2	9·9	2·1	81	69·3	33·9	2·2	8·3	0·017	1·2	vP : sP, ssN : vP
26	Greatest Declination N.	29·211	48·1	39·2	8·9	42·8	+ 2·0	40·1	36·9	5·9	9·9	3·2	80	79·1	32·5	4·4	8·3	0·004	6·8	wP : mP, mN : sP
27	..	29·605	43·3	35·0	8·3	39·0	− 1·8	36·6	33·4	5·6	9·2	3·4	81	63·8	26·7	4·2	8·2	0·000	0·0	sP
28	..	29·841	41·7	30·8	10·9	37·9	− 3·0	34·7	30·4	7·5	10·6	4·8	75	59·0	23·5	3·0	8·1	0·000	0·0	sP
29	..	29·627	45·4	32·3	13·1	41·1	+ 0·1	39·7	37·9	3·2	5·3	0·7	89	49·1	24·1	0·0	8·2	0·258	0·0	sP, vvN : wN, vP : vP
30	..	29·860	42·6	34·1	8·5	39·6	− 1·6	38·5	37·1	2·5	5·1	1·0	91	54·4	27·0	0·5	8·1	0·024	0·0	vP, vN : sP
Means	..	29·521	48·7	38·4	10·3	43·8	+ 1·1	41·7	39·2	4·7	8·4	1·8	84·0	71·4	32·8	1·9	8·8	Sum 2·199	4·0	..
Number of Column for Reference	1	2	3	4	5	6	7	8	9	10	11	12	13	14	15	16	17	18	19	20

The results apply to the civil day.

The mean reading of the Barometer (Column 2) and the mean temperatures of the Air and Evaporation (Columns 6 and 8) are deduced from the photographic records. The average temperature (Column 7) is that determined from the reduction of the photographic records from 1849 to 1868. The temperature of the Dew Point (Column 9) and the Degree of Humidity (Column 13) are deduced from the corresponding temperatures of the Air and Evaporation by means of Glaisher's Hygrometrical Tables. The mean difference between the Air and Dew Point Temperatures (Column 10) is the difference between the numbers in Columns 6 and 9, and the Greatest and Least Differences (Columns 11 and 12) are deduced from the 24 hourly photographic measures of the Dry-bulb and Wet-bulb Thermometers. The result on November 23 for Evaporation Temperature depends partly on values derived from eye-observations, on account of accidental loss of photographic register.

The values given in Columns 3, 4, 5, 14, and 15 are derived from eye-readings of self-registering thermometers.

The mean reading of the *Barometer* for the month was 29^{in}·521, being 0^{in}·230 *lower* than the average for the 20 years, 1854–1873.

TEMPERATURE OF THE AIR.

The highest in the month was 60°·1 on November 5; the lowest in the month was 24°·4 on November 18; and the range was 35°·7.

The mean of all the highest daily readings in the month was 48°·7, being 0°·1 *lower* than the average for the 41 years, 1841–1881.

The mean of all the lowest daily readings in the month was 38°·4, being 1°·0 *higher* than the average for the 41 years, 1841–1881.

The mean of the daily ranges was 10°·3, being 1°·2 *less* than the average for the 41 years, 1841–1881.

The mean for the month was 43°·8, being 1°·1 *higher* than the average for the 20 years, 1849–1868.

MONTH and DAY. 1882.	WIND AS DEDUCED FROM SELF-REGISTERING ANEMOMETERS. OSLER'S. General Direction. A.M.	P.M.	Pressure on the Square Foot. Greatest.	Least.	Mean of 24 Hourly Measures.	ROBINSON'S. Horizontal Movement of the Air.	CLOUDS AND WEATHER. A.M.	P.M.
			lbs.	lbs.	lbs.	miles.		
Nov. 1	SSE : S	SSW : SW : WSW	14·5	0·0	3·2	567	p.-cl : 10, w	9,cu,cu.-s,ci.-cu,sc,st.-w : p.-cl, st.-w, oc.-shs
2	SW : SSW	SSW	7·5	0·0	1·8	511	v, li.-cl : 8, th.-cl, cu.-s	10, sc, shs.-r, w : v, r
3	SSW : SW : WSW	SW : WSW	12·5	0·0	2·4	566	v, th.-cl, ci.-s : 0 : 1, li.-cl	s,cu,ci.-cu,ci,th.-cl : 10,sh.-r,st.-w : 10,r,fq.-hy.-sqs
4	SW	WSW	13·5	0·3	4·0	758	10, st.-w : 4, ci.-cu, ci.-s, st.-w	[illegible],ci.-cu,cu.-s,cu.-sh.-r,st.-w : 0 : 0
5	SW	SW : WSW	15·0	0·2	3·8	722	p.-cl : 10, sc, w	8, ci-cu, st.-w : 10,st.-w,oc.-slt.-r : p.-cl, sh.-r
6	WSW : SW	SW : SE : SSW	2·7	0·0	0·3	242	0 : 2, ci.-s, li.-cl	10, r : 10, fq.-r : 10, fq.-r
7	SW : NW : WSW	SW : SSE : SSW	5·0	0·0	1·1	381	10 : 10	10 : v, r, sqs
8	SW	SW : SSW	7·3	0·0	2·0	522	v : p.-cl	1, w : 1, slt.-r, w : 0, l, w
9	SW : WSW	W : WSW	7·1	0·1	2·0	538	0 : 0 : p.-cl	8, ci.-cu, li.-cl, sc : 0
10	WSW	WSW : SW	3·6	0·0	1·0	416	0, d : 0	6,ci.-cu,cu.-s,cu,shs.-r : v, sc
11	WSW : WNW	WNW : W : SW	3·5	0·0	1·0	400	0 : 0	3, cu, ci.-cu, h : v, li.-cl, f, ho.-fr
12	SW : Calm	E : ENE	1·0	0·0	0·1	131	v : tk.-f, ho.-fr	0, slt.-f : 1, m, h
13	E	NE	8·0	0·3	1·7	474	p.-cl : 10, sc, r	10, sc, oc.-shs, w : 10, sc, w
14	NNE : NE	NNE : N	7·0	0·4	2·7	613	10, w : 10, w	10, w : v : 10
15	N	NW : SW : ESE	4·3	0·0	1·3	355	10 : 10, oc.-th.-r	6, cu.-s, cu, ci.-cu : 10, r, sl
16	E : N	N	5·4	0·0	2·1	467	10, r : 10, r, sn, sc	10, c.-r, sc : 10, slt.-r, w
17	N : NNW	NNW : NNE	3·6	0·0	0·7	280	10 : v, ci	8, ci, ci.-s, ci.-cu, sc : 0, ho.-fr, a
18	SW : SE	SE : S	4·1	0·0	0·2	176	0 : 0, ho.-fr, f	p.-cl,ci.-s,li.-cl,slt.-f : 10, r : 10, r
19	SW : WNW : W	WSW : SW	4·5	0·0	1·9	493	10, slt.-r : p.-cl : 0, m	v,st.-glm,hy.-sh,hl : 0 : p.-cl
20	SW : WNW : WSW	W : WSW	3·7	0·0	1·0	394	p.-cl : th.-cl, m : 6, th.-cl, m	10, sc, r : 8, oc.-r : p.-cl,h,lu.-ha
21	NNE : NNW : WNW	NW : W : WSW	2·0	0·0	0·3	262	10 : v, s, ho.-fr : 0, h, m	6,th.-cl,h,so.-ha,m : 10, m : 10
22	SSW : WSW	WSW	10·2	0·1	2·5	596	10, r : 10, sc	10, sc, w : 10, sc, w
23	W : WSW	SW	5·0	0·1	2·1	537	10 : v, s, ci	10, sc, r : 10, sc, r
24	WSW	WSW : SW	6·5	0·2	2·1	579	10, shs.-r : v : p.-cl, slt.-r	8, cu.-s, cu, ci.-cu, w : 6, oc.-slt.-r
25	SW : WSW	WSW : SW	3·0	0·0	0·9	397	p.-cl : 4, ci	9, sc, r : 10, oc.-r : p.-cl
26	SW : WSW	WSW	4·7	0·0	1·9	557	0 : 0, slt.-h	9, cu.-s, slt.-r : v, li.-cl
27	WSW : W : WNW	W : WSW : WNW	5·0	0·0	1·3	498	0, ho.-fr : 0, h, m	5, ci.-cu : v, slt.-r : 1, li.-cl
28	WNW : NNW	NW : SW	7·7	0·0	1·7	463	1, li.-cl, w : 3, ci.-cu	2, ci, ci.-cu, so.-ha : li.-cl, lu.-ha, ho.-fr
29	SSW : SSE : NW	NW : NNW	3·1	0·0	0·7	331	li.-cl,lu.-ha, r : 10, c.-r : 10,slt.-r,glm	10, sc, slt.-r, glm : 10, oc.-slt.-r
30	NNW : N	N : NNW	2·5	0·0	0·3	254	10 : 10, slt.-r	8, cu, cu.-s, ci.-cu : 1, ho.-fr
Means	...	...	..	..	1·6	449		
Number of Column for Reference.	21	22	23	24	25	26	27	28

The mean *Temperature of Evaporation* for the month was 41°·7, being 0°·5 *higher* than
The mean *Temperature of the Dew Point* for the month was 39°·2, being 0°·1 *lower* than
The mean *Degree of Humidity* for the month was 84·0, being 3·3 *less* than
The mean *Elastic Force of Vapour* for the month was 0^in·239, being 0^in·001 *less* than
The mean *Weight of Vapour in a Cubic Foot of Air* for the month was 2^grs·8, being *the same as*
The mean *Weight of a Cubic Foot of Air* for the month was 543 grains, being 6 grains *less* than
} the average for the 20 years, 1849–1868.

The mean amount of *Cloud* for the month (a clear sky being represented by 0 and an overcast sky by 10) was 6·5.

The mean proportion of *Sunshine* for the month (constant sunshine being represented by 1) was 0·22. The maximum daily amount of *Sunshine* was 5·2 hours on November 8 and 10.

The highest reading of the *Solar Radiation Thermometer* was 100°·8 on November 6; and the lowest reading of the *Terrestrial Radiation Thermometer* was 18°·2 on November 18.

The mean daily distribution of *Ozone* was, for the 12 hours ending 9 a.m., 2·1; for the 6 hours ending 3 p.m., 1·0; and for the 6 hours ending 9 p.m., 0·9.

The *Proportions of Wind* referred to the cardinal points were N. 5, E. 3, S. 9, and W. 13.

The *Greatest Pressure of the Wind* in the month was 15^lbs·0 on the square foot on November 5. The mean daily *Horizontal Movement of the Air* for the month was 449 miles; the greatest daily value was 758 miles on November 4; and the least daily value 131 miles on November 12.

Rain fell on 19 days in the month, amounting to 2^in·199, as measured by gauge No. 6 partly sunk below the ground; being 0^in·030 *less* than the average fall for the 41 years, 1841–1881.

MONTH and DAY, 188[illegible].	Phases of the Moon.	BAROMETER. Mean of 24 Hourly Values (corrected and reduced to 32° Fahrenheit).	TEMPERATURE. Of the Air. Highest.	Lowest.	Daily Range.	Mean of 24 Hourly Values.	Excess of Mean above Average of 20 Years.	Of Evaporation. Mean of 24 Hourly Values.	Of the Dew Point. Deduced Mean Daily Value.	Difference between the Air Temperature and Dew Point Temperature. Mean Daily Value.	Greatest of 24 Hourly Values.	Least of 24 Hourly Values.	Degree of Humidity (Saturation = 100).	TEMPERATURE. Highest in the Sun's Rays as shown by a Self-Registering Maximum Thermometer with blackened bulb in vacuo placed on the Grass.	Lowest on the Grass as shown by a Self-Registering Minimum Thermometer.	Daily Duration of Sunshine.	Sun above Horizon.	Rain collected in Gauge No. 6, whose receiving surface is 5 inches above the Ground.	Daily Amount of Ozone.	Electricity.
		in.	°	°	°	°	°	°	°	°	°	°		°	°	hours	hours	in.		
Dec. 1	..	29·812	34·1	28·0	6·1	30·9	−10·6	30·7	30·1	0·8	2·9	0·0	96	40·9	21·6	0·0	8·1	0·000	0·0	sP : ssP : sP
2	Last Qr.	29·832	36·4	27·3	9·1	31·6	−10·2	31·2	30·3	1·3	5·2	0·0	94	40·4	27·3	0·0	8·1	0·009	2·2	vP : sP : vP
3	In Equator	29·293	51·2	34·0	17·2	43·4	+ 1·3	42·5	41·4	2·0	3·2	0·8	93	63·0	33·4	0·0	8·0	0·058	6·8	vN, wP : —
4	Apogee	28·913	51·2	37·4	13·8	43·5	+ 1·1	40·9	37·8	5·7	9·5	2·3	80	66·8	32·8	3·8	8·0	0·000	0·0	— : mP
5	..	28·914	39·4	34·8	4·6	37·2	− 5·4	35·5	33·1	4·1	6·8	2·2	86	42·4	31·2	0·0	8·0	0·004	0·0	vP : wN, vP
6	..	28·997	37·0	29·0	8·0	34·6	− 8·1	32·9	30·1	4·5	6·5	2·5	83	37·0	26·0	0·0	8·0	0·000	0·0	wN, vP
7	..	28·970	33·4	25·5	7·9	31·4	−11·4	30·8	29·4	2·0	4·0	1·1	91	35·2	20·5	0·0	7·9	0·425	0·0	vP : sP, ssN
8	..	29·130	36·1	32·3	3·8	34·6	− 8·2	33·6	32·0	2·6	3·5	0·9	90	43·0	29·9	0·0	7·9	0·003	0·0	wN, wP : wP : vP, w[illegible]
9	..	29·494	38·7	28·8	9·9	34·3	− 8·5	33·0	30·8	3·5	6·2	1·7	86	51·4	23·8	1·6	7·9	0·000	0·0	mP : mP : sP
10	New Greatest Dec. S	29·580	29·1	23·6	5·5	26·9	−15·8	26·9	26·9	0·0	1·7	0·0	100	34·2	20·3	0·0	7·9	0·000	0·0	sP : — : —
11	..	29·585	30·1	22·2	7·9	26·7	−15·8	26·7	26·7	0·0	1·6	0·0	100	30·1	21·9	0·0	7·8	0·000	2·2	..
12	..	29·522	32·7	22·9	9·8	30·1	−12·1	29·4	27·3	2·8	4·4	1·1	89	36·0	20·9	0·0	7·8	0·000	6·8	— : sP
13	..	29·395	44·4	32·4	12·0	37·7	− 4·1	36·6	35·1	2·6	6·2	1·0	91	56·0	30·3	2·2	7·8	0·035	0·0	vP : sP
14	..	29·528	39·9	35·8	4·1	38·1	− 3·4	37·9	37·6	0·5	1·1	0·0	98	42·1	30·9	0·0	7·8	0·005*	0·0	mP
15	..	29·686	39·9	36·6	3·3	38·0	− 3·1	37·8	37·5	0·5	1·2	0·0	98	43·7	36·6	0·0	7·8	0·028	0·0	vP : mP, wN : m[illegible]
16	..	29·711	45·1	38·4	6·7	42·3	+ 1·3	41·7	41·0	1·3	2·0	0·5	95	47·6	31·0	0·0	7·8	0·012	3·2	wP
17	In Equator First Quarter	29·673	49·3	44·5	4·8	46·5	+ 6·0	45·6	44·6	1·9	4·0	0·0	94	56·0	41·6	0·0	7·7	0·005	9·5	wP
18	Perigee	29·507	46·8	36·3	10·5	44·1	+ 3·9	43·0	41·7	2·4	4·0	0·7	91	53·8	30·6	0·0	7·7	0·012	4·5	wP : mP
19	..	29·863	50·5	36·6	13·9	42·0	+ 2·0	40·9	39·6	2·4	7·1	0·5	91	72·2	29·2	3·1	7·7	0·000	0·0	wP : mP
20	..	30·103	47·5	29·7	17·8	38·5	− 1·3	37·7	36·6	1·9	3·5	0·8	94	48·6	27·4	1·6	7·7	0·016	0·5	mP : sP : vP
21	..	29·783	48·3	38·3	10·0	44·8	+ 5·2	42·7	40·3	4·5	9·9	0·8	85	62·1	32·1	2·2	7·7	0·022	1·5	wP, wN : sP
22	..	29·538	44·9	36·7	8·2	39·8	+ 0·4	38·5	36·8	3·0	6·8	0·5	90	67·2	29·5	3·5	7·7	0·027	0·0	mP : sP : vP, vN
23	Greatest Declination N	29·397	42·3	33·7	8·6	39·4	+ 0·1	37·3	34·6	4·8	7·9	0·5	83	50·3	28·5	0·0	7·7	0·019	0·0	mN, mP : sP, wN : m[illegible]
24	Full	29·662	37·8	29·8	8·0	34·5	− 4·8	32·8	30·0	4·5	8·1	0·7	83	40·2	25·8	0·0	7·7	0·000	0·0	sP
25	..	29·418	52·4	37·8	14·6	46·6	+ 7·4	45·5	44·3	2·3	6·2	0·4	92	52·4	35·0	0·0	7·7	0·126	1·5	vP : wP
26	..	29·303	53·4	48·8	4·6	50·4	+11·3	49·4	48·3	2·1	5·2	0·6	93	62·5	45·5	0·0	7·8	0·355	12·5	wP : vP, wN
27	..	29·410	56·9	48·4	8·5	53·4	+14·4	52·3	51·2	2·2	4·6	1·0	92	59·8	46·8	0·0	7·8	0·051	1·3	wP
28	..	29·562	55·1	49·8	5·3	53·0	+14·2	50·5	48·0	5·0	7·4	2·8	83	58·3	48·1	0·0	7·8	0·000	3·[illegible]	wP : mP
29	..	29·428	53·8	49·1	4·7	51·2	+12·5	49·9	48·6	2·6	4·4	1·2	91	61·7	47·7	0·0	7·8	0·000	1·5	wP
30	In Equator	29·518	53·4	47·6	5·8	50·4	+11·9	49·5	48·6	1·8	3·4	0·6	94	57·1	44·7	0·1	7·8	0·461	5·5	wP : wN, wP : mP
31	Apogee	29·694	52·3	45·8	6·5	49·5	+11·2	48·9	48·3	1·2	2·4	0·6	96	57·2	44·0	0·0	7·8	0·098	1·3	wP
Means	..	29·492	44·0	35·5	8·4	40·2	− 0·6	39·1	37·7	2·5	4·9	0·8	91·0	50·6	32·1	0·6	7·8	Sum 1·771	2·1	..
Number of Column for Reference.	1	2	3	4	5	6	7	8	9	10	11	12	13	14	15	16	17	18	19	20

The results apply to the civil day.

The mean reading of the Barometer (Column 2) and the mean temperatures of the Air and Evaporation (Columns 6 and 8) are deduced from the photographic records. The average temperature (Column 7) is that determined from the reduction of the photographic records from 1849 to 1868. The temperature of the Dew Point (Column 9) and the Degree of Humidity (Column 13) are deduced from the corresponding temperatures of the Air and Evaporation by means of Glaisher's Hygrometrical Tables. The mean difference between the Air and Dew Point Temperatures (Column 10) is the difference between the numbers in Columns 6 and 9, and the Greatest and Least Differences (Columns 11 and 12) are deduced from the 24 hourly photographic measures of the Dry-bulb and Wet-bulb Thermometers. The results on December 18 for Air and Evaporation Temperatures depend partly on values inferred from eye-observations, on account of accidental loss of photographic register.

The values given in Columns 3, 4, 5, 14, and 15 are derived from eye-readings of self-registering thermometers.

* Rainfall (Column 18). The amount given for December 14 is derived from dew.

The mean reading of the *Barometer* for the month was 29in·492, being 0in·299 *lower* than the average for the 20 years, 1854–1873.

TEMPERATURE OF THE AIR.

The highest in the month was 56°·9 on December 27; the lowest in the month was 22°·2 on December 11; and the range was 34°·7.
The mean of all the highest daily readings in the month was 44°·0, being 0°·4 *lower* than the average for the 41 years, 1841–1881.
The mean of all the lowest daily readings in the month was 35°·5, being 0°·8 *higher* than the average for the 41 years, 1841–1881.
The mean of the daily ranges was 8°·4, being 1°·0 *less* than the average for the 41 years, 1841–1881.
The mean for the month was 40°·2, being 0°·6 *lower* than the average for the 20 years, 1849–1868.

MONTH and DAY. 1882.	WIND AS DEDUCED FROM SELF-REGISTERING ANEMOMETERS. Osler's. General Direction. A.M.	P.M.	Pressure on the Square Foot. Greatest.	Least.	Mean of 24 Hourly Measures.	Robinson's. Horizontal Movement of the Air.	CLOUDS AND WEATHER. A.M.	P.M.
			lbs.		lbs.	miles		
Dec. 1	Calm : SW : E	NE	0·0	0·0	0·0	73	ho.-fr : 10, f, ho.-fr	10, f : 10, tk.-f, fr
2	N : SE : Calm	SSE : SSW	2·4	0·0	0·1	136	10, tk.-f, ho.-fr : 10, f, ho.-fr	10, slt.-f, slt.-m : 10, slt.-r
3	S : SSW	S : SW	4·8	0·0	0·8	401	10, r : 10	10, slt.-r : 10, oc.-r
4	W : WSW	WSW : SW	3·9	0·1	1·2	512	v : 1, li.-cl, h	5, cu, ci.-cu, cu.-s : 9, th.-cl
5	SW : W	W : NNW	4·1	0·0	0·4	326	10 : p.-cl, ci.-s, cu.-s, m, sn	10, glm : 10, slt.-r
6	NNW : NW	NW : W : SW : S	3·0	0·0	0·5	360	10 : 10, glm, m, m.-r, slt.-sn	10, glm, slt.-sn : 10 : v, ho.-fr
7	SE : E : NE	N : NNE	2·3	0·0	0·3	273	o, ho.-fr : 10, sn	10, sn : 10, sn
8	NE : N	NNW : NW	1·3	0·0	0·2	287	10, slt.-sn : 9	9, ci.-cu, s, sc : 10
9	W : WSW	WSW : SW	1·0	0·0	0·1	246	10 : 10	9 : v : li.-cl, ho.-fr
10	SW : Calm	Calm : SW	0·0	0·0	0·0	44	ho.-fr : 10, tk.-f, ho.-fr	10, tk.-f, glm : 10, tk.-f, ho.-fr
11	Calm	ESE	0·0	0·0	0·0	30	10, tk.-f, ho.-fr : 10, tk.-f, ho.-fr	10, tk.-f : 10, f, ho.-fr
12	ESE	E	1·3	0·0	0·0	165	10, ho.-fr : 10, ho.-fr	10 : 10
13	E : SE	SE : NE	0·6	0·0	0·0	135	10, r : p.-cl	5, ci.-cu, ci, th.-cl : v, f
14	SE : NE	NNE : N	0·0	0·0	0·0	122	p.-cl, f : 10, f	10, f, glm : 10, f
15	N : NE	Calm : SE	0·0	0·0	0·0	47	10, slt.-f : 10, tk.-f, m.-r	10, slt.-f, m.-r : 10, slt.-f, m.-r
16	SE	SE : SSE	1·5	0·0	0·0	206	10 : 10	10 : 10, oc.-r
17	S	ESE : SE	1·6	0·0	0·1	231	10, slt.-r : 10, m.-r	10 : 10
18	SE	SE : ESE : E	3·6	0·0	0·2	256	10 : 10, slt.-r, sc	7, cu.-s, ci.-s, ci, so.-ha : 3, li.-cl, d
19	E : ESE	ESE	0·0	0·0	0·0	115	li.-cl, d : 9, slt.-r	1, li.-cl, ci, ci.-cu, cu.-s : o, slt.-f, d : o, slt.-f, ho.-fr
20	ESE : Calm	S : SSW	1·7	0·0	0·1	151	o, ho.-fr, tk.-f : o, tk.-f	3, th.-cl, slt.-f : 10, oc.-m.-r
21	SSW : SW : WSW	WSW	5·1	0·0	1·0	465	10, slt.-r : p.-cl, ci, cu.-s, sc	2, ci.-cu, cu.-s : o, hy.-d
22	SW : WSW	SW : SSE : WSW	1·9	0·0	0·3	244	o, ho.-fr : 1, s, li.-cl, ho.-fr	3, ci.-s, ci.-cu, li.-cl : 10, slt.-f, m.-r : 10, oc.-r, m
23	W : WNW	WNW	7·0	0·0	1·1	447	10, r : ho.-fr : 10	9, cu.-s, ci.-cu, w : o, lu.-ha, ho.-fr
24	WSW : NW	NW : SW : SSW	0·5	0·0	0·0	234	li.-cl, lu.-ha : 2, ci, ho.-fr, m	3, th.-cl, h : 10, th.-cl, lu.-ha
25	SSW : SW	WSW	6·0	0·0	1·3	465	10, oc.-r : 10, oc.-r	10, sc, oc.-r : 10, sc, oc.-r
26	WSW	W : SW : S	5·0	0·0	1·4	462	10, slis.-r : 10, hy.-r : 10, sc, r	10, sc, oc.-r : 10, r
27	WSW	WSW	7·1	0·0	2·0	580	10, r : 10, sc, w	10, sc, slt.-r : 10, sc, fq.-r : 10, sc, m.-r
28	WSW	SW	9·3	0·0	2·5	661	10, w : 10, sc, w	10, sc, m.-r : 10, oc.-m.-r
29	SW	SW	6·6	0·0	2·6	616	10 : 10, sc	10, sc : vv, w
30	WSW : SSW	SW : WSW : NE	4·9	0·0	1·2	422	v : 10, r, glm : 10, hy.-r	10, sc, fq.-m.-r : v : 10
31	SSE : S : SSW	SE : SW	0·6	0·0	0·0	184	10 : 10, r	10, fq.-th.-r : 10, fq.-th.-r : 10, r
Means	...	...	..	..	0·6	288		
Number of Column for	21	22	23	24	25	26	27	28

HIGHEST and LOWEST READINGS of the BAROMETER, reduced to 32° Fahrenheit, as extracted from the PHOTOGRAPHIC RECORDS.

MAXIMA.			MINIMA.			MAXIMA.			MINIMA.		
Approximate Greenwich Mean Solar Time, 1882.		Reading.	Approximate Greenwich Mean Solar Time, 1882.		Reading.	Approximate Greenwich Mean Solar Time, 1882.		Reading.	Approximate Greenwich Mean Solar Time, 1882.		Reading.
	d h m	in.		d h m	in.		d h m	in.		d h m	in.
January	1. 10. 30	29·715	January	1. 5. 23	29·611	April	26. 23. 25	29·611	April	25. 7. 20	28·891
	4. 6. 55	29·838		2. 16. 38	29·009		28. 17. 30	29·385		27. 20. 35	29·044
	5. 10. 10	29·675		5. 1. 50	29·493		29. 22. 0	29·643		29. 5. 20	28·825
	7. 14. 40	30·095		6. 1. 20	29·464	May	2. 8. 45	29·784		30. 15. 45:	29·510
	9. 11. 25	30·180		8. 16. 20	29·658		5. 10. 0	29·736	May	3. 17. 20	29·443
	17. 22. 20	30·790		10. 17. 5	29·954		8. 21. 40	30·254		5. 16. 55	29·671
	24. 9. 30	30·576		22. 17. 0	30·360		13. 9. 35	30·176		11. 13. 20	29·969
	31. 10. 50	30·533		29. 6. 30:	29·874		16. 19. 45:	30·306		14. 16. 35:	30·049
February	2. 22. 10	30·445	February	1. 18. 0	30·330		21. 10. 10	29·780		20. 16. 10	29·642
	6. 23. 10	30·393		5. 3. 27:	30·260		24. 10. 40	29·365		23. 15. 20	29·294
	12. 11. 55	29·969		11. 15. 0	29·656		29. 9. 10	30·164		25. 0. 0	29·149
	14. 4. 35	30·082		13. 3. 20	29·815		31. 12. 35	30·173		30. 4. 35	30·054
	15. 18. 30	30·265		14. 20. 30	29·557	June	3. 17. 15	29·580	June	3. 5. 50	29·494
	17. 9. 15	30·169		16. 17. 40	30·024		5. 6. 0	29·655		4. 3. 0	29·512
	19. 20. 0	30·655		18. 4. 40	29·953		7. 20. 30	29·711		6. 13. 45	29·519
	21. 13. 20	30·545		20. 16. 10	30·413		11. 1. 0	29·867		8. 23. 40	29·258
	27. 19. 30	29·435		26. 4. 30	28·897		12. 23. 0	29·824		12. 0. 10	29·618
March	4. 18. 55	29·616		28. 16. 10:	28·656		16. 0. 20	30·044		14. 7. 30	29·588
	6. 13. 45	30·090	March	5. 11. 15	29·404		20. 10. 5	29·770		18. 4. 25	29·433
	8. 21 10	30·193		7. 6. 0	30·025		23. 20. 0	29·825		22. 6. 5	29·526
	13. 21. 10	30·421		9. 16. 20	30·100		25. 11. 55	29·919		24. 14. 10	29·743
	15. 21. 10	30·475		14. 5. 20:	30·185		28. 10. 45	30·015		26. 4. 55	29·781
	22. 13. 0	30·104		21. 8. 30	29·495	July	2 10. 25	29·962	July	1. 6. 25	29·895
	24. 21. 50	29·609		24. 7. 30	29·420		10. 9. 20	29·608		6. 5. 50	29·160
	27. 21. 15	30·040		25. 18. 0	28·789		12. 11. 0	29·809		11. 9. 0	29·220
April	4. 10. 30	29·932		30. 15. 25	29·342		17. 0. 50:	29·696		15. 2. 0	29·299
	7. 19. 30	30·181	April	5. 1. 45	29·877		19. 22. 10:	30·015		17. 13. 30	29·617
	15. 21. 45	29·630		13. 10. 25	28·867		26. 18. 50	30·298		22. 23. 15	29·427
	18. 11. 45	29·905		17. 5. 50	29·163		30. 21. 45	30·130		30. 3. 30	29·872
	20. 11. 50	30·123		19. 17. 35	29·705	August	4. 9. 40	30·105	August	2. 6. 35	29·850
	24. 3. 40	29·377		22. 20. 0	29·070		10. 0. 10	30·095		6. 6. 30	29·912

HIGHEST and LOWEST READINGS of the BAROMETER, reduced to 32° Fahrenheit, as extracted from the PHOTOGRAPHIC RECORDS—*continued*.

MAXIMA.			MINIMA.			MAXIMA.			MINIMA.		
Approximate Greenwich Mean Solar Time, 1882.		Reading.	Approximate Greenwich Mean Solar Time, 1882.		Reading.	Approximate Greenwich Mean Solar Time, 1882.		Reading.	Approximate Greenwich Mean Solar Time, 1882.		Reading.
	d h m	in.		d h m	in.		d h m	in.		d h m	in.
August	13. 20. 0	29·706	August	11. 17. 55	29·385	November	4. 13. 30	29·846	November	3. 15. 25	29·424
	18. 9. 0	29·830		13. 17. 20	29·363		5. 21. 10	29·965		5. 6. 40	29·654
	19. 22. 0	29·853		19. 0. 0	29·753		6. 22. 40	29·698		6. 15. 10	29·468
	21. 21. 0	29·669		21. 3. 0	29·547		9. 21. 50	29·515		8. 17. 20	29·012
	24. 9. 0	29·463		22. 21. 0	29·103		11. 22. 0	29·926		10. 10. 10	29·329
	27. 8. 0	29·624		25. 3. 0	29·174		17. 20. 55	29·865		13. 18. 40	28·920
	30. 12. 15	29·940		29. 0. 0	29·236		21. 3. 35	29·692		19. 17. 20	29·104
September	4. 9. 10	30·058	September	1. 19. 15	29·340		22. 21. 40	29·414		22. 3. 15	29·321
	8. 10. 25	30·223		5. 12. 0	29·960		24. 9. 50	29·256		23. 15. 55	29·030
	12. 20. 30	29·515		11. 17. 0	29·435		26. 22. 50	29·684		25. 10. 35	29·115
	17. 20. 55	29·854		14. 1. 10	29·430		28. 7. 30	30·006		27. 6. 45	29·609
	23. 11. 0	29·871		19. 17. 50	29·489		30. 6. 35	29·962		28. 20. 30:	29·530
	28. 2. 20	29·532		26. 17. 50	29·032	December	1. 23. 10	29·938	December	1. 3. 0	29·747
	29. 23. 25	29·768		28. 19. 20	29·092		4. 6. 25	28·945		3. 16. 30	28·874
October	4. 10. 55	30·334	October	1. 5. 0	29·392		5. 21. 0	29·046		4. 19. 0	28·883
	8. 19. 35	29·989		6. 16. 10	29·865		10. 22. 5	29·604		7. 12. 30	28·935
	14. 6. 0	29·840		11. 15. 35	29·306		13. 14. 15	29·746		12. 17. 20	29·351
	17. 22. 0	29·971		16. 7. 45:	29·413		19. 21. 50	30·153		17. 19. 0	29·465
	20. 6. 10	29·672		19. 13. 15	29·336		24. 4. 0	29·716		22. 13. 0	29·234
	23. 10. 55	29·420		21. 17. 30	28·952		26. 7. 55	29·459		25. 19. 5	29·155
	25. 9. 20	29·416		24. 0. 0	28·610		28. 6. 15	29·622		26. 18. 40	29·345
	29. 13. 50	29·785		27. 1. 10	29·201		29. 18. 45	29·367		29. 5. 30	29·360
	30. 22. 40	29·837		30. 7. 55	29·535		30. 15. 40	29·762		30. 1. 30	29·420
November	1. 21. 30	29·678	November	1. 5. 30	29·270					31. 5. 0	29·613
	2. 22. 40	29·720		2. 7. 25	29·580						

The readings in the above table are accurate, but the times are occasionally liable to uncertainty, as the barometer will sometimes remain at its extreme reading without sensible change for a considerable interval of time. In such cases the time given is the middle of the stationary period, the symbol : denoting that the reading has been sensibly the same through a period of more than one hour. The reading at March 23^{d}. 18^{h}. 0^{m}. has been inferred from comparison with the Kew register on account of loss of photographic register from 16^{h}. to $18\frac{1}{2}^{h}$., and the readings from August 18 to August 29 are taken from the eye-observations, on account of temporary interruption of the photographic registration.

ABSOLUTE MAXIMA AND MINIMA READINGS OF THE BAROMETER for each Month in the YEAR 1882.

[Extracted from the preceding Table.]

1882. MONTH.	Readings of the Barometer.		Range of Reading in each Month.
	Maxima.	Minima.	
	in.	in.	in.
January	30·790	29·009	1·781
February	30·655	28·656	1·999
March	30·475	28·789	1·686
April	30·181	28·825	1·356
May	30·306	29·149	1·157
June	30·044	29·258	0·786
July	30·298	29·160	1·138
August	30·105	29·103	1·002
September	30·223	29·052	1·171
October	30·334	28·610	1·724
November	30·006	28·920	1·086
December	30·155	28·874	1·281

The highest reading in the year was 30^{in}·790 on January 18. The lowest reading in the year was 28^{in}·610 on October 24.

The range of reading in the year was 2^{in}·180.

MONTHLY RESULTS of METEOROLOGICAL ELEMENTS for the YEAR 1882.

1882, Month.	Mean Reading of the Barometer.	Temperature of the Air. Highest.	Lowest.	Range in the Month.	Mean of all the Highest.	Mean of all the Lowest.	Mean of the Daily Ranges.	Monthly Mean.	Excess of Mean above Average of 20 Years.	Mean Temperature of Evaporation.	Mean Temperature of the Dew Point.	Mean Degree of Humidity. (Saturation = 100.)
	in.	°	°	°	°	°	°	°	°	°	°	
January ..	30·180	52·9	25·4	27·5	44·4	35·3	9·1	40·5	+ 1·8	39·2	37·6	89·6
February..	30·060	55·4	24·8	30·6	47·7	36·2	11·5	42·0	+ 2·3	40·4	38·5	88·3
March	29·834	65·0	28·8	36·2	55·1	37·6	17·5	46·2	+ 4·6	43·7	40·9	82·2
April	29·605	65·7	31·8	33·9	57·6	39·8	17·9	48·0	+ 0·5	45·3	42·4	81·5
May	29·873	76·5	34·5	42·0	66·2	44·2	22·0	54·5	+ 1·4	50·5	46·7	75·5
June	29·732	74·1	40·9	33·2	66·3	48·9	17·4	56·7	− 3·1	53·3	50·2	79·4
July	29·697	78·7	45·7	33·0	71·1	52·5	18·6	60·5	− 2·3	56·4	53·0	77·2
August ...	29·742	81·0	44·0	37·0	70·5	51·7	18·8	59·9	− 1·9	56·3	53·1	78·5
September.	29·687	71·1	36·7	34·4	64·0	46·6	17·4	54·6	− 2·9	52·0	49·5	83·3
October ...	29·660	71·1	30·6	40·5	57·7	44·7	12·9	51·0	0·0	49·4	47·7	88·9
November .	29·521	60·1	24·4	35·7	48·7	38·4	10·3	43·8	+ 1·1	41·7	39·2	84·0
December .	29·492	56·9	22·2	34·7	44·0	35·5	8·4	40·2	− 0·6	39·1	37·7	91·0
Means	29·757	Highest. 81·0	Lowest. 22·2	Annual Range. 58·8	57·8	42·6	15·2	49·8	+ 0·1	47·3	44·7	83·3

1882, Month.	Mean Elastic Force of Vapour.	Mean Weight of Vapour in a Cubic Foot of Air.	Mean Weight of a Cubic Foot of Air.	Mean Amount of Ozone.	Mean Amount of Cloud. (0–10.)	Rain. Number of Rainy Days.	Amount collected in Gauge No. 6 whose receiving Surface is 5 Inches above the Ground.	Wind. From Osler's Anemometer. Number of Hours of Prevalence of each Wind, referred to different Points of Azimuth. N.	N.E.	E.	S.E.	S.	S.W.	W.	N.W.	Number of Calm or nearly Calm Hours.	Mean Daily Pressure on the Square Foot.	From Robinson's Anemometer. Mean Daily Horizontal Movement of the Air.
	in.	grs.	grs.				in.	h	h	h	h	h	h	h	h	h	lbs.	miles.
January...	0·225	2·6	559	2·6	8·2	10	1·352	8	17	32	99	109	345	50	12	72	0·55	265
February..	0·233	2·7	555	3·2	8·0	9	1·153	33	39	46	63	105	188	60	54	84	0·46	289
March	0·256	3·0	546	3·9	5·6	11	1·144	44	20	11	14	50	413	88	54	50	0·88	348
April.....	0·271	3·1	540	7·5	6·4	13	2·403	51	110	100	66	105	138	94	33	3	0·70*	354
May......	0·319	3·6	538	5·4	5·5	11	1·367	57	170	108	43	110	189	28	16	23	0·30	268
June......	0·364	4·1	532	6·5	8·1	19	2·356	26	62	34	38	104	257	127	55	17	0·38	325
July......	0·403	4·5	528	6·9	6·5	19	2·451	35	41	15	38	143	369	61	33	9	0·27*	290
August ...	0·404	4·5	529	4·2	7·0	15	1·159	49	48	50	32	61	238	147	112	7	0·36*	303
September.	0·353	4·0	534	2·7	6·9	14	2·405	130	119	53	57	72	181	52	37	19	0·32	228
October...	0·331	3·7	537	3·4	7·6	23	5·421	68	115	69	93	120	176	53	23	27	0·65	269
November.	0·239	2·8	543	4·0	6·5	19	2·199	79	38	28	24	48	308	124	63	8	1·60	449
December .	0·226	2·6	547	2·1	8·2	17	1·771	44	54	68	105	69	225	92	43	44	0·56	288
Sums.....	..	..	..	..	..	180	25·181	624	833	614	672	1096	3047	976	535	363	..	..
Means	0·302	3·4	541	4·4	7·0	..		..	..	..	..					..	0·39	306

The greatest recorded pressure of the wind on the square foot in the year was 49·5 lbs. on April 29.
The greatest recorded daily horizontal movement of the air " " 758 miles on November 4.
The least recorded daily horizontal movement of the air " " 30 miles on December 11.

* The mean daily pressures of the wind for April, July, and August are derived from the results for 25, 26, and 27 days respectively.

MONTHLY MEAN READING of the BAROMETER at every HOUR of the DAY, as deduced from the PHOTOGRAPHIC RECORDS.

Hour, Greenwich Mean Solar Time (Civil reckoning).	1882. January.	February.	March.	April.	May.	June.	July.	August.	September.	October.	November.	December.	Yearly Means.
	in.	in.	in.	in.	in.	in.	in.	in.	in.	in.	in.	in.	in.
Midnight	30·175	30·097	29·825	29·617	29·878	29·735	29·697	29·906	29·695	29·668	29·509	29·499	29·775
1h. a.m.	30·170	30·093	29·822	29·613	29·871	29·732	29·692	29·899	29·691	29·666	29·501	29·492	29·770
2 "	30·171	30·087	29·818	29·608	29·865	29·726	29·688	29·890	29·684	29·662	29·496	29·492	29·766
3 "	30·168	30·078	29·811	29·605	29·860	29·724	29·684	29·882	29·679	29·656	29·490	29·488	29·760
4 "	30·159	30·072	29·810	29·602	29·859	29·724	29·688	29·879	29·674	29·657	29·490	29·486	29·758
5 "	30·156	30·070	29·812	29·602	29·863	29·727	29·693	29·877	29·675	29·655	29·494	29·482	29·759
6 "	30·159	30·067	29·813	29·607	29·868	29·731	29·699	29·880	29·679	29·656	29·499	29·482	29·762
7 "	30·165	30·063	29·829	29·611	29·874	29·735	29·707	29·884	29·682	29·662	29·509	29·486	29·768
8 "	30·175	30·071	29·842	29·614	29·878	29·742	29·711	29·890	29·687	29·665	29·524	29·492	29·774
9 "	30·185	30·073	29·851	29·618	29·879	29·743	29·710	29·888	29·692	29·664	29·535	29·502	29·778
10 "	30·195	30·076	29·856	29·618	29·879	29·742	29·710	29·888	29·692	29·662	29·542	29·508	29·781
11 "	30·196	30·077	29·856	29·615	29·876	29·743	29·708	29·882	29·690	29·657	29·545	29·504	29·779
Noon	30·186	30·069	29·854	29·608	29·870	29·741	29·705	29·879	29·690	29·650	29·542	29·495	29·774
1h. p.m.	30·176	30·056	29·845	29·602	29·869	29·738	29·701	29·875	29·685	29·650	29·538	29·487	29·768
2 "	30·171	30·045	29·835	29·594	29·866	29·734	29·697	29·872	29·682	29·652	29·532	29·483	29·764
3 "	30·173	30·037	29·829	29·586	29·861	29·732	29·691	29·868	29·679	29·651	29·532	29·484	29·760
4 "	30·175	30·033	29·825	29·583	29·859	29·726	29·687	29·864	29·677	29·652	29·532	29·489	29·759
5 "	30·179	30·035	29·826	29·583	29·861	29·724	29·683	29·860	29·680	29·657	29·534	29·488	29·759
6 "	30·187	30·040	29·833	29·583	29·865	29·722	29·685	29·861	29·686	29·663	29·535	29·490	29·763
7 "	30·194	30·041	29·840	29·595	29·872	29·726	29·688	29·865	29·693	29·664	29·531	29·492	29·767
8 "	30·200	30·040	29·844	29·604	29·884	29·728	29·694	29·871	29·697	29·668	29·528	29·494	29·771
9 "	30·202	30·038	29·847	29·610	29·893	29·733	29·702	29·875	29·700	29·669	29·525	29·496	29·774
10 "	30·203	30·036	29·850	29·614	29·896	29·732	29·705	29·879	29·699	29·671	29·518	29·495	29·775
11 "	30·207	30·036	29·850	29·617	29·899	29·732	29·706	29·880	29·698	29·671	29·518	29·495	29·776
Means	30·180	30·060	29·834	29·605	29·873	29·732	29·697	29·879	29·687	29·660	29·521	29·492	29·768
Number of Days employed.	31	28	31	30	31	30	31	18	30	31	30	31	..

MONTHLY MEAN TEMPERATURE of the AIR at every HOUR of the DAY, as deduced from the PHOTOGRAPHIC RECORDS.

Hour, Greenwich Mean Solar Time (Civil reckoning).	1882. January.	February.	March.	April.	May.	June.	July.	August.	September.	October.	November.	December.	Yearly Means.
Midnight	39°·5	40°·4	43°·0	43°·9	48°·5	52°·5	55°·6	56°·1	51°·2	49·3	43°·0	39°·5	46°·9
1h. a.m.	39·3	40·0	42·6	43·7	48·1	52·2	55·2	55·4	50·8	48·8	42·8	39·2	46·5
2 "	39·3	40·1	42·5	43·6	47·4	51·7	54·9	54·9	50·2	48·6	42·7	39·2	46·3
3 "	39·2	40·0	42·1	43·3	47·1	51·3	54·4	54·7	49·9	48·4	42·8	39·2	46·0
4 "	39·2	39·8	41·9	43·1	46·9	51·1	54·3	54·4	49·7	48·2	42·8	39·0	45·9
5 "	39·1	39·8	41·6	42·8	47·3	51·6	54·5	54·6	49·5	47·9	42·1	39·0	45·8
6 "	39·2	39·9	41·3	43·2	49·3	53·0	55·8	55·1	49·8	47·8	41·8	39·1	46·3
7 "	39·2	39·9	41·1	45·1	52·1	55·1	57·6	56·9	50·8	48·2	41·7	39·3	47·3
8 "	39·2	40·3	42·8	47·5	55·3	57·0	59·7	58·8	52·8	49·1	41·8	39·3	48·6
9 "	39·8	41·0	45·7	49·8	58·0	58·8	61·8	60·9	55·7	50·8	42·6	39·4	50·4
10 "	40·8	42·2	47·9	51·3	59·2	60·0	63·3	62·5	57·7	53·3	44·1	39·9	51·8
11 "	41·4	43·4	49·9	52·4	61·5	60·8	65·1	63·7	59·2	54·5	45·8	41·0	53·2
Noon	42·4	44·7	51·7	53·6	62·9	61·3	65·9	64·7	60·1	55·4	46·4	41·6	54·2
1h. p.m.	42·9	45·0	52·6	54·1	63·4	61·4	66·6	65·9	60·7	55·3	47·1	42·1	54·8
2 "	43·2	45·6	52·9	54·2	63·3	62·2	67·0	66·0	60·8	55·4	47·1	42·2	55·0
3 "	43·0	45·6	52·8	54·3	63·4	62·2	67·2	66·4	60·5	54·7	46·6	41·8	54·9
4 "	42·4	45·1	52·0	53·2	62·9	61·8	66·3	66·0	59·8	53·9	45·3	41·1	54·2
5 "	41·7	44·1	50·7	52·2	61·9	60·8	65·6	64·9	58·5	52·8	44·7	40·5	53·2
6 "	41·1	43·0	48·8	50·3	59·4	59·7	63·9	63·3	56·3	51·8	44·3	40·4	51·9
7 "	40·7	42·4	47·3	48·4	56·8	57·9	62·0	61·4	54·7	51·0	44·0	40·4	50·6
8 "	40·4	41·8	46·0	46·9	53·7	56·1	59·6	59·5	53·7	50·4	43·5	40·2	49·3
9 "	40·1	41·5	44·8	45·6	51·9	54·9	57·9	58·3	53·0	50·0	43·3	40·2	48·5
10 "	39·9	41·1	44·0	44·8	50·7	54·0	57·0	57·4	52·6	49·5	43·1	40·3	47·9
11 "	39·7	40·9	43·4	44·3	49·6	53·2	56·4	56·5	51·8	49·3	42·6	40·1	47·3
Means	40·5	42·0	46·2	48·0	55·0	56·7	60·3	59·9	54·6	51·0	43·8	40·2	49·9
Number of Days employed.	31	28	31	30	24	30	31	31	30	31	30	31	..

MONTHLY MEAN TEMPERATURE of EVAPORATION at every HOUR of the DAY, as deduced from the PHOTOGRAPHIC RECORDS.

Hour, Greenwich Mean Solar Time (Civil reckoning).	1882. January.	February.	March.	April.	May.	June.	July.	August.	September.	October.	November.	December.	Yearly Means.
	°	°	°	°	°	°	°	°	°	°	°	°	°
Midnight	38·5	39·3	41·9	42·5	47·1	51·1	54·2	54·4	50·1	48·3	41·3	38·5	45·6
1h, a.m.	38·3	39·0	41·6	42·2	47·0	51·0	53·9	54·0	49·8	47·9	41·2	38·4	45·4
2 "	38·3	39·0	41·7	42·3	46·5	50·7	53·6	53·7	49·3	47·[illegible]	41·1	38·4	45·2
3 "	38·3	39·0	41·3	41·9	46·4	50·4	53·4	53·4	48·9	47·5	41·2	38·3	45·0
4 "	38·3	38·9	41·1	41·7	46·3	50·2	53·1	53·2	48·8	47·4	41·2	38·0	44·9
5 "	38·2	38·8	40·9	41·6	46·8	50·7	53·4	53·2	48·6	47·2	40·6	38·1	44·8
6 "	38·2	38·9	40·5	42·0	48·3	51·7	54·1	53·7	48·7	47·1	40·3	38·2	45·1
7 "	38·2	38·9	40·3	43·3	50·2	53·0	55·2	54·9	49·4	47·3	40·1	38·4	45·8
8 "	38·3	39·3	41·5	45·3	51·8	53·9	56·5	55·8	50·9	48·0	40·2	38·4	46·7
9 "	38·7	39·8	43·5	46·7	52·9	54·8	57·4	56·8	53·0	49·4	40·8	38·5	47·7
10 "	39·4	40·7	44·9	47·6	53·6	55·2	58·2	57·6	54·2	51·0	41·8	39·0	48·6
11 "	40·0	41·4	45·8	48·1	54·7	55·5	58·9	58·1	54·8	51·7	42·8	39·8	49·3
Noon	40·6	42·2	46·8	48·9	55·2	55·7	59·2	58·8	55·1	52·1	43·2	40·2	49·8
1h, p.m.	40·9	42·5	47·4	49·4	55·2	55·6	59·4	59·2	55·3	52·0	43·7	40·4	50·1
2 "	41·0	42·8	47·4	49·5	54·9	56·0	59·6	59·4	55·3	52·0	43·7	40·6	50·2
3 "	40·8	42·9	47·6	49·7	55·3	56·1	59·7	59·5	55·2	51·6	43·3	40·3	50·2
4 "	40·6	42·5	47·2	49·2	54·7	55·6	59·3	59·3	54·9	51·1	42·7	39·9	49·7
5 "	40·1	42·0	46·4	48·3	54·3	55·1	58·9	58·9	54·3	50·7	42·4	39·4	49·2
6 "	39·7	41·3	45·4	47·1	53·3	54·6	58·1	58·2	53·4	50·0	42·2	39·4	48·6
7 "	39·4	40·9	44·5	45·8	51·7	53·9	57·1	57·2	52·4	49·6	41·9	39·4	47·8
8 "	39·1	40·5	43·8	44·5	50·2	53·1	55·9	56·2	51·9	49·3	41·6	39·3	47·1
9 "	39·0	40·1	43·2	43·7	49·2	52·5	55·2	55·6	51·5	49·0	41·4	39·2	46·6
10 "	38·8	39·9	42·7	43·2	48·4	52·2	54·8	55·3	51·1	48·6	41·3	39·3	46·3
11 "	38·6	39·8	42·2	42·9	47·9	51·7	54·6	54·7	50·5	48·1	41·0	39·2	45·9
Means	39·2	40·4	43·7	45·3	50·9	53·3	56·4	56·3	52·0	49·4	41·7	39·1	47·3
Number of Days employed.	31	28	31	30	24	30	31	31	30	31	30	31	..

MONTHLY MEAN TEMPERATURE of the DEW POINT at every HOUR of the DAY, as deduced by GLAISHER'S TABLES from the corresponding AIR and EVAPORATION TEMPERATURES.

Hour, Greenwich Mean Solar Time (Civil reckoning).	1882. January.	February.	March.	April.	May.	June.	July.	August.	September.	October.	November.	December.	Yearly Means.
	°	°	°	°	°	°	°	°	°	°	°	°	°
Midnight	37·2	37·9	40·6	40·8	45·6	49·7	52·9	52·8	49·0	47·2	39·3	37·2	44·2
1h, a.m.	37·0	37·7	40·4	40·4	45·8	49·8	52·6	52·6	48·8	46·9	39·3	37·4	44·1
2 "	37·0	37·6	40·7	40·7	45·5	49·7	52·3	52·5	48·3	46·7	39·2	37·4	44·0
3 "	37·1	37·7	40·3	40·2	45·6	49·5	52·4	52·1	47·9	46·5	39·3	37·1	43·8
4 "	37·1	37·7	40·1	40·0	45·7	49·3	51·9	52·0	47·9	46·5	39·3	36·7	43·7
5 "	37·0	37·5	40·0	40·2	46·2	49·8	52·3	51·8	47·7	46·4	38·8	36·9	43·7
6 "	36·9	37·6	39·5	40·6	47·2	50·4	52·5	52·3	47·6	46·3	38·4	37·0	43·9
7 "	36·9	37·6	39·3	41·2	48·3	51·0	53·0	53·1	47·9	46·3	38·3	37·2	44·2
8 "	37·1	38·0	39·9	42·9	48·5	51·0	53·7	53·1	49·0	46·8	38·2	37·2	44·6
9 "	37·3	38·3	41·0	43·4	48·3	51·2	53·6	53·3	50·3	47·9	38·7	37·3	45·1
10 "	37·7	38·9	41·7	43·8	48·6	51·0	53·9	53·4	51·0	48·7	39·1	37·8	45·5
11 "	38·2	39·0	41·5	43·7	48·8	50·9	53·8	53·4	50·9	49·0	39·5	38·3	45·6
Noon	38·4	39·3	41·8	44·3	48·6	50·9	53·7	53·9	50·7	48·9	39·6	38·4	45·7
1h, p.m.	38·6	39·6	42·2	44·8	48·3	50·6	53·6	53·7	50·6	48·8	39·9	38·3	45·7
2 "	38·4	39·6	41·9	44·0	47·8	50·6	53·7	54·0	50·5	48·7	39·9	38·7	45·7
3 "	38·2	39·8	42·4	45·2	48·5	50·8	53·7	53·9	50·6	48·6	39·6	38·4	45·8
4 "	38·4	39·5	42·3	45·2	47·7	50·3	53·5	53·8	50·6	48·4	39·7	38·4	45·6
5 "	38·1	39·5	41·9	44·3	47·8	50·2	53·4	53·9	50·5	48·6	39·7	38·0	45·5
6 "	37·9	39·3	41·7	43·7	47·9	50·1	53·3	53·9	50·5	48·2	39·7	38·1	45·4
7 "	37·8	39·1	41·4	43·0	47·0	50·3	52·9	53·6	50·2	48·2	39·4	38·1	45·1
8 "	37·5	38·9	41·3	41·8	46·8	50·3	52·6	53·3	50·2	48·1	39·4	38·2	44·9
9 "	37·6	38·3	41·4	41·5	46·5	50·2	52·8	53·2	50·0	47·9	39·1	37·9	44·7
10 "	37·4	38·4	41·1	41·4	46·0	50·4	52·8	53·4	49·6	47·7	39·1	38·0	44·6
11 "	37·2	38·3	40·8	41·3	46·1	50·2	52·9	53·1	49·2	46·8	39·1	38·0	44·4
Means	37·6	38·6	41·0	42·5	47·2	50·3	53·1	53·2	49·6	47·7	39·3	37·7	44·8

MONTHLY MEAN DEGREE of HUMIDITY (Saturation = 100) at every HOUR of the DAY, as deduced by GLAISHER'S TABLES from the corresponding AIR and EVAPORATION TEMPERATURES.

Hour, Greenwich Mean Solar Time (Civil reckoning)	1882. January.	February.	March.	April.	May.	June.	July.	August.	September.	October.	November.	December.	Yearly Means.
Midnight	92	91	91	89	90	91	91	89	92	93	86	92	91
1h, a.m.	92	92	92	88	92	92	91	91	93	94	87	94	91
2 "	92	91	94	90	94	93	91	92	94	94	87	94	92
3 "	93	92	94	89	93	94	93	91	93	94	87	93	92
4 "	93	93	94	89	96	94	92	92	94	94	87	92	93
5 "	93	92	95	90	96	94	92	90	94	95	88	93	93
6 "	93	92	94	90	93	91	89	91	92	95	89	93	92
7 "	92	92	94	87	87	87	85	87	90	94	89	93	90
8 "	93	92	90	83	78	80	82	82	87	92	88	93	87
9 "	91	90	84	79	71	76	75	76	84	90	86	93	83
10 "	89	88	80	76	68	72	72	73	79	84	82	93	80
11 "	89	84	73	73	63	69	67	70	74	81	79	90	76
Noon	86	81	69	71	59	69	65	68	71	80	78	89	74
1h, p.m.	85	81	68	70	58	68	63	65	69	79	77	87	73
2 "	83	80	67	71	58	66	62	66	69	79	77	88	72
3 "	83	81	68	71	59	67	62	64	69	79	78	89	72
4 "	86	81	70	74	57	67	63	65	71	81	81	90	74
5 "	88	83	73	73	60	68	65	68	75	86	83	91	76
6 "	89	86	77	79	66	70	69	72	80	87	84	92	79
7 "	90	88	81	82	70	76	73	76	85	90	83	92	82
8 "	90	90	85	83	77	81	78	81	88	92	85	93	85
9 "	91	89	88	86	82	84	83	83	89	93	85	92	87
10 "	91	91	90	88	83	87	86	86	90	94	86	92	89
11 "	91	91	90	89	89	90	88	88	91	92	87	93	90
Means	90	88	83	82	77	80	78	79	84	89	84	92	84

TOTAL AMOUNT of SUNSHINE registered in each HOUR of the DAY in each MONTH, as derived from the Records of CAMPBELL'S SELF-REGISTERING INSTRUMENT, for the YEAR 1882.

1882, Month.	Registered Duration of Sunshine in the Hour ending 5h. a.m.	6h. a.m.	7h. a.m.	8h. a.m.	9h. a.m.	10h. a.m.	11h. a.m.	Noon.	1h. p.m.	2h. p.m.	3h. p.m.	4h. p.m.	5h. p.m.	6h. p.m.	7h. p.m.	8h. p.m.	Total registered Duration of Sunshine in each Month.	Corresponding aggregate Period during which the Sun was above Horizon.	Mean Altitude of the Sun at Noon.
	h	h	h	h	h	h	h	h	h	h	h	h	h	h	h	h	h	h	°
January ..	..	..	..	..	0·2	1·7	1·7	4·5	3·0	2·9	1·8	..	..	..	..	..	15·8	259·1	18
February .	..	..	..	..	2·9	2·7	4·7	6·9	5·3	6·5	6·1	0·9	..	..	..	..	36·0	277·9	26
March ...	..	..	0·1	5·1	11·5	13·5	15·5	16·7	15·8	14·6	14·7	12·1	7·6	0·7	..	..	127·9	366·9	37
April	..	2·3	9·5	13·0	12·2	14·8	14·4	14·2	14·1	14·2	12·4	11·6	11·8	6·4	0·5	..	151·4	414·9	48
May	0·4	5·9	13·4	16·6	19·0	18·4	20·3	21·8	21·6	20·0	17·6	18·5	18·5	14·0	9·4	0·4	237·8	482·1	57
June . ..	0·1	5·1	10·6	9·0	9·7	8·6	9·9	9·7	9·2	9·9	9·7	9·5	8·2	8·1	4·0	0·1	121·4	494·5	62
July	0·1	6·6	11·0	12·2	14·3	16·0	17·8	17·5	17·9	17·8	17·3	16·9	14·1	11·3	3·8	0·1	194·7	496·8	60
August ..	..	1·0	6·6	7·2	8·4	10·5	9·5	10·0	11·9	12·4	12·7	12·8	11·1	10·3	1·9	..	126·3	449·1	52
September	..	..	1·4	7·2	9·7	10·9	10·2	9·2	10·3	11·7	8·8	9·4	8·5	2·1	..	..	99·4	376·9	41
October		..	..	0·9	2·9	7·8	9·0	10·9	10·1	8·9	6·0	2·7	0·9	..		..	60·1	328·7	30
November		..	..	..	1·7	7·7	12·2	12·9	10·1	6·1	4·8	0·6	..	..		..	56·1	264·4	20
December		..	..	..	..	1·9	4·2	4·0	4·4	2·9	0·7		..	..		..	18·1	242·7	16

The hours are reckoned from apparent noon.

The total registered duration of sunshine during the year was 1245·0 hours; the corresponding aggregate period during which the Sun was above the horizon was 4454·0 hours; the mean proportion for the year (constant sunshine = 1) was therefore 0·280.

(I.)—Reading of a Thermometer whose bulb is sunk to the depth of 25·6 feet (24 French feet) below the surface of the soil, at Noon on every Day of the Year.

1882.

Days of the Month.	January.	February.	March.	April.	May.	June.	July.	August.	September.	October.	November.	December.
d	°	°	°	°	°	°	°	°	°	°	°	°
1	51·98	51·34	50·67	49·98	49·57	49·47	49·73	50·33	51·14	51·94	52·45	52·53
2	51·98	51·30	50·65	49·97	49·56	49·47	49·76	50·38	51·17	51·95	52·46	52·53
3	51·95	51·30	50·63	49·94	49·56	49·48	49·78	50·38	51·19	51·97	52·47	52·55
4	51·92	51·25	50·58	49·92	49·54	49·48	49·78	50·41	51·23	51·99	52·49	52·53
5	51·93	51·24	50·58	49·90	49·55	49·49	49·80	50·44	51·26	52·00	52·50	52·52
6	51·93	51·21	50·55	49·90	49·54	49·48	49·82	50·45	51·27	52·03	52·51	52·51
7	51·87	51·20	50·54	49·88	49·54	49·50	49·83	50·44	51·31	52·05	52·49	52·49
8	51·87	51·17	50·53	49·87	49·52	49·50	49·83	50·51	51·28	52·07	52·50	52·49
9	51·85	51·14	50·50	49·85	49·52	49·50	49·86	50·52	51·35	52·12	52·50	52·50
10	51·83	51·12	50·47	49·83	49·51	49·50	49·90	50·55	51·39	52·12	52·52	52·46
11	51·83	51·11	50·44	49·81	49·50	49·50	49·88	50·57	51·41	52·13	52·51	52·45
12	51·80	51·10	50·41	49·80	49·51	49·50	49·92	50·62	51·43	52·14	52·50	52·45
13	51·77	51·08	50·38	49·77	49·50	49·53	49·94	50·63	51·45	52·16	52·53	52·47
14	51·75	51·06	50·36	49·76	49·50	49·54	49·96	50·66	51·47	52·17	52·53	52·44
15	51·73	51·00	50·34	49·75	49·48	49·55	49·97	50·68	51·52	52·19	52·54	52·42
16	51·71	51·00	50·33	49·74	49·48	49·55	50·01	50·60	51·55	52·18	52·52	52·43
17	51·67	50·97	50·30	49·73	49·48	49·56	50·03	50·75	51·57	52·22	52·55	52·44
18	51·65	50·96	50·27	49·70	49·48	49·56	50·04	50·75	51·60	52·24	52·52	52·42
19	51·64	50·93	50·26	49·70	49·48	49·57	50·06	50·79	51·61	52·26	52·56	52·41
20	51·63	50·89	50·24	49·70	49·47	49·60	50·07	50·81	51·65	52·27	52·56	52·37
21	51·58	50·89	50·20	49·68	49·47	49·60	50·10	50·83	51·66	52·29	52·55	52·38
22	51·57	50·85	50·17	49·66	49·48	49·61	50·11	50·85	51·70	52·29	52·58	52·35
23	51·54	50·82	50·15	49·66	49·47	49·63	50·13	50·87	51·71	52·30	52·60	52·33
24	51·52	50·80	50·14	49·64	49·47	49·64	50·15	50·91	51·73	52·31	52·58	52·30
25	51·48	50·77	50·11	49·62	49·45	49·66	50·17	50·93	51·77	52·34	52·58	52·31
26	51·46	50·76	50·08	49·60	49·48	49·66	50·21	50·96	51·81	52·35	52·57	52·30
27	51·46	50·73	50·07	49·60	49·47	49·67	50·23	50·98	51·83	52·35	52·56	52·31
28	51·45	50·70	50·06	49·59	49·47	49·71	50·25	51·03	51·84	52·36	52·56	52·28
29	51·43		50·05	49·57	49·48	49·72	50·27	51·04	51·86	52·37	52·57	52·26
30	51·39		50·02	49·58	49·48	49·72	50·29	51·08	51·89	52·42	52·56	52·23
31	51·36		49·99		49·47		50·32	51·12		52·43		52·21
Means.	51·69	51·02	50·32	49·76	49·50	49·56	50·01	50·71	51·52	52·19	52·53	52·41

The mean of the twelve monthly values is 50°·93.

(II.)—Reading of a Thermometer whose bulb is sunk to the depth of 12·8 feet (12 French feet) below the surface of the soil, at Noon on every Day of the Year.

1882.

Days of the Month.	January.	February.	March.	April.	May.	June.	July.	August.	September.	October.	November.	December.
d	°	°	°	°	°	°	°	°	°	°	°	°
1	50·40	48·60	47·38	47·59	48·33	49·92	51·95	54·12	55·74	55·80	54·90	52·59
2	50·32	48·31	47·37	47·59	48·39	50·09	52·03	54·22	55·81	55·74	54·84	52·50
3	50·21	48·49	47·35	47·60	48·41	50·10	52·11	54·22	55·80	55·70	54·79	52·46
4	50·10	48·40	47·30	47·60	48·41	50·18	52·13	54·31	55·80	55·65	54·72	52·37
5	50·09	48·37	47·32	47·60	48·49	50·26	52·20	54·40	55·81	55·62	54·67	52·24
6	50·00	48·30	47·31	47·65	48·50	50·30	52·24	54·48	55·81	55·60	54·58	52·16
7	49·89	48·28	47·36	47·67	48·54	50·41	52·30	54·53	55·86	55·59	54·47	52·03
8	49·83	48·21	47·37	47·68	48·53	50·48	52·38	54·57	55·88	55·57	54·42	51·97

(II.)—Reading of a Thermometer whose bulb is sunk to the depth of 12·8 feet (12 French feet) below the surface of the soil, at Noon on every Day of the Year—*concluded.*

1882.												
Days of the Month.	January.	February.	March.	April.	May.	June.	July.	August.	September.	October.	November.	December.
d	°	°	°	°	°	°	°	°	°	°	°	°
9	49·73	48·17	47·34	47·69	48·58	50·55	52·47	54·62	55·87	55·59	54·32	51·90
10	49·68	48·11	47·35	47·70	48·60	50·61	52·55	54·67	55·90	55·51	54·28	51·77
11	49·61	48·09	47·32	47·73	48·69	50·70	52·60	54·75	55·88	55·50	54·20	51·68
12	49·53	48·00	47·33	47·76	48·70	50·80	52·70	54·88	55·83	55·43	54·10	51·61
13	49·48	47·96	47·34	47·78	48·74	50·88	52·76	54·90	55·86	55·41	54·11	51·56
14	49·40	47·92	47·37	47·80	48·78	50·95	52·88	54·97	55·83	55·40	54·03	51·44
15	49·36	47·81	47·34	47·82	48·82	51·01	52·90	55·00	55·91	55·37	53·98	51·31
16	49·30	47·79	47·39	47·85	48·87	51·09	53·00	55·02	55·93	55·30	53·90	51·26
17	49·26	47·77	47·38	47·90	48·93	51·10	53·08	55·09	55·96	55·31	53·84	51·18
18	49·20	47·70	47·40	47·90	48·98	51·21	53·14	55·19	55·94	55·29	53·76	51·08
19	49·18	47·61	47·40	47·95	49·05	51·30	53·22	55·24	55·90	55·30	53·73	50·95
20	49·11	47·59	47·40	48·00	49·10	51·40	53·28	55·30	55·93	55·29	53·64	50·82
21	49·08	47·58	47·40	48·02	49·18	51·41	53·34	55·31	55·93	55·27	53·53	50·73
22	49·05	47·54	47·40	48·05	49·23	51·47	53·40	55·37	55·92	55·20	53·53	50·63
23	49·01	47·50	47·42	48·09	49·30	51·53	53·49	55·40	55·88	55·20	53·46	50·52
24	48·98	47·48	47·48	48·11	49·37	51·59	53·53	55·46	55·89	55·18	53·33	50·40
25	48·90	47·47	47·48	48·13	49·38	51·63	53·60	55·48	55·88	55·15	53·24	50·38
26	48·88	47·44	47·48	48·15	49·49	51·70	53·68	55·53	55·87	55·11	53·10	50·29
27	48·87	47·40	47·50	48·19	49·58	51·73	53·72	55·57	55·83	55·08	52·99	50·23
28	48·81	47·39	47·53	48·26	49·64	51·80	53·82	55·62	55·80	55·03	52·88	50·13
29	48·78		47·53	48·27	49·72	51·84	53·93	55·61	55·76	55·00	52·83	50·08
30	48·70		47·54	48·30	49·80	51·89	54·00	55·70	55·75	54·98	52·72	49·98
31	48·64		47·56		49·87		54·05	55·73		54·94		49·89
Means.	49·40	47·91	47·40	47·88	48·97	50·99	52·98	55·01	55·86	55·36	53·90	51·23

The mean of the twelve monthly values is 51°·41.

(III.)—Reading of a Thermometer whose bulb is sunk to the depth of 6·4 feet (6 French feet) below the surface of the soil, at Noon on every Day of the Year.

1882.												
Days of the Month.	January.	February.	March.	April.	May.	June.	July.	August.	September.	October.	November.	December.
d	°	°	°	°	°	°	°	°	°	°	°	°
1	47·32	46·02	46·26	47·69	49·70	53·77	56·06	58·99	59·36	57·30	54·11	50·12
2	47·32	46·00	46·35	47·75	49·69	53·92	56·21	59·14	59·31	57·18	54·08	49·97
3	47·28	46·02	46·44	47·80	49·70	54·11	56·38	59·11	59·25	57·09	53·96	49·84
4	47·26	45·96	46·51	47·90	49·69	54·22	56·43	59·24	59·20	57·06	53·91	49·68
5	47·29	45·89	46·59	47·98	49·78	54·32	56·60	59·36	59·14	57·03	53·88	49·48
6	47·29	45·78	46·59	48·10	49·90	54·40	56·75	59·40	59·19	57·03	53·83	49·33
7	47·27	45·65	46·58	48·19	50·06	54·56	56·93	59·48	59·19	57·00	53·77	49·21
8	47·27	45·53	46·58	48·29	50·19	54·63	57·08	59·46	59·21	56·96	53·71	49·10
9	47·21	45·43	46·60	48·36	50·32	54·70	57·19	59·50	59·19	56·93	53·66	48·96
10	47·20	45·39	46·61	48·45	50·50	54·80	57·28	59·53	59·20	56·85	53·62	48·73
11	47·18	45·34	46·70	48·54	50·70	54·89	57·29	59·63	59·11	56·80	53·50	48·50
12	47·13	45·29	46·80	48·63	50·80	54·91	57·38	59·69	59·01	56·77	53·32	48·35
13	47·15	45·27	46·90	48·70	50·90	54·93	57·39	59·78	59·00	56·77	53·23	48·17
14	47·13	45·28	47·03	48·78	51·07	54·94	57·48	59·80	58·90	56·76	53·02	47·91
15	47·20	45·30	47·10	48·82	51·22	54·90	57·50	59·80	58·89	56·73	52·71	47·70

(III.)—Reading of a Thermometer whose bulb is sunk to the depth of 6·4 feet (6 French feet) below the surface of the soil, at Noon on every Day of the Year—*concluded.*

1882.												
Days of the Month.	January.	February.	March.	April.	May.	June.	July.	August.	September.	October.	November.	December.
d	°	°	°	°	°	°	°	°	°	°	°	°
16	47·21	45·36	47·19	48·90	51·40	54·89	57·58	59·82	58·79	56·66	52·56	47·53
17	47·23	45·48	47·21	48·98	51·58	54·90	57·69	59·90	58·63	56·62	52·32	47·40
18	47·23	45·57	47·28	49·00	51·70	54·80	57·78	59·99	58·46	56·53	52·04	47·30
19	47·20	45·62	47·33	49·05	51·80	54·83	57·90	60·00	58·24	56·45	51·84	47·26
20	47·17	45·70	47·39	49·10	51·90	54·91	58·01	59·98	58·19	56·33	51·57	47·24
21	47·08	45·78	47·40	49·13	52·03	54·93	58·12	59·90	58·08	56·18	51·29	47·28
22	46·99	45·82	47·48	49·19	52·21	54·99	58·22	59·89	58·00	55·94	51·12	47·27
23	46·91	45·82	47·55	49·28	52·39	55·10	58·35	59·83	57·82	55·84	50·92	47·24
24	46·82	45·90	47·62	49·38	52·52	55·29	58·43	59·83	57·79	55·75	50·70	47·20
25	46·70	45·96	47·60	49·50	52·62	55·28	58·53	59·79	57·68	55·56	50·57	47·20
26	46·59	46·00	47·54	49·58	52·90	55·40	58·66	59·74	57·60	55·40	50·52	47·11
27	46·48	46·06	47·56	49·67	53·09	55·50	58·79	59·67	57·50	55·25	50·52	47·06
28	46·30	46·11	47·60	49·72	53·20	55·63	58·79	59·61	57·42	54·87	50·48	47·00
29	46·18		47·60	49·70	53·33	55·77	58·86	59·49	57·33	54·40	50·44	47·02
30	46·06		47·60	49·70	53·47	55·88	58·89	59·49	57·30	54·42	50·30	47·16
31	46·01		47·61		53·60		58·92	59·42		54·21		47·24
Means.	46·99	45·69	47·07	48·80	51·42	54·87	57·66	59·62	58·53	56·28	52·38	48·08

The mean of the twelve monthly values is 52°·28.

(IV.)—Reading of a Thermometer whose bulb is sunk to the depth of 3·2 feet (3 French feet) below the surface of the soil, at Noon on every Day of the Year.

1882.												
Days of the Month.	January.	February.	March.	April.	May.	June.	July.	August.	September.	October.	November.	December.
d	°	°	°	°	°	°	°	°	°	°	°	°
1	43·42	42·68	45·08	46·83	48·72	56·90	59·08	62·10	59·90	56·18	50·80	45·55
2	43·53	42·46	45·20	46·98	48·90	56·90	59·25	62·49	59·94	56·48	51·10	45·18
3	43·70	42·00	45·09	47·13	49·23	57·00	59·60	62·45	60·10	56·74	51·29	44·74
4	44·02	41·70	44·77	47·46	49·71	57·02	60·03	62·40	60·23	56·77	51·51	44·64
5	43·89	41·40	44·48	47·70	50·37	57·12	60·50	62·28	60·33	56·51	51·75	44·87
6	43·80	41·05	44·40	47·85	50·68	57·11	60·52	62·18	60·39	56·22	51·86	44·77
7	44·09	41·10	44·60	47·95	51·10	57·20	60·33	62·20	60·32	56·16	51·79	44·48
8	44·10	41·11	44·69	48·11	51·40	57·21	60·00	62·40	60·25	56·20	51·63	43·93
9	43·80	41·33	45·00	48·29	51·60	57·30	59·90	62·49	60·10	56·34	51·20	43·52
10	44·00	41·38	45·38	48·40	51·68	57·11	59·81	62·44	60·03	56·40	50·88	43·13
11	43·88	41·40	45·79	48·50	51·90	56·80	59·71	62·41	59·88	56·49	50·31	42·70
12	44·10	41·42	46·00	48·46	52·21	56·42	59·72	62·45	59·65	56·54	49·80	42·30
13	44·31	41·89	46·20	48·49	52·75	56·18	59·70	62·46	59·36	56·50	49·24	41·96
14	44·48	42·29	46·09	48·60	53·11	55·95	59·90	62·73	58·78	56·23	48·74	41·80
15	44·49	42·78	45·91	48·70	53·28	55·80	60·10	62·74	58·25	56·19	48·37	41·81
16	44·38	43·30	46·00	48·70	53·31	55·79	60·52	62·71	57·67	55·83	47·91	42·10
17	44·30	43·28	46·09	48·55	53·22	55·80	60·78	62·39	57·50	55·38	47·39	42·33
18	44·06	43·31	46·21	48·53	53·20	55·98	61·00	62·12	57·50	55·02	46·98	42·83
19	43·68	43·53	46·32	48·60	53·50	56·28	61·23	61·91	57·44	54·63	46·49	43·27
20	43·40	43·50	46·50	48·71	53·87	56·42	61·30	61·92	57·30	54·22	46·24	43·37

(IV.)—Reading of a Thermometer whose bulb is sunk to the depth of 3·2 feet (3 French feet) below the surface of the soil, at Noon on every Day of the Year—*concluded.*

	1882.											
Days of the Month.	January.	February.	March.	April.	May.	June.	July.	August.	September.	October.	November.	December.
d	°	°	°	°	°	°	°	°	°	°	°	°
21	43·32	43·50	46·60	49·01	54·25	56·61	61·40	61·82	57·20	54·16	46·00	43·26
22	43·13	43·58	46·69	49·32	54·62	56·92	61·56	61·85	57·01	54·02	45·88	43·38
23	42·93	43·68	46·32	49·72	55·10	57·20	61·80	61·50	56·82	53·79	45·97	43·27
24	42·63	43·81	45·92	49·83	55·40	57·19	61·80	61·32	56·70	53·49	46·58	43·10
25	42·30	43·88	45·95	49·86	55·42	57·39	61·76	60·90	56·59	52·90	47·13	42·78
26	41·68	44·10	46·09	49·63	55·49	57·81	61·63	60·70	56·70	52·41	47·20	42·70
27	41·52	44·60	46·20	49·33	55·41	58·20	61·59	60·49	56·75	51·90	46·98	43·37
28	41·50	44·90	46·09	49·08	55·72	58·47	61·47	60·43	56·70	51·51	46·59	44·11
29	41·90		46·10	48·90	56·13	58·80	61·62	60·21	56·33	51·00	46·14	44·92
30	42·31		46·40	48·80	56·50	59·00	61·70	60·17	56·21	50·80	45·75	45·47
31	42·60		46·62		56·83		61·91	60·06		50·69		45·90
Means.	43·40	42·68	45·77	48·33	53·05	57·00	60·68	61·83	58·40	54·76	48·65	43·60

The mean of the twelve monthly values is 51°·53.

(V.)—Reading of a Thermometer whose bulb is sunk to the depth of 1 inch below the surface of the soil, at Noon on every Day of the Year.

	1882.											
Days of the Month.	January.	February.	March.	April.	May.	June.	July.	August.	September.	October.	November.	December.
d	°	°	°	°	°	°	°	°	°	°	°	°
1	44·0	37·3	46·0	48·0	49·0	58·3	59·7	65·2	60·4	58·8	50·6	38·0
2	43·3	35·0	44·8	49·0	50·2	59·6	62·8	66·4	62·0	57·2	50·7	36·7
3	44·9	38·5	42·3	48·7	52·3	61·2	65·3	62·1	61·0	55·7	51·0	40·6
4	39·3	35·1	39·4	48·3	53·1	60·0	64·0	61·8	60·9	54·1	52·1	43·0
5	43·7	35·2	44·0	48·0	53·3	59·5	63·0	63·3	60·3	54·0	52·4	39·8
6	46·1	35·3	45·0	50·2	53·4	58·2	61·3	62·8	59·2	55·4	50·8	39·3
7	42·2	39·2	45·3	48·4	55·6	60·0	59·2	65·4	58·8	55·4	49·1	35·2
8	42·3	39·4	47·3	49·2	52·1	59·0	60·0	63·3	58·3	55·3	46·7	36·3
9	42·9	38·0	48·3	49·0	51·4	57·3	60·0	62·3	58·6	56·8	45·0	37·4
10	40·8	38·3	49·0	48·7	54·6	55·7	60·3	62·4	59·0	56·0	45·3	33·9
11	45·2	42·0	48·8	47·0	58·3	54·0	59·0	62·9	58·4	57·3	44·2	33·7
12	43·8	43·0	46·5	49·2	56·3	53·5	60·4	64·4	55·0	54·8	40·4	34·3
13	44·5	43·4	44·3	50·2	55·1	53·2	60·5	66·2	53·2	53·5	43·3	38·3
14	42·2	46·3	44·2	50·0	53·7	53·2	62·5	65·9	52·2	55·0	42·3	38·5
15	41·3	44·3	46·3	49·4	53·3	55·2	63·2	65·1	52·8	53·8	41·7	39·0
16	41·6	40·8	46·3	46·0	52·7	55·1	63·1	60·1	53·7	51·3	40·2	40·2
17	38·9	44·1	46·3	49·3	52·7	57·3	64·0	60·4	55·3	51·4	40·7	43·1
18	37·9	43·0	45·0	48·0	54·2	58·3	63·7	61·9	56·0	50·7	37·6	43·8
19	38·3	42·7	46·3	49·2	56·2	57·0	63·3	63·9	53·7	51·3	42·2	42·0
20	40·3	40·3	48·3	51·4	57·4	59·0	62·3	61·4	56·4	52·0	40·7	38·4
21	38·5	44·3	47·2	52·0	58·2	60·0	63·5	61·7	55·3	52·7	39·5	43·2
22	39·1	44·5	42·3	53·2	60·0	59·8	64·0	65·1	55·0	53·0	43·7	40·1
23	37·1	43·6	40·6	52·3	61·3	58·3	63·1	59·3	53·0	49·4	48·3	40·2
24	37·0	42·9	47·0	50·1	58·7	59·9	63·0	58·8	55·0	49·8	47·8	36·8
25	34·8	46·3	46·7	49·3	56·2	60·0	61·2	59·3	55·9	47·2	45·2	46·2

(V.)—Reading of a Thermometer whose bulb is sunk to the depth of 1 inch below the surface of the soil, at Noon on every Day of the Year—*concluded.*

1882.												
Days of the Month.	January.	February.	March.	April.	May.	June.	July.	August.	September.	October.	November.	December.
d	°	°	°	°	°	°	°	°	°	°	°	°
26	35·0	48·3	44·8	47·4	57·6	61·9	61·3	59·2	56·8	45·3	44·3	46·0
27	38·7	47·1	44·8	46·3	59·0	61·0	62·6	59·4	55·5	47·4	41·4	48·7
28	42·1	45·0	46·0	48·0	62·6	62·7	63·2	59·1	53·0	48·4	41·9	49·3
29	43·0		49·1	47·6	59·8	63·5	63·3	58·0	54·3	47·5	41·3	48·8
30	42·1		47·6	45·5	61·3	60·8	64·0	57·9	53·4	47·8	41·7	48·3
31	40·7		46·3		60·2		62·9	58·6		53·3		48·3
Means.	41·0	41·6	45·7	49·0	55·8	58·5	62·2	62·1	56·4	52·6	44·7	40·9

The mean of the twelve monthly values is 50°·87.

(VI.)—Reading of a Thermometer within the case covering the deep-sunk Thermometers, whose bulb is placed on a level with their scales, at Noon on every Day of the Year.

1882.												
Days of the Month.	January.	February.	March.	April.	May.	June.	July.	August.	September.	October.	November.	December.
d	°	°	°	°	°	°	°	°	°	°	°	°
1	47·8	38·4	48·6	56·7	56·2	62·4	67·2	67·7	64·6	67·8	55·5	33·3
2	47·9	31·8	49·2	57·1	57·2	62·4	70·2	75·7	68·1	65·0	57·1	32·4
3	45·9	41·3	46·5	50·3	60·3	69·8	74·2	62·4	66·2	58·9	54·8	45·0
4	37·3	34·2	38·6	53·2	53·8	66·2	65·2	66·2	64·1	56·9	55·6	46·1
5	50·2	35·2	49·2	49·2	61·1	64·2	66·2	69·8	60·0	57·0	58·9	36·3
6	51·9	36·0	47·7	59·4	57·5	59·4	61·8	69·8	63·4	58·2	54·9	34·5
7	43·2	42·4	50·9	56·1	63·5	66·2	62·8	70·7	64·9	60·1	45·3	31·3
8	45·5	40·2	52·0	58·6	57·4	60·3	59·9	66·1	65·6	61·8	47·9	36·0
9	43·3	36·8	53·3	56·5	52·8	58·4	63·7	63·8	64·0	66·8	47·4	36·5
10	42·8	42·1	51·9	55·6	60·2	56·3	65·3	61·2	66·5	60·8	49·8	27·8
11	49·4	48·4	50·2	53·3	69·7	57·0	59·8	65·4	61·2	60·0	44·9	28·0
12	45·5	49·2	49·5	56·0	63·3	53·8	65·9	74·5	52·2	53·0	37·3	30·8
13	47·3	47·4	48·4	52·7	63·0	53·8	61·8	69·4	53·6	54·8	43·4	43·0
14	41·7	52·4	54·8	56·1	59·9	58·5	68·9	71·3	50·0	54·8	39·6	38·7
15	40·0	40·9	49·9	53·6	56·3	56·4	63·4	65·9	58·1	55·2	41·4	39·2
16	42·3	41·9	58·2	50·7	58·6	60·7	67·2	60·2	60·0	48·3	38·2	41·3
17	33·9	47·8	54·2	54·6	59·8	65·9	68·2	60·6	62·3	49·5	40·2	48·7
18	32·9	49·5	53·8	49·3	62·3	59·2	66·8	67·3	61·5	49·8	35·3	45·9
19	39·2	45·4	53·3	54·1	64·3	61·1	68·9	68·2	52·1	53·4	44·9	45·8
20	40·0	40·8	57·2	59·4	62·3	68·2	67·9	67·6	58·3	58·3	42·0	36·3
21	37·0	50·2	49·7	61·1	66·8	63·2	68·0	64·4	59·9	55·2	38·1	46·3
22	39·9	50·3	43·7	54·7	69·0	63·2	66·7	63·7	59·2	52·0	50·2	42·7
23	36·8	43·1	45·3	55·8	70·2	65·3	67·5	60·2	54·2	53·7	53·6	40·4
24	38·3	43·5	52·3	52·3	61·8	67·4	65·1	62·3	60·0	51·4	50·0	34·4
25	30·9	52·4	49·5	51·7	55·0	63·0	63·8	58·6	60·0	51·0	47·0	48·1
26	32·0	52·3	45·6	49·3	64·8	67·0	66·9	63·0	61·6	51·3	47·4	52·8
27	43·7	50·8	48·8	46·1	66·3	68·7	73·0	60·8	58·4	50·0	41·3	55·2
28	47·5	47·1	53·1	53·3	70·9	69·3	66·7	64·6	59·5	48·4	41·6	33·3
29	46·4		55·8	48·4	68·5	67·9	71·2	57·8	54·1	48·8	43·8	52·4
30	41·8		54·4	54·4	70·4	61·3	69·2	63·0	55·6	50·9	42·2	50·9
31	39·2		50·9		67·4		68·8	64·9		49·4		50·7
Means.	42·0	44·0	50·5	54·0	62·3	62·5	66·5	65·4	60·0	55·2	46·3	41·4

The mean of the twelve monthly values is 54°·17.

ABSTRACT of the CHANGES of the DIRECTION of the WIND, as derived from the Records of OSLER'S ANEMOMETER.

1882, Month.	Direction of the Wind. At beginning of Month.	Direction of the Wind. At end of Month.	Apparent Motion.	Times of Shifts of the Recording Pencil.	Amount of Motion.	Monthly Excess of Motion. Direct.	Monthly Excess of Motion. Retrograde.
			°	d h m	°	°	
January.	S.S.W.	E.	+ 247½	12. 21. 0	− 360		
				17. 21. 0	+ 360		
				18. 21. 0	+ 360		
				20. 0. 0	+ 360		
				22. 7. 45	− 360	607½	
February	E.	S.S.E.	+ 67½	2. 0. 0	+ 360		
				2. 8. 45	+ 360		
				3. 0. 0	+ 360		
				3. 21. 0	− 360		
				5. 0. 0	− 360		
				5. 21. 0	+ 720		
				9. 0. 0	+ 360		
				23. 21. 10	+ 360		
				28. 8. 40	(+ 360)	1867½	
March ..	S.S.E.	S.S.E.	− 360	1. 0. 0	+ 360		
				3. 9. 30	− 360		
				4. 0. 0	+ 360		
				7. 0. 0	+ 360		
				16. 0. 0	+ 360		
				17. 2. 45	− 720		
				30. 9. 15	+ 360	360	
April ...	S.S.E.	S.S.E.	0	1. 0. 0	− 360		
				3. 9. 40	(− 360)		
				7. 8. 30	(− 360)		
				9. 7. 30	(− 360)		
				10. 8. 10	+ 360		
				15. 0. 0	(+ 360)		
				16. 0. 0	+ 360		
				16. 8. 10	(− 360)		
				18. 8. 50	− 360		
				19. 0. 0	+ 360		
				21. 8. 45	− 360		
				23. 0. 0	+ 360		
				25. 9. 30	+ 360	720	
May	S.S.E.	N.E.	+ 267½	1. 8. 40	(+ 360)		
				3. 0. 0	− 360		
				3. 8. 45	+ 360		
				4. 2. 40	+ 360		
				5. 2. 50	(− 360)		
				5. 21. 10	+ 360		
				6. 1. 50	(− 360)		
				7. 7. 30	(− 360)		
				7. 21. 5	+ 360		
				9. 0. 0	+ 360		
				11. 0. 0	+ 360		
				13. 1. 50	(+ 360)		
				18. 0. 0	(+ 360)		
May—*cont.*				18. 1. 50	(+ 360)		
				20. 1. 30	(− 360)		
				21. 0. 0	(− 360)		
				21. 21. 15	(− 360)		
				22. 2. 45	+ 360		
				23. 0. 0	(− 360)		
				29. 9. 45	(+ 360)		
				31. 0. 0	(− 360)	2427½	
June	N.E.	N.N.E.	− 382½	15. 21. 5	+ 360		
				16. 8. 55	+ 360		
				17. 9. 10	(+ 360)		
				20. 0. 0	(− 360)		
				24. 9. 20	(+ 360)		
				26. 0. 0	(− 360)		
				26. 9. 55	(− 360)		
				29. 0. 0	+ 360	697½	
July	N.N.E.	W.S.W.	+ 225	1. 9. 45	(+ 360)		
				2. 0. 0	− 360		
				2. 7. 30	(+ 720)		
				8. 2. 0	(− 360)		
				16. 1. 30	(− 360)		
				18. 0. 0	(− 360)		
				25. 7. 55	+ 360		
				26. 0. 0	− 360		
				26. 21. 5	+ 360		
				27. 0. 15	(+ 360)		
				27. 2. 40	(+ 360)		
				31. 8. 45	(− 360)	225	
August ..	W.S.W.	S.S.E.	− 90	9. 2. 55	− 360		
				11. 0. 0	{ + 360 (+ 360)		
				12. 0. 0	(− 360)		
				12. 2. 0	(− 360)		
				22. 21. 0	(− 360)		90
Sept.	S.S.E.	S.W.	+ 67½	4. 8. 55	+ 360		
				10. 0. 0	(− 360)		
				11. 9. 55	− 360		
				12. 21. 0	+ 360		
				13. 2. 40	(− 360)		
				16. 9. 30	+ 360		
				17. 0. 0	+ 360		
				17. 8. 40	(− 360)	1147½	
October .	S.W.	S.S.E.	− 67½	7. 0. 0	+ 360		
				7. 9. 15	(− 360)		
				13. 9. 30	+ 360		
				15. 0. 0	+ 360		

The sign + implies that the change in the direction of the wind has taken place in the order N., E., S., W., N., &c., or in *direct* motion; the sign − implies that the change has taken place in the order N., W., S., E., N., &c., or in *retrograde* motion.

The times of shifts of the recording pencil, as given above, refer to the shifts made by hand, when, by the turning of the vane, the tracer tends to travel or has travelled out of range. Amounts of Motion produced by turnings of the vane which appear to be of an accidental nature, and not due to real changes of direction of the wind, are placed in brackets, and have been omitted in the formation of the "whole excess."

ABSTRACT of the CHANGES of the DIRECTION of the WIND, as derived from the Records of OSLER'S ANEMOMETER—*concluded*.

1882, Month.	Direction of the Wind.		Apparent Motion.	Times of Shifts of the Recording Pencil.	Amount of Motion.	Monthly Excess of Motion.		1882, Month.	Direction of the Wind.		Apparent Motion.	Times of Shifts of the Recording Pencil.	Amount of Motion.	Monthly Excess of Motion.	
	At beginning of Month.	At end of Month.				Direct.	Retrograde.		At beginning of Month.	At end of Month.				Direct.	Retrograde.
			°	d h m	°	°	°				°	d h m	°	°	°
October —*cont.*				17. 0. 0	− 360			December	N.N.W.	S.S.W.	− 135	7. 0. 0	− 360		
				17. 2. 40	(− 360)							10. 0. 0	+ 720		
				23. 2. 45	+ 360							10. 21. 0	− 360		
				28. 1. 45	− 360	652½						14. 0. 0	− 360		
												16. 0. 0	+ 360		
												20. 0. 0	− 360		
November	S.S.E.	N.N.W.	+ 180	16. 0. 0	− 360		180					31. 0. 0	+ 360		135

The sign + implies that the change in the direction of the wind has taken place in the order N., E., S., W., N., &c., or in *direct* motion; the sign − implies that the change has taken place in the order N., W., S., E., N., &c., or in *retrograde* motion.

The times of shifts of the recording pencil, as given above, refer to the shifts made by hand, when, by the turning of the vane, the trace tends to travel or has travelled out of range. Amounts of Motion produced by turnings of the vane which appear to be of an accidental nature, and not due to real changes of direction of the wind, are placed in brackets, and have been omitted in the formation of the "whole excess."

The whole excess of direct motion for the year was 8300°.

The revolution-counter which is attached to the vertical spindle of the vane, whose readings increase with *direct* changes, and decrease with *retrograde* changes, gave the following readings:—

	revs.
On 1881, December 31ᵈ. 12ʰ	49·00
On 1882, December 31ᵈ. 12ʰ	60·05

Implying an apparent excess of direct motion, during the year, of 11·05 revolutions or 3978°, but eliminating the amounts due to accidental shifts of the vane, as shown in the table above, the true annual excess of direct motion becomes 23·05 revolutions or 8298°.

MEAN HOURLY MEASURES of the HORIZONTAL MOVEMENT of the AIR in each Month, and GREATEST and LEAST HOURLY MEASURES, as derived from the Records of ROBINSON'S ANEMOMETER.

Hour ending	1881.												Mean for the Year.
	January.	February.	March.	April.	May.	June.	July.	August.	September.	October.	November.	December.	
	Miles.	Miles.	Miles.	Miles.	Miles.	Miles.	Miles.	Miles.	Miles.	Miles.	Miles.	Miles.	Miles.
1 a.m.	10·2	10·7	13·4	12·9	8·8	11·7	10·1	10·6	8·3	9·1	17·6	11·5	11·2
2 a.m.	10·5	11·1	12·5	13·2	8·4	10·8	9·7	10·1	8·0	9·6	17·4	41·1	11·0
3 a.m.	10·2	10·9	12·5	13·7	8·4	10·8	9·6	10·1	8·2	9·3	18·0	12·3	11·2
4 a.m.	10·0	10·9	11·8	12·8	7·9	11·2	9·5	9·6	8·0	8·9	18·2	12·3	10·9
5 a.m.	10·4	11·3	11·5	12·6	7·7	11·0	9·7	9·7	7·9	8·7	17·0	12·1	10·8
6 a.m.	10·3	10·6	11·8	12·8	7·8	12·1	9·5	10·0	8·2	8·9	16·6	12·0	10·9
7 a.m.	10·8	11·3	12·8	12·6	9·4	12·6	10·5	10·5	8·3	9·6	16·8	12·1	11·4
8 a.m.	10·6	11·4	13·5	13·5	10·7	13·4	11·2	12·8	8·6	9·9	17·0	11·8	12·0
9 a.m.	10·9	11·2	14·3	14·5	12·2	14·3	11·6	13·0	9·5	10·2	17·4	11·1	12·5
10 a.m.	10·7	11·2	14·8	14·3	12·0	13·8	12·2	13·6	10·2	11·0	17·8	11·5	12·8
11 a.m.	10·8	12·5	16·7	15·7	12·7	15·1	13·1	14·4	11·0	12·9	18·9	11·9	13·8
Noon.	12·0	13·3	17·5	17·1	13·5	16·2	13·9	15·2	11·2	13·7	20·8	12·4	14·7
1 p.m.	12·6	13·2	18·1	16·8	13·9	16·5	14·7	15·2	10·7	14·3	20·8	12·7	15·0
2 p.m.	12·8	13·6	18·5	16·6	14·3	16·2	13·9	15·3	11·9	15·2	20·6	13·1	15·3
3 p.m.	12·2	13·8	17·8	16·7	14·5	16·2	15·5	15·5	11·2	14·0	21·1	12·3	15·1
4 p.m.	12·1	13·6	18·0	17·3	15·0	16·4	15·8	16·3	11·2	13·2	20·5	11·6	15·1
5 p.m.	11·4	12·1	16·3	17·4	14·3	16·3	15·0	15·3	10·8	12·6	19·7	11·9	14·4
6 p.m.	11·5	12·7	15·7	16·8	12·9	15·9	14·5	14·6	10·2	12·5	19·2	11·7	14·0
7 p.m.	11·6	12·3	14·6	15·4	12·6	14·2	13·1	13·7	9·2	11·6	19·4	12·1	13·3
8 p.m.	11·5	12·4	13·4	15·1	11·6	12·7	11·5	11·6	9·0	11·3	19·6	11·5	12·6
9 p.m.	11·0	12·9	13·2	15·1	10·2	12·1	10·7	12·0	8·6	10·9	19·2	12·1	12·3
10 p.m.	10·7	12·3	13·4	13·6	9·9	12·3	10·7	11·3	9·5	10·8	19·5	12·3	12·2
11 p.m.	10·7	12·0	12·7	14·1	9·6	11·7	10·5	11·4	9·6	11·0	18·2	12·1	12·0
Midnight.	10·0	11·3	13·4	13·4	9·1	11·1	10·7	11·5	9·1	10·1	18·0	11·9	11·6
Means	11·1	12·0	14·5	14·7	11·1	13·5	12·1	12·6	9·5	11·2	18·7	12·0	12·6
Greatest Hourly Measures	41	38	40	59	31	33	30	41	32	64	45	34	..
Least Hourly Measures	0	0	0	1	0	1	0	1	0	0	0	0	..

MEAN ELECTRICAL POTENTIAL of the ATMOSPHERE, from THOMSON'S ELECTROMETER, for each CIVIL DAY.

(Each result is the Mean of Twenty-four Hourly Ordinates from the Photographic Register. The scale employed is arbitrary; the zero reading is 10·000, and numbers greater than 10·000 indicate positive potential.)

1882.

Days of the Month.	January.	February.	March.	April.	May.	June.	July.	August.	September.	October.	November.	December.
d												
1	10·042	10·621	10·126	10·382	10·140	10·084	10·226	10·173	10·027	10·076	10·112	10·840
2	10·039	10·508	10·241	10·217	10·186	10·010	10·166	10·168	10·160	10·312	10·116	10·537
3	..	10·360	10·297	10·240	10·180	10·061	10·160	10·159	10·193	10·277	10·197	..
4	10·536	10·354	10·322	10·307	10·145	10·123	10·301	10·101	10·139	10·263	10·201	..
5	10·124	10·297	10·177	10·383	10·027	..	9·958	10·147	10·146	10·194	10·123	10·260
6	10·174	10·248	10·256	10·347	10·089	..	10·201	10·268	10·318	10·095	10·153	10·133
7	10·332	10·215	10·227	10·345	10·359	10·148	10·160	10·147	10·261	10·183	10·239	9·954
8	10·222	10·327	10·125	10·446	10·250	10·095	10·105	10·216	10·240	10·279	10·410	10·171
9	10·145	10·261	10·079	10·448	10·181	9·722	10·034	10·372	10·141	10·371	10·386	10·414
10	10·324	10·384	10·064	10·319	10·020	9·960	10·084	10·190	10·040	10·163	10·445	..
11	10·268	10·241	10·030	10·269	10·248	10·078	10·059	10·383	10·045	10·063	10·332	..
12	10·150	10·146	10·095	10·353	10·320	9·943	10·048	10·301	10·040	10·024	10·472	..
13	10·391	10·079	10·167	10·034	10·283	9·843	10·218	10·175	10·005	10·121	10·076	10·486
14	10·419	10·200	10·304	10·375	10·407	10·062	10·110	10·201	9·897	10·155	10·360	10·335
15	10·445	10·130	10·248	10·252	10·352	9·900	10·069	10·240	10·428	10·136	10·366	10·268
16	10·557	10·300	10·220	10·423	10·405	10·000	10·162	9·989	10·263	9·908	9·467	10·130
17	10·715	10·212	10·205	10·090	10·598	10·177	10·144	10·095	10·336	10·085	10·240	10·050
18	10·300	10·140	10·267	10·190	10·493	9·900	10·121	10·234	10·298	10·219	10·261	10·160
19	10·225	10·468	10·505	10·221	10·282	9·938	10·168	10·130	10·076	10·082	10·280	10·323
20	10·162	10·425	10·458	10·178	10·078	10·211	10·193	10·214	10·135	10·305	10·272	10·391
21	10·264	10·182	10·153	10·476	10·393	10·089	10·302	9·993	10·301	10·108	10·312	10·435
22	10·234	10·160	10·529	10·170	10·277	10·030	10·183	10·060	10·423	10·220	9·991	10·587
23	10·453	10·194	10·564	9·962	10·138	10·203	10·272	10·168	10·241	10·364	10·129	10·278
24	10·713	10·264	10·165	10·099	10·136	10·133	10·085	10·051	10·221	..	10·178	10·771
25	10·484	10·035	10·200	9·479	10·138	10·253	10·093	10·088	10·237	10·193	10·383	10·167
26	10·352	10·048	10·237	9·820	10·190	10·056	10·187	9·993	10·314	10·270	10·435	10·115
27	10·119	9·996	10·462	10·104	10·205	10·090	10·221	10·223	10·166	10·024	10·715	10·117
28	10·071	10·031	10·350	10·062	10·261	10·108	10·260	10·119	10·339	9·828	10·683	10·155
29	10·039		10·215	10·085	10·118	10·051	10·242	10·103	10·027	10·414	10·222	10·130
30	10·095		10·274	10·348	10·192	10·088	10·239	10·318	10·279	..	10·450	10·109
31	10·229		10·260		10·295		10·085	10·267		..		10·082
Means -	10·287	10·244	10·252	10·214	10·238	10·048	10·157	10·171	10·191	10·169	10·267	10·284

The mean of the twelve monthly values is 10·210.

MONTHLY MEAN ELECTRICAL POTENTIAL of the ATMOSPHERE, from THOMSON'S ELECTROMETER, at every HOUR of the DAY.

(The results depend on the Photographic Register, using all days of complete record. The scale employed is arbitrary; the zero reading is 10·000, and numbers greater than 10·000 indicate positive potential.)

Hour, Greenwich Mean Solar Time (Civil reckoning).	1882.												Yearly Means.
	January.	February.	March.	April.	May.	June.	July.	August.	September.	October.	November.	December.	
Midnight	10·288	10·304	10·325	10·257	10·264	10·123	10·260	10·274	10·221	10·180	10·181	10·239	10·243
1h. a.m.	10·252	10·265	10·278	10·253	10·242	10·090	10·228	10·272	10·171	10·162	10·144	10·278	10·220
2 ,,	10·255	10·216	10·254	10·226	10·277	10·093	10·177	10·231	10·161	10·109	10·182	10·262	10·204
3 ,,	10·245	10·191	10·251	10·222	10·258	10·124	10·149	10·185	10·142	10·144	10·168	10·235	10·193
4 ,,	10·227	10·178	10·221	10·229	10·263	10·135	10·143	10·174	10·152	10·134	10·185	10·225	10·189
5 ,,	10·209	10·167	10·225	10·234	10·253	10·150	10·120	10·179	10·144	10·127	10·129	10·233	10·181
6 ,,	10·199	10·157	10·229	10·197	10·265	10·066	10·126	10·160	10·119	10·135	10·161	10·235	10·171
7 ,,	10·213	10·170	10·223	10·201	10·272	10·121	10·123	10·191	10·120	10·130	10·205	10·228	10·183
8 ,,	10·222	10·169	10·186	10·209	10·275	10·103	10·136	10·203	10·144	10·125	10·225	10·225	10·185
9 ,,	10·207	10·135	10·187	10·199	10·245	10·047	10·128	10·188	10·172	10·127	10·237	10·276	10·179
10 ,,	10·206	10·136	10·190	10·067	10·163	9·976	10·094	10·081	10·113	10·121	10·294	10·289	10·144
11 ,,	10·253	10·139	10·168	10·144	10·120	10·037	10·086	10·062	10·136	10·101	10·316	10·307	10·156
Noon	10·301	10·172	10·214	10·108	10·089	9·891	10·046	10·035	10·173	10·126	10·312	10·280	10·147
1h. p.m.	10·329	10·221	10·230	10·132	10·120	9·863	10·018	10·044	10·160	10·193	10·348	10·314	10·164
2 ,,	10·310	10·254	10·224	10·099	10·120	9·972	10·038	10·016	10·216	10·197	10·339	10·345	10·179
3 ,,	10·333	10·291	10·244	10·133	10·126	9·793	10·094	10·049	10·145	10·065	10·224	10·296	10·149
4 ,,	10·360	10·315	10·254	10·181	10·183	9·942	10·066	10·030	10·224	10·247	10·333	10·297	10·204
5 ,,	10·365	10·349	10·158	10·160	10·150	9·956	10·126	10·062	10·232	10·242	10·379	10·370	10·212
6 ,,	10·360	10·313	10·221	10·250	10·246	9·956	10·133	10·181	10·208	10·239	10·397	10·361	10·239
7 ,,	10·373	10·341	10·360	10·265	10·319	10·001	10·201	10·234	10·315	10·273	10·378	10·321	10·282
8 ,,	10·363	10·344	10·368	10·361	10·363	10·136	10·301	10·276	10·370	10·208	10·387	10·257	10·311
9 ,,	10·342	10·325	10·340	10·378	10·387	10·168	10·305	10·294	10·273	10·214	10·362	10·292	10·307
10 ,,	10·334	10·364	10·345	10·322	10·383	10·223	10·340	10·336	10·253	10·257	10·321	10·333	10·318
11 ,,	10·334	10·336	10·339	10·314	10·338	10·196	10·304	10·299	10·225	10·223	10·198	10·330	10·288
Means	10·287	10·244	10·252	10·214	10·238	10·048	10·157	10·171	10·191	10·169	10·267	10·284	10·210
Number of Days employed	30	28	31	30	31	28	31	31	30	28	30	26	..

MONTHLY MEAN ELECTRICAL POTENTIAL of the ATMOSPHERE, from THOMSON'S ELECTROMETER, on RAINY DAYS, at every HOUR of the DAY.

(The results depend on the Photographic Register, using all days on which the rainfall amounted to or exceeded 0in·020. The scale employed is arbitrary; the zero reading is 10·000, and numbers greater than 10·000 indicate positive potential.)

Hour, Greenwich Mean Solar Time (Civil reckoning).	1882.												Yearly Means.
	January.	February.	March.	April.	May.	June.	July.	August.	September.	October.	November.	December.	
Midnight	10·173	10·085	10·267	9·991	10·060	10·184	10·236	10·243	10·102	10·133	10·063	10·310	10·154
1h. a.m.	10·130	10·063	10·247	10·068	10·015	10·019	10·199	10·237	10·012	10·115	9·980	10·274	10·113
2 "	10·138	10·057	10·219	10·076	10·147	10·036	10·144	10·217	10·024	10·044	10·105	10·237	10·120
3 "	10·118	10·042	10·217	10·098	10·075	10·081	10·105	10·186	10·000	10·111	10·049	10·159	10·103
4 "	10·088	10·045	10·221	10·119	10·107	10·105	10·124	10·178	10·043	10·111	10·087	10·172	10·117
5 "	10·085	10·040	10·207	10·128	10·070	10·128	10·106	10·169	10·057	10·118	9·967	10·188	10·105
6 "	10·098	10·040	10·204	10·019	10·089	10·004	10·124	10·115	10·023	10·128	10·007	10·180	10·086
7 "	10·112	10·048	10·194	10·073	10·074	10·091	10·119	10·197	10·043	10·121	10·065	10·163	10·108
8 "	10·112	10·032	10·123	10·115	10·116	10·076	10·143	10·198	10·071	10·104	10·074	10·169	10·111
9 "	10·117	10·013	10·122	10·103	10·092	10·019	10·123	10·185	10·076	10·103	10·063	10·217	10·103
10 "	10·137	9·997	10·174	9·797	10·009	9·967	10·068	9·970	9·972	10·085	10·183	10·254	10·051
11 "	10·148	10·007	10·173	10·001	9·991	10·049	10·037	9·967	10·025	10·057	10·237	10·240	10·079
Noon	10·165	10·083	10·170	9·840	10·015	9·806	9·969	9·976	10·146	10·070	10·212	10·224	10·056
1h. p.m.	10·130	10·080	10·229	9·727	10·089	9·779	9·920	9·885	10·086	10·163	10·228	10·289	10·050
2 "	10·078	10·063	10·244	9·763	10·084	9·926	9·992	9·885	10·182	10·163	10·234	10·350	10·080
3 "	9·998	10·110	10·280	9·882	10·143	9·812	10·051	9·996	9·966	10·043	10·191	10·181	10·054
4 "	10·078	10·138	10·272	9·949	10·222	9·993	9·985	10·000	10·112	10·195	10·257	10·108	10·109
5 "	10·067	10·137	10·070	9·971	10·077	9·949	10·093	10·128	10·102	10·172	10·334	10·365	10·122
6 "	10·100	10·105	10·166	10·104	10·259	9·964	10·074	10·167	10·010	10·142	10·363	10·382	10·153
7 "	10·152	10·147	10·342	10·046	10·376	9·946	10·193	10·223	10·147	10·187	10·329	10·307	10·200
8 "	10·185	10·153	10·273	10·232	10·389	10·157	10·296	10·273	10·284	10·093	10·306	10·091	10·228
9 "	10·193	10·063	10·174	10·167	10·395	10·153	10·287	10·252	10·228	10·108	10·272	10·178	10·206
10 "	10·193	10·093	10·138	9·999	10·353	10·232	10·322	10·247	10·264	10·150	10·219	10·257	10·206
11 "	10·183	10·118	10·228	10·153	10·249	10·180	10·287	10·231	10·287	10·136	9·954	10·270	10·191
Means	10·124	10·073	10·206	10·018	10·146	10·027	10·126	10·131	10·094	10·119	10·157	10·232	10·121
Number of Days employed	6	6	9	10	10	17	18	11	11	19	16	10	..

MONTHLY MEAN ELECTRICAL POTENTIAL of the ATMOSPHERE, from THOMSON'S ELECTROMETER, on NON-RAINY DAYS, at every HOUR of the DAY.

(The results depend on the Photographic Register, using only those days on which no rainfall was recorded. The scale employed is arbitrary: the zero reading is 10·000, and numbers greater than 10·000 indicate positive potential.)

Hour, Greenwich Mean Solar Time (Civil reckoning).	1882.												Yearly Means.
	January.	February.	March.	April.	May.	June	July.	August.	September.	October.	November.	December.	
Midnight	10·316	10·374	10·335	10·406	10·359	10·169	10·318	10·299	10·255	10·357	10·363	10·317	10·324
1ʰ. a.m.	10·277	10·326	10·294	10·359	10·347	10·212	10·283	10·301	10·228	10·333	10·404	10·280	10·304
2 "	10·290	10·277	10·275	10·318	10·331	10·194	10·235	10·252	10·211	10·307	10·322	10·349	10·280
3 "	10·282	10·240	10·276	10·299	10·341	10·182	10·230	10·211	10·203	10·271	10·379	10·347	10·272
4 "	10·267	10·219	10·226	10·302	10·334	10·167	10·186	10·197	10·208	10·224	10·360	10·301	10·249
5 "	10·244	10·213	10·240	10·303	10·331	10·183	10·157	10·219	10·187	10·176	10·370	10·329	10·246
6 "	10·219	10·204	10·245	10·299	10·345	10·171	10·154	10·226	10·169	10·174	10·388	10·307	10·242
7 "	10·224	10·215	10·240	10·276	10·374	10·157	10·143	10·225	10·156	10·159	10·428	10·331	10·244
8 "	10·230	10·222	10·219	10·261	10·343	10·139	10·124	10·246	10·165	10·177	10·450	10·290	10·239
9 "	10·204	10·178	10·226	10·259	10·316	10·106	10·146	10·213	10·215	10·193	10·468	10·336	10·238
10 "	10·194	10·183	10·203	10·263	10·230	10·059	10·137	10·142	10·187	10·226	10·430	10·336	10·216
11 "	10·271	10·192	10·168	10·247	10·168	10·068	10·144	10·107	10·197	10·226	10·386	10·384	10·213
Noon	10·342	10·224	10·244	10·262	10·114	10·073	10·161	10·079	10·193	10·281	10·423	10·404	10·233
1ʰ. p.m.	10·368	10·281	10·245	10·331	10·127	10·070	10·162	10·127	10·215	10·270	10·494	10·436	10·260
2 "	10·383	10·327	10·227	10·272	10·126	10·061	10·155	10·092	10·246	10·283	10·504	10·451	10·261
3 "	10·414	10·383	10·240	10·292	10·092	9·977	10·149	10·079	10·240	10·077	10·441	10·451	10·236
4 "	10·439	10·399	10·256	10·322	10·142	10·011	10·177	10·052	10·261	10·397	10·456	10·483	10·283
5 "	10·443	10·451	10·197	10·292	10·163	10·006	10·150	10·063	10·269	10·450	10·417	10·419	10·277
6 "	10·434	10·475	10·250	10·357	10·227	10·030	10·194	10·187	10·295	10·513	10·470	10·431	10·322
7 "	10·429	10·459	10·385	10·432	10·281	10·063	10·199	10·243	10·395	10·531	10·429	10·453	10·358
8 "	10·425	10·447	10·436	10·475	10·338	10·094	10·304	10·298	10·410	10·533	10·492	10·499	10·396
9 "	10·398	10·437	10·432	10·489	10·367	10·167	10·361	10·334	10·257	10·503	10·483	10·496	10·394
10 "	10·416	10·478	10·451	10·446	10·383	10·214	10·392	10·409	10·208	10·477	10·546	10·514	10·411
11 "	10·404	10·416	10·435	10·358	10·376	10·230	10·345	10·349	10·177	10·481	10·522	10·539	10·386
Means -	10·330	10·317	10·282	10·330	10·273	10·117	10·209	10·206	10·231	10·317	10·434	10·395	10·287
Number of Days employed -	19	16	20	16	19	9	10	16	15	7	9	7	..

AMOUNT OF RAIN COLLECTED IN EACH MONTH OF THE YEAR 1882.

1882. MONTH.	Number of Rainy Days.	Monthly Amount of Rain collected in each Gauge.							
		Self-registering Gauge of Osler's Anemometer.	Second Gauge at Osler's Anemometer.	On the Roof of the Octagon Room.	On the Roof of the Magnetic Observatory.	On the Roof of the Photographic Thermometer Shed.	Gauges partly sunk in the ground.		
		No. 1.	No. 2.	No. 3.	No. 4.	No. 5.	No. 6.	No. 7.	No. 8.
		in.	in.	in.	in.	in.	in.	in.	in.
January	10	0·626	0·599	0·935	1·074	1·238	1·352	1·278	1·238
February	9	0·586	0·586	0·802	0·954	1·090	1·153	1·121	1·127
March	11	0·533	0·561	0·751	0·943	1·092	1·144	1·051	1·070
April	13	1·302	1·349	1·587	1·968	2·263	2·403	2·114	2·190
May	11	1·075	1·104	1·183	1·222	1·330	1·367	1·226	1·262
June	19	1·367	1·407	1·778	2·038	2·252	2·356	2·114	2·123
July	19	1·806	1·804	1·949	2·201	2·348	2·451	2·180	2·249
August	13	0·651	0·606	0·833	0·921	1·078	1·159	1·024	1·003
September	14	1·736	1·753	2·052	2·217	2·396	2·405	2·344	2·348
October	23	3·656	3·833	4·282	4·943	5·333	5·421	5·297	5·337
November	19	1·124	1·127	1·616	1·831	2·095	2·199	2·112	2·179
December	17	0·835	0·847	1·379	1·472	1·678	1·771	1·758	1·770
Sums	180	13·297	13·376	19·147	21·784	24·193	25·181	23·619	23·896
Height of receiving Surface above the ground.	..	ft. in. 50. 8	ft. in. 50. 8	ft. in. 38. 4	ft. in. 21. 9	ft. in. 10. 0	ft. in. 0. 5	ft. in. 0. 5	ft. in. 0. 5
Height of receiving Surface above mean sea level.	..	ft. in. 205. 6	ft. in. 205. 6	ft. in. 193. 2	ft. in. 176. 7	ft. in. 164. 10	ft. in. 155. 3	ft. in. 155. 3	ft. in. 155. 3

OBSERVATIONS OF AURORA BOREALIS IN THE YEAR 1882

h m

1882, October 2. at 6 I could see no trace of Aurora. On looking at the sky at [illegible]^{h}. 15^{m} there was extended and diffused light along the northern horizon.

" 16 Three bright irregularly shaped luminous patches (forming a broken arch of great width) were observed, two below Andromeda and Pegasus, varying rapidly in brightness, and another (a bright white patch, also of varying brilliancy) a few degrees below Aquila. In the north below Ursa Major there is extended bluish or greenish white light, with dusky brownish masses beneath (probably auroral cloud) and dark lateral streaks.

" 24 The eastern mass of light has moved more to the southward and is now below α Pegasi, and in the south-west there is now a bright patch of light also (although not so large or intense as those in the south-east), and a very faint white streamer appears to be shooting from this mass.

7 29 An intense patch has developed itself below γ Piscium; the other patches have faded, although they brighten up from time to time.

7 31 Phosphorescent patch, very large and very intense in east-south-east just below γ Pegasi, moving slowly westwards; at 7^{h}. 34^{m} its centre was south-south-east over ι Pegasi; at 7^{h}. 36^{m} it faded away somewhat rapidly. The stars shone through this patch with diminished brightness.

7 45 Nothing but diffused light now, low in the north. A thin veil of haze; stars dim for some minutes.

8 Haze now gone, stars brilliant again; diffused light remains below Ursa Major, and so continued till 9^{h}.; at times between 8^{h}. and 8^{h}. 15^{m} clouds passed over.

9 Light intensified below Ursa Major, with dark transversal streaks.

9 8 Short streamers shooting up through and near Ursa Major, varying in length and brightness; at times they are seen as far westward as Boötes and as far eastward as Auriga.

9 15 Streamers numerous and very brilliant.

9 18 Ruddy appearance above and to the left of Ursa Major. Streamers continued to appear till 9^{h}. 25^{m}.

9 30 Nothing now visible except diffused light, but clouds have appeared, which are tinged with ruddy light in the north. The light of the rising Moon had now become powerful, and nothing further was seen.

WILLIAM C. NASH.

h m

1882, October 2. at 6 48½ Aurora now first seen, when streamers were numerous from north-east to north-west, reaching to α Cygni; they appeared to meet in Cygnus. Splendid red light near Arcturus.

6 51 Streamers reaching to α Cygni, and cutting through Cassiopeia and Ursa Major.

6 52 Red tinge near Arcturus; two bluish-white masses in the east and west.

6 53½ Light in the east and west, throwing streamers which meet in Cygnus.

6 58 Streamers very numerous.

7 1 Fine streamers to above Polaris. Auroral light in the south (like a bank of cloud) stretching across sky from east to west, cutting through a point near Aquila. An arch near northern horizon has been noticeable all through, of a bluish-white colour; in the north-east it nearly reached Capella; at times it appears to throw out clouds of auroral light.

7 2 Wavy motion perceived in the north-east (only noticed at this time).

7 5 Red tinge above Arcturus.

7 7 Streamers forming in the west. Light in the east and west still seen.

7 9 Northern arch very intense, especially near Capella.

7 13 Northern arch very intense.

7 15 Streamers observed; tinged with red in Perseus.

7 17 Streamers in north-west, reaching to Cassiopeia; red light still above Arcturus.

7 19 Thin but intense streamer, reaching a point between Polaris and Cassiopeia.

OBSERVATIONS OF AURORA BOREALIS IN THE YEAR 1882—*continued.*

	h m	
1882, October 2— (*continued*)	7 21	Streamers, reaching to Polaris.
	7 22½	Streamers, reaching to Polaris.
	7 24	Still red below Arcturus.
	7 25	Broad streamers, reaching to Polaris.
	7 26	Broad streamers, reaching to Polaris.
	7 27	Clouding up in north-east (clouds of a brownish colour). Auroral light stretching across from east to west.
	7 29	Northern arch fainter. Cloud increasing from south-west, tinged with light as it approaches.

WILLIAM HUGO.

	h m	
1882, November 17, at	5 14	Bright red light in zenith, fainter towards horizon. The mass of red light is increasing: it is brightest a little below Lyra.
	5 17	The light to the east of zenith now fainter; remaining brighter towards the west.
	6 4	Bright streak of phosphorescent light (about 25° long) appeared in the east-north-east, and passed over a little above the Moon to the west; it faded away in about ½ a minute, shortly before reaching the western horizon. The whole horizon from west-north-west to north-east is now illuminated with bright light.
	6 11	Bright streamer due north, extending to above Polaris and remaining visible about 2 minutes.
	6 15	Well-defined streamer a few degrees west of north, reaching almost to the zenith and remaining visible about ½ minute.
	After 6 15	The light in the north faded until about 6h. 30m, when it began again to brighten, but by 7h. it had disappeared.

FRANK FINCH.

1882, November 17. The Aurora, when first seen, consisted principally of a ruddy glow extending all over the north-west. About 5h. 30m a brilliant arm shot up from the northern horizon to the zenith, principally red but with a green vein in it. The rosy colour disappeared soon after this. The principal red display lay between α Lyræ and ε and η Ursæ Majoris, a broad band of light; a fainter band, at right angles to the first, went down to Boötes, (α Coronæ Borealis shining in the centre of it), and upward toward and nearly to the zenith.

The green Aurora, during the time of observation, consisted, with one marvellous exception, of little else than a pale-green light fringing the upper edge of the London smoke-cloud. The exception was the sudden appearance of a magnificent streak of light, which, rising in the east-north-east, and slowly mounting, seemed to follow a parallel of declination; it passed just above the Moon, and sank with an even regular motion down to the west, fading somewhat after passing the meridian, and disappearing at 6h. 5m. 59s. It took about two minutes to cross the sky. It had risen some 20° when first seen, and slowly increased in length up to meridian passage; decreasing afterwards. Its greatest length was perhaps about 30°.

EDWARD W. MAUNDER.

1882, November 17. The aurora was again seen at 11h. 45m. The appearance was then that of an arch, with faint streamers shooting upwards a short distance. At 11h. 55m the arch had an irregular shape, with brilliant streamers reaching to within a few degrees of the zenith; it extended from about north-north-east to about north-west, the most brilliant part being about north-north-west. At 12h. 10m it was scarcely visible.

J. W. H. PEAD.

ROYAL OBSERVATORY, GREENWICH.

OBSERVATIONS

OF

LUMINOUS METEORS

1882.

Month and Day. 1882.		Greenwich Mean Solar Time.	Observer.	Apparent Size of Meteor in Star-Magnitudes.	Colour of Meteor.	Duration of Meteor in Seconds of Time.	Appearance and Duration of Train.	Length of Meteor's Path in Degrees.	No. for Reference.
		h m s				s		°	
June	14	10. 43. ±	N.	Venus	White	1·5	Fine	..	1
July	6	9. 58. ±	N.	Venus	Bluish-white	2	Fine	..	2
July	9	10. 37. 0	N.	1	White	0·5	Train	5	3
July	19	11. 47. 0	H.	1	Bluish-white	1	Fine	15	4
August	7	9. 36. 30	N.	Jupiter	White	1	Fine	12	5
August	8	10. 4. 57	M.	2	Bluish-white	0·5	Slight	..	6
	,,	10. 51. 22	M.	1	Bluish-white	0·6	Slight	..	7
	,,	10. 59. 36	M.	2	Bluish-white	0·4	None	..	8
	,,	11. 27. 34	M.	3	Bluish-white	0·7	None	7	9
	,,	11. 43. 40	M.	1	Yellow	0·8	Slight	10	10
	,,	11. 49. 39	M.	2	Bluish-white	0·4	Slight	8	11
	,,	12. 4. 27	M.	1	Bluish-white	0·6	Fine	12	12
	,,	12. 8. 58	M.	Jupiter	Bluish-white	1·0	Fine; 3ˢ	18	13
	,,	12. 12. 50	M.	1	Yellow	0·9	Fine; 2ˢ	10	14
	,,	12. 27. 15	M.	2	Bluish-white	0·6	Slight	8	15
	,,	12. 31. 43	M.	Venus	Bluish-white	1·5	Splendid; 2ˢ	20	16
	,,	14. 24. 31	N.	Jupiter	Bluish-white	2·0	Fine	30	17
August	9	10. 13. 52	G. & F.	3	Bluish-white	0·5	Slight	10	18
	,,	10. 13. 57	G. & F.	4	Bluish-white	0·5	None	..	19
	,,	10. 19. 30	G. & F.	4	Bluish-white	0·3	None	20	20
	,,	10. 19. 54	G. & F.	3	Bluish-white	0·4	None	..	21
	,,	10. 32. 46	G. & F.	3	Bluish-white	0·3	Slight	..	22
	,,	10. 41. 51	N.	2	Bluish-white	0·5	Slight	12	23
	,,	10. 44. 27	G.	2	White	0·8	Slight	10	24
	,,	10. 54. 57	G.	2	Bluish-white	0·8	None	20	25
	,,	10. 57. 12	F.	4	Bluish-white	0·4	None	..	26
August	11	9. 19. 15	N.	1	Bluish-white	..	Fine	15	27
	,,	9. 20. 21	N.	3	Bluish-white	..	None	4	28
	,,	10. 8. 49	M.	1	Bluish-white	0·6	Slight	9	29
	,,	10. 19. 4	M.	Jupiter	Bluish-white	1	Fine	20	30
	,,	10. 20. 20	F.	2	Bluish-white	0·5	Slight	..	31
	,,	10. 23. 39	F.	3	Bluish-white	0·7	None	8	32
	,,	10. 25. 18	F.	3	Bluish-white	0·3	None	6	33
	,,	10. 27. 55	M.	1	Bluish-white	0·7	Slight	8	34
	,,	10. 31. 59	F.	2	Bluish-white	0·8	Slight	7	35
	,,	10. 32. 42	N.	3	...	0·5	Train	7	36
	,,	10. 32. 50	M.	2	Bluish-white	0·4	None	8	37
	,,	10. 33. 9	N.	..	White	0·3	Train	5	38
	,,	10. 38. 53	F.	1	Bluish-white	0·8	Fine	..	39
	,,	10. 39. 37	M.	2	Bluish-white	0·4	None	7	40
	,,	10. 41. 48	M.	2	Bluish-white	0·5	Slight	8	41
	,,	10. 41. 54	N.	1	Bluish-white	0·7	Train	15	42
	,,	10. 44. 50	F.	1	Bluish-white	1	Slight	7	43
	,,	10. 46. 9	M.	1	Bluish-white	0·6	None	10	44
	,,	10. 58. 42	M.	2	Bluish-white	0·3	None	8	45
	,,	10. 59. 20	F.	1	Bluish-white	0·7	None	..	46
	,,	11. 1. 38	M.	1	Bluish-white	0·8	Slight	9	47
	,,	11. 3. 42	F.	1	Bluish-white	1·5	Fine	9	48
	,,	11. 5. 2	M.	> 1	Bluish-white	0·9	Fine	16	49
	,,	11. 6. 55	F.	1	Yellow	0·6	Slight	..	50
	,,	11. 8. 48	F.	1	Bluish-white	0·7	Fine	..	51
	,,	11. 9. 13	M.	2	Bluish-white	0·4	None	6	52
	,,	11. 9. 46	F.	1	Bluish-white	1	Fine	..	53
	,,	11. 15. 14	M.	1	Bluish-white	0·7	Train	10	54
	,,	11. 21. 41	M.	1	Bluish-white	0·8	Fine	10	55
	,,	11. 22. 25	N.	2	Bluish-white	0·5	Train	7	56

August 9. 11ʰ. Clouds began to appear, and soon afterwards the sky became overcast.

August 10. Sky cloudy.

No. for Reference.	Path of Meteor through the Stars.
1	Passed across ζ Cygni and ζ Cassiopeiæ.
2	From direction of Polaris passed near α Cephei almost to ζ Cygni.
3	From near β Ophiuchi moved parallel to line joining α and ι Ophiuchi.
4	From direction of δ Ursæ Majoris shot across a point about 1° below β Ursæ Majoris.
5	Moved from direction of α Andromedæ, passing a few degrees to left of α Pegasi towards β Piscium.
6	From β Cassiopeiæ to a point to south of ζ Cephei.
7	From a point midway between γ Andromedæ and β Persei disappeared beyond α Trianguli.
8	From δ Persei passed between β and ε Persei.
9	From near ι Piscium disappeared about midway between 77 Pegasi and ω Piscium.
10	Appeared near Capella, and disappeared a little above ν Aurigæ.
11	From near ε Persei disappeared a few degrees to left of ζ Persei.
12	Appeared near γ Andromedæ, and disappeared a little beyond θ Persei.
13	From direction of η Piscium disappeared a few degrees beyond ω Piscium.
14	From near γ Andromedæ to α Arietis.
15	Appeared near γ Andromedæ, and disappeared near β Persei.
16	From 41 Arietis passed across and disappeared below the Pleiades.
17	From direction of Aries moved nearly to β Ceti.
18	From direction of γ Cassiopeiæ towards β Andromedæ.
19	From β Andromedæ towards γ Cassiopeiæ.
20	Shot from α Pegasi towards γ Persei.
21	From γ Camelopardali towards Polaris.
22	From Polaris towards β Ursæ Minoris.
23	Passed above β Cassiopeiæ, moving towards ι Cygni.
24	From about midway between α and γ Cassiopeiæ towards γ Persei.
25	From near Polaris towards γ Persei.
26	From α Andromedæ to α Pegasi.
27	Moved towards α Capricorni from direction of ε Pegasi.
28	From direction of α Cassiopeiæ moved towards γ Andromedæ.
29	From direction of τ Ursæ Majoris to α Ursæ Majoris.
30	Appeared near Polaris, and disappeared near ζ Ursæ Majoris.
31	Appeared near 51 Andromedæ, and disappeared near α Andromedæ.
32	Appeared near κ Draconis, and disappeared near ζ Ursæ Majoris.
33	Appeared near γ Pegasi, and disappeared near ω Piscium.
34	Shot from direction of ε Cassiopeiæ to Polaris.
35	Appeared near β Andromedæ, and disappeared near ζ Andromedæ.
36	Passed between Polaris and β Ursæ Minoris, moving towards δ Draconis.
37	From direction of Polaris passed across and disappeared beyond β Ursæ Minoris
38	Passed between γ Cephei and Polaris (nearer the former), moving from α Persei.
39	Appeared near θ Pegasi, and disappeared near β Delphini.
40	Appeared near γ Cephei, and disappeared near β Cassiopeiæ.
41	From ξ Cephei to γ Cephei.
42	Passed midway between Delphinus and γ Equulei from direction of Lacerta.
43	Appeared near ω Andromedæ, and disappeared near β Andromedæ.
44	Appeared near η Pegasi, and disappeared beyond α Pegasi.
45	From α Cassiopeiæ towards γ Andromedæ.
46	Appeared near θ Pegasi, and disappeared near δ Aquilæ.
47	Shot from direction of γ Andromedæ, and disappeared near α Arietis.
48	Appeared near Polaris, and disappeared near λ Draconis.
49	Appeared near α Andromedæ, and disappeared near β Arietis.
50	Appeared near β Persei, and moved perpendicularly downwards.
51	Appeared near β Camelopardali, and disappeared near κ Draconis.
52	Shot from direction of β Andromedæ, and disappeared a little above α Arietis.
53	Appeared near γ Andromedæ, and disappeared near φ Piscium.
54	Shot from a point a little to the left of α Persei, and disappeared near Capella.
55	Appeared near δ Persei, and disappeared a little to the right of the Pleiades.
56	From direction of β Cassiopeiæ passed nearly to δ Cephei.

Month and Day, 1882.		Greenwich Mean Solar Time.	Observer.	Apparent Size of Meteor in Star-Magnitudes.	Colour of Meteor.	Duration of Meteor in Seconds of Time.	Appearance and Duration of Train.	Length of Meteor's Path in Degrees.	No. for Reference.
		h m s				s		°	
August	11	11. 23. 41	F.	1	Bluish-white	1	Fine	..	1
"		11. 24. 44	M.	2	Bluish-white	0·5	None	6	2
"		11. 26. 43	N.	3	...	0·3	...	5	3
"		11. 31. 38	N.	3	...	0·5	Train	7	4
"		11. 46. 37	F.	3	Yellow	0·8	None	7	5
"		11. 50. 28	M.	3	Bluish-white	0·4	None	5	6
"		11. 51. 55	M.	2	Bluish-white	0·8	Slight	11	7
"		12. 2. 19	F.	1	Bluish-white	1·5	Fine	..	8
"		12. 6. 40	M.	1	Bluish-white	1	Fine	10	9
"		12. 13. 27	M.	> 1	Bluish-white	1·2	Fine	14	10
"		12. 20. 3	M.	> 1	Bluish-white	1·2	Fine	12	11
"		12. 21. 45	F.	1	Bluish-white	1	Slight	6	12
"		12. 25. 17	M.	Jupiter	White	1·6	Fine; 2°	28	13
"		12. 29. 12	M.	1	Bluish-white	1	Fine	12	14
"		12. 37. 27	M.	2	Bluish-white	0·7	Slight	8	15
"		12. 38. 49	F.	> 1	Yellow	1	Fine	8	16
"		12. 45. 44	M.	1	Bluish-white	1·1	Fine	12	17
"		12. 48. 5	F.	3	Bluish-white	0·5	None	6	18
"		12. 49. 40	M.	Saturn	Yellow	1·3	Fine	14	19
"		12. 50. 55	F.	Jupiter	Bluish-white	1·2	Fine; 4°·5	..	20
"		12. 55. 27	M.	> 1	Bluish-white	1	Fine	10	21
"		12. 56. 50	F.	2	Yellow	0·6	None	6	22
"		12. 59. 23	M.	2	Bluish-white	0·8	Slight	9	23
"		13. 1. 11	F.	1	Bluish-white	1·2	Slight	..	24
"		13. 3. 43	M.	2	Bluish-white	0·7	Slight	10	25
"		13. 5. 5	F.	1	Bluish-white	0·7	Slight	7	26
"		13. 7. 17	M.	1	Bluish-white	0·9	Fine	..	27
"		13. 14. 39	F.	3	Yellow	0·5	None	8	28
"		13. 15. 4	M.	> Jupiter	Bluish-white	1·7	Very fine; 3s	20	29
September	20	11. 2. 55	N.	1	Bluish-white	1	Fine		30
October	2	11. 14. 5	N.	> 1	White	1·5	Fine and enduring.		31
October	3	10. 28. 13	F.	2	Bluish-white	0·5	None	..	32
"		10. 53. 35	F.	1	Bluish-white	0·7	Slight	..	33
"		11. 1. 36	F.	3	Bluish-white	1	None	9	34
October	24	16. 17. ±	E.	2	Reddish	..		10	35
November	10	11. 39. 30	N.	2	White	0·7	Train	12	36
November	30	9. 50.	G.	2	Bluish-white	0·7	Slight	20	37
"		10. 20.	G.	2	Bluish-white	1	None	15	38
"		10. 40.	G.	2	Bluish-white	0·7	Train	..	39

August 11. It was estimated by Mr. Nash that the meteors were appearing at the rate of 30 per hour.

No. for Reference.	Path of Meteor through the Stars.
1	Appeared near ι Cassiopeiæ, and disappeared near α Camelopardali.
2	From near α Draconis disappeared a little beyond ζ Ursæ Majoris.
3	Passed about 5° to left of the Pleiades, moving from ζ Persei.
4	Appeared 3° or 4° above α Pegasi, and moved parallel to line joining α and ζ Pegasi.
5	Appeared near 48 Cassiopeiæ, and disappeared near β Camelopardali.
6	From direction of α Ursæ Majoris disappeared a little below β Ursæ Majoris.
7	Appeared near γ Ursæ Minoris, and disappeared a little to left of ζ Ursæ Majoris.
8	Appeared near α Lacertæ, and disappeared in Delphinus.
9	From a point a few degrees below ι Pegasi disappeared near ζ Aquarii.
10	Appeared near β Andromedæ, passed between and disappeared a little below α and β Arietis.
11	Appeared near β Andromedæ, and disappeared near β Persei.
12	Appeared near ι Cassiopeiæ, and disappeared near 50 Cassiopeiæ.
13	Shot from Polaris, and disappeared about 4° to right of α Ursæ Majoris.
14	From α Pegasi disappeared near α Aquarii.
15	From direction of β Trianguli disappeared near λ Arietis.
16	Appeared near γ Persei, and disappeared near Piazzi III. 51 (Camelopardalus).
17	Appeared near α Persei, and disappeared a little to left of Capella.
18	Appeared near Piazzi III. 51 (Camelopardalus), and disappeared near Piazzi III. 7 (Cassiopeia).
19	Shot from near Polaris, and disappeared near ι Draconis.
20	Appeared near β Camelopardali, and disappeared near Polaris.
21	Appeared near γ Cygni, and disappeared about 3° to right of α Lyræ.
22	Appeared near γ Andromedæ, and disappeared near β Andromedæ.
23	Shot from direction of γ Pegasi, passed between and disappeared near ι and θ Piscium.
24	Appeared near γ Andromedæ, and disappeared near θ Cassiopeiæ.
25	Appeared near β Andromedæ, and disappeared near α Arietis.
26	Appeared near α Trianguli, and disappeared near γ Andromedæ.
27	Shot from α Andromedæ, and disappeared about 2° to left of γ Andromedæ.
28	Appeared near α Trianguli, and disappeared near β Arietis.
29	From near θ Cassiopeiæ disappeared about 4° to right of Polaris.
30	From ι Aurigæ moved almost to the Pleiades.
31	From near λ Draconis passed across α Draconis and several degrees beyond.
32	From ζ Cephei to κ Cygni.
33	From a point a little below ι Cassiopeiæ to a point a few degrees above and north of Capella.
34	From a little below β Camelopardali disappeared near Capella.
35	Appeared at a point 10° to right and 5° below Sirius, and moved towards right on a path inclined to the horizon by an angle of 30°. (Sky not clear.)
36	Passed midway between γ Ursæ Minoris and α Draconis, and between θ and ι Draconis.
37	From near α Draconis towards γ Draconis.
38	Shot from α Draconis, and passed about 5° above ι Draconis.
39	From direction of β Orionis passed a little below ε Leporis.

www.ingramcontent.com/pod-product-compliance
Lightning Source LLC
Chambersburg PA
CBHW032151160426
43197CB00008B/868

9783337869380